The Cadottes

THE CADOTTES

*A Fur Trade Family
on Lake Superior*

ROBERT SILBERNAGEL

WISCONSIN HISTORICAL SOCIETY PRESS

Published by the Wisconsin Historical Society Press
Publishers since 1855

The Wisconsin Historical Society helps people connect to the past by collecting, preserving, and sharing stories. Founded in 1846, the Society is one of the nation's finest historical institutions.
Join the Wisconsin Historical Society: wisconsinhistory.org/membership

Printed in Wisconsin, USA
Cover design by Tom Heffron
Typesetting by Kristyn Kalnes
27 26 25 24   3 4 5 6

Library of Congress Cataloging-in-Publication Data
Names: Silbernagel, Robert, 1952– author.
Title: The Cadottes : a fur trade family on Lake Superior / Robert Silbernagel.
Other titles: Fur trade family on Lake Superior
Description: Madison, WI : Wisconsin Historical Society Press, [2020] | Includes bibliographical references and index.
Identifiers: LCCN 2019046352 (print) | LCCN 2019046353 (e-book) | ISBN 9780870209406 (hardcover) | ISBN 9780870209413 (e-book)
Subjects: LCSH: Cadotte family. | Cadot, Jean-Baptiste, Sr., 1723–1800—Family. | Fur traders—Québec (Province)—History. | Fur traders—Superior, Lake, Region— History. | Fur trader—Québec (Province)—History. | Fur trader—Superior, Lake, Region—History. | French—Superior, Lake, Region—Genealogy. | Québec (Province)—Genealogy. | Superior, Lake, Region—Genealogy.
Classification: LCC CS71.C125 2020 (print) | LCC CS71.C125 (e-book) | DDC 971.4092 [B]— dc23
LC record available at https://lccn.loc.gov/2019046352. LC e-book record available at https://lccn.loc.gov/2019046353

This book is dedicated to families.

First, there is my own family: my wife, Judy; our children, Derek and Kara; my five siblings; and my mother, all of whom encouraged me in this project and, in a number of instances, took an active role assisting me in my research. Sometimes, they simply joined me on visits to Lake Superior.

Additionally, there is the Cadotte family. They were the inspiration and primary reason for this book, of course. But their descendants living today— and their extended families—have also been inspirational, graciously sharing family stories with me and demonstrating their ongoing love for their heritage while serving their communities in a multitude of ways.

CONTENTS

THE CADOTTE

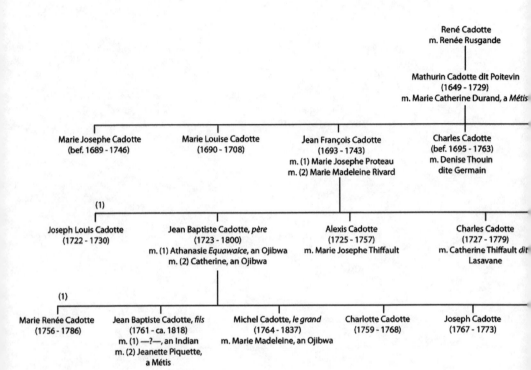

René Cadotte
m. Renée Rusgande

Mathurin Cadotte dit Poitevin
(1649 - 1729)
m. Marie Catherine Durand, a *Métis*

Marie Josephe Cadotte
(bef. 1689 - 1746)

Marie Louise Cadotte
(1690 - 1708)

Jean François Cadotte
(1693 - 1743)
m. (1) Marie Josephe Proteau
m. (2) Marie Madeleine Rivard

Charles Cadotte
(bef. 1695 - 1763)
m. Denise Thouin
dite Germain

(1)

Joseph Louis Cadotte
(1722 - 1730)

Jean Baptiste Cadotte, *père*
(1723 - 1800)
m. (1) Athanasie *Equawaice,* an Ojibwa
m. (2) Catherine, an Ojibwa

Alexis Cadotte
(1725 - 1757)
m. Marie Josephe Thiffault

Charles Cadotte
(1727 - 1779)
m. Catherine Thiffault *dit*
Lasavane

(1)

Marie Renée Cadotte
(1756 - 1786)

Jean Baptiste Cadotte, *fils*
(1761 - ca. 1818)
m. (1) —?—, an Indian
m. (2) Jeanette Piquette,
a Métis

Michel Cadotte, *le grand*
(1764 - 1837)
m. Marie Madeleine, an Ojibwa

Charlotte Cadotte
(1759 - 1768)

Joseph Cadotte
(1767 - 1773)

FAMILY TREE

Marie Jeanne Cadotte	René Cadotte	Mathurin Cadotte
(1697 - 1759)	(bef. 1699 - 1749)	(1701 - 1777)
m. Jacques Thiffault	m. Marie Louise Proteau	m. (1) Marie Felicite Ayotte
dit Despres		m. (2) Angélique Gaudry

Augustin Cadotte	Michel Cadotte	Marie Joseph Cadotte
(1728 - 1772)	(1729 - 1784)	(1730 - 1737)
m. Marie Josephe Cossette	m. Marie Anne Cossette	

(2)

Augustin Cadotte	Charlotte Cadotte	Joseph Cadotte	Marie Cadotte
(ca. 1770 - 1825)	(ca. 1779 - 1851)	(ca. 1788 - ca. 1836)	(ca. 1791 - bef. 1851)
m. Madeleine, an Ojibwa	m. (1) Séraphin Trullier	m. Angelica Constons,	m. (1) John Warren Dease
	dit Lacombe	a Métis	m. (2) Joachim La Rivière
	m. (2) Jean-Baptiste Pelletier		

CADOTTE FAMILY TREE © 2015 BY JOHN P. DULONG. PREVIOUSLY PUBLISHED IN *MICHIGAN'S HABITANT HERITAGE*. USED WITH PERMISSION.

TIMELINE

1395—The earliest of several dates given for when ancestors of the Ojibwe arrive at western end of Lake Superior and Madeline Island.

1534—Jacques Cartier explores the Gulf of St. Lawrence.

1608—Samuel De Champlain establishes Québec City.

1649—Mathurin Cadot is born in France.

1659—Médard de Groseilliers visits Lake Superior and Chequamegon Bay, possibly accompanied by his brother-in-law Pierre-Esprit Radisson.

1670—Hudson's Bay Company is founded.

1671—Saint Lusson plants a flag at Sault Ste. Marie and negotiates a treaty with multiple Native nations. Mathurin Cadot is probably present.

1713—France cedes Hudson Bay and Acadia to the British in the Treaty of Utrecht.

1723—Jean-Baptiste Cadot Sr. is born in Bastican, Québec.

1741—Jean-Baptiste Sr. enters the fur trade as a voyageur.

1750—Jean-Baptiste Sr. and Athanasie are living at Sault Ste. Marie when French military officers arrive.

1756—Jean-Baptiste Sr. and Athanasie are married at Michilimackinac.

1761—Jean-Baptiste Cadotte Jr. is born at Sault St. Marie.

1762—Alexander Henry visits the Sault for the first time, signaling the arrival of the British.

1764—Michel Cadotte is born at Sault Ste. Marie.

1765—Jean-Baptiste Sr. and Alexander Henry enter into a fur-trade partnership, establishing a post at Chequamegon Bay.

1776—The British colonies in southern North America issue the Declaration of Independence.

1783—The Revolutionary War ends with the signing of the Treaty of Paris and the establishment of the United States. The southern portion of Lake Superior, including Madeline Island, officially becomes part of the new nation.

1784—The North West Company is formed.

1787—Michel Cadotte Jr. is born while Michel and Equaysayway are trading near Chippewa Falls.

1795—Jean-Baptiste Jr. begins working as an independent trader for the North West Company.

1796—Jean-Baptiste Sr. retires from the fur trade and turns his business over to his sons.

1798—Michel begins working as an independent trader for the North West Company.

1800—Jean-Baptiste Sr. dies at Sault Ste. Marie. Approximate date that Michel and Equaysayway Cadotte establish a permanent home on Madeline Island.

1801—Jean-Baptiste Jr. becomes a partner in the North West Company.

1803—Jean-Baptiste Jr. is dismissed from the North West Company.

1807—Michel's business is severely harmed when Ojibwe warriors who support the Shawnee Prophet ransack his Lac Courte Oreilles trading post.

1808—John Jacob Astor establishes the American Fur Company.

1812–1814—The War of 1812 is fought by Great Britain and United States. The Treaty of Ghent is signed in December of 1814, ending the war.

1817—Congress passes a law banning foreign fur traders from operating in the United States.

1818—Jean-Baptiste Jr. dies in Canada.

1820—Michel becomes a US citizen and begins trading with the American Fur Company.

1821—Lyman and Truman Warren marry Michel and Equasayway's daughters. Hudson's Bay Company takes over the North West Company.

1823—Lyman and Truman buy Michel's fur trade business.

1837—Michel dies on Madeline Island.

1840—William Warren begins gathering stories on Ojibwe history.

1850—Hundreds of Ojibwe perish in the Sandy Lake Tragedy.

1854—Treaty of 1854, signed at La Pointe, guarantees Lake Superior Ojibwe can remain in their homeland; establishes major Wisconsin reservations and some in Upper Michigan and Minnesota.

1855—The first ship goes through the locks at Sault Ste. Marie.

Introduction

M y first encounter with Michel Cadotte, one of the most important fur traders of his time, occurred around 2005, nearly 170 years after his death. It was during a trip to Madeline Island when my wife, Judy, and I visited the old Catholic cemetery there. We saw Cadotte's unremarkable gravestone with this inscription:

> Sacred to the Memory of Michel Cadotte, who departed this
> Earth July 8, 1837, Aged 72 years, 11 months & 16 days

The grave marker was intriguing to me because it related to someone who had lived a long life during an era when fur trading was the principal industry in the region, someone who had died on this isolated island but whose name suggested that he wasn't American or British. I wanted to know more about Michel Cadotte's life and the history of the area. As I read contemporary books about Lake Superior and Madeline Island and perused journals from some of the early traders and explorers, I found something else of interest: the name "Cadotte" kept showing up, often tied to important historical events.

I eventually came to know a great deal about Michel Cadotte, his wife, Equaysayway, his father, brother, and other relatives. But I still feel as though I am looking at the Cadottes through a veil. The picture remains blurry, even if it sits on a solid foundation of historical documentation. Neither Michel nor Equaysayway, and not even Michel's father or brother, left journals that historians have discovered. Although a family account book includes entries written by Michel Cadotte or dictated by his illiterate father, there are no known letters by their hands or written statements from them. Most of what is known about them comes second-hand, or even third-hand, from people who interacted with the Cadottes or learned their stories later.

At least five generations of Cadottes were involved in the fur trade around Lake Superior, spanning nearly two centuries. And they were equally involved with the Lake Superior Ojibwe as partners, spouses, and relatives. The earliest member of the family to arrive at the big lake was Mathurin Cadot (the family name later morphed into "Cadotte"). He was born in France in 1649 but traveled to the New World as a young man, and soon became involved in the fur business, first as a *coureur de bois* (an itinerant, unlicensed fur trader). Later, he operated legally under the French system when he obtained a license from the government of New France.

Mathurin Cadot is believed to have been present in 1671 for one of the critical events during the early days of French rule when, at the eastern end of Lake Superior, a representative of King Louis XIV formally declared the lake and its surroundings under French control and received proclamations of loyalty from various Indian nations living near the lake. Mathurin Cadot remained involved in the fur trade until 1690, before retiring to a farm near Montreal. Two of his three sons also participated in the fur trade for a time, but it was his grandson Jean-Baptiste Cadot Sr. who really established the family as important to the trade on and around Lake Superior.

Working initially for the French, then joining the British after they won control of Canada in 1763, Jean-Baptiste Cadot Sr. was an interpreter and a critical connection between the Ojibwe of the region and the Europeans who sought to trade with them. He partnered with Alexander Henry, the first British subject given official permission to trade on Lake Superior, and was also an ally of the British during the Revolutionary War. Based at his headquarters at Sault Ste. Marie, he established fur-trading posts along the southern shore of Lake Superior as far west as Chequamegon Bay. He also married an Ojibwe woman with important familial connections to Ojibwe leaders. The couple had two sons who also became key players in the fur trade on and around Lake Superior: Jean-Baptiste Cadotte Jr. and the aforementioned Michel Cadotte. Throughout the last decades of the eighteenth century and well into the nineteenth, the brothers were significant players in the fur business, especially in the regions we now call northern Wisconsin and northern Minnesota. Michel Cadotte remained in the business longer than his brother, and with his wife, Equaysayway, established himself as a trader to be reckoned with at the western end of Lake Superior, with both the British and the Americans.

Three of Michel and Equaysayway's sons also served important roles in the fur trade and in the War of 1812. The couple's son-in-law Lyman Warren eventually took over their fur trade post on Madeline Island and helped it become the primary regional post for the American Fur Company. Moreover, Michel and Equaysayway's grandchildren gained renown as interpreters and educators after the heyday of the fur trade. They assisted in treaty negotiations between the US government and the Ojibwe and served as intermediaries between the government and the nation once reservations were established. One grandchild, William Warren, became a territorial legislator and the author of the first written book-length account of the Ojibwe: *History of the Ojibway People* (1885).

Other people with the surname Cadotte, most of them descended from Mathurin Cadot, were involved in the fur trade near Lake Superior, in Canada, and elsewhere. Nonetheless, I have chosen to focus on Jean-Baptiste Cadot Sr.; his sons Jean-Baptiste Cadotte Jr. and Michel Cadotte; and Michel and Equaysayway's children and grandchildren because they played the most significant roles along the southern shores of Lake Superior and in what would eventually become Wisconsin and Minnesota.

The fur trade that developed around Lake Superior could be boisterous and sometimes brutal. Indeed, the fur-trade era was characterized by revelry and celebration, tedium, drudgery, and occasional danger. It was a time of unfettered adventure and uncommon exploration. And while the fur trade created immense wealth for a few, many of its workers lived little more than subsistence lives.

The trade created partnerships and conflict among Europeans and Native people, and it led to innumerable marriages and children of mixed ancestry. It also exacerbated enmity between different Indian nations, which European leaders frequently sought to prevent. Fur trading further altered the ways in which many Native peoples lived, changing the tools they used, the food they ate, and the animals they hunted. It brought devastating disease and shifting alliances. But unlike the changes wrought by the widespread settlement, agriculture, and industry that would come later, traditional Native cultures and their seasonal patterns of life were not obliterated by the fur trade. Indians continued to hunt, fish, and live in communities much as they had before the Europeans arrived.[1]

Fur traders didn't ply their trade only around Lake Superior. They worked from the Atlantic Coast to Hudson Bay to the Ohio River Valley, pushing westward to the Mississippi and Missouri Rivers, the Saskatchewan, and the Athabasca. Eventually, the trade would extend to the Rocky

Mountains and on to the Pacific Ocean. But for nearly two hundred years—longer by far than most other regions engaged in the trade—Lake Superior was a critical area for fur trappers, traders, and merchants. First, independent Frenchmen sought furs from Native people. Later, they would be followed by Scottish traders, Englishmen, and Americans, who continued to work with French Canadians and the Native people of the region, especially the Ojibwe—the primary nation involved along the southern shores of Lake Superior during the fur-trade era from roughly the 1670s to the 1840s.

During the heyday of the fur trade—about 1783 to the War of 1812—when the Montreal-based North West Company monopolized the northern Great Lakes region and beyond, great flotillas of large canoes left Montreal each spring and headed westward across rivers, lakes, and portages until they reached Lake Superior. From Sault Ste. Marie at the east end of the lake, the canoes—laden with dried corn and peas, clothing and blankets, knives, guns, powder, axes, traps, rum, and brandy—were paddled nearly four hundred miles to Grand Portage at the far west end of the lake in what is now Minnesota. Later, they went to Fort William at today's Thunder Bay in Canada, a move demanded by military and political events.

In midsummer, at either Grand Portage or Fort William, there would be a rendezvous with those who had spent the winter far inland, trapping and trading for furs. The winterers would restock their larders for the coming season and hand their furs off to those from the east, who would ferry them back to Montreal for eventual shipment to Europe and other parts of the globe. But before the winterers headed back to the forests and the Montrealers paddled eastward, there would be several weeks of feasting, drinking, and company meetings.

Most of the partners of the North West Company were Scottish, English, or Irish. A few of the French Canadians also became partners. One such man was Jean-Baptiste Cadotte Jr., although his partnership in the company proved to be short-lived. His brother Michel was never a partner of the North West Company, but he did work with it as a contract clerk and an independent trader for much longer than his brother. He continued in the fur trade along the southern shores of Lake Superior after the Americans assumed control of the region and new economic and political alliances formed.

The Cadottes: A Fur Trade Family on Lake Superior is about several generations of a family that successfully navigated the geography of the Lake Superior region, as well as a variety of cultural, political, and economic upheavals from the seventeenth century up to the present day. Because of the historical haze through which I view the Cadottes, I wanted to gain an understanding of the places where they lived, the geography through which they traveled, and the activities in which they engaged. Consequently, a number of chapters in this book involve my own attempts to follow some of their pathways or activities or to learn from other people who have done so.

The French were the first Europeans to interact with Native people in this part of North America. The people who would later become known as French Canadians, many of whom married Native people, were critical in the development of the fur trade in the Great Lakes region. They also brought cultural changes to the Native peoples who had long inhabited the region—sometimes collaborating with the French Roman Catholic priests who arrived at the same time and at other times ignoring or outright opposing the religious strictures that the priests hoped to impose.

Indeed, the French government sought trade with the Indians around Lake Superior, not conquest, and the French Canadians who spent much of their lives in the backcountry with the Native inhabitants married into their families and lived with them. Their story isn't better known in the United States because they were not English, Scottish, or American. Additionally, only a handful of those who spent their time trading with Indians and living in the backcountry provided written documentation of their lives, and those are mostly in French. But the development of the Lake Superior region, particularly northern Wisconsin and Minnesota and Michigan's Upper Peninsula, cannot be fully understood without examining the role played by the French Canadians.

While trapping animals for their furs may seem like an historical anomaly to modern Americans, it's easy to underestimate what a potent economic driver the fur trade was for a long time on much of the North American continent. The Pilgrims at Plymouth Rock and other early settlers along the Eastern Seaboard supplemented their agricultural activities with fur trapping, at least until the area became largely trapped out. The government of New France depended heavily on the fur trade to keep its small colonies economically stable, and, once the English gained control, the fur trade became the dominant economic activity of Britain's northern lands—what would become Canada and the Upper Great Lakes region that's now part of the United States. America's first multimillionaire, John Jacob Astor, gained his wealth from the fur trade mostly in the Great Lakes region, aided in no small part by a near monopoly for his business decreed by the US government. For the first centuries of European involvement in North America, the fur trade was one of the most profitable of economic activities, especially in the Upper Great Lakes and Canada. Only much later would endeavors such as agriculture, mining, shipping, and manufacturing surpass the fur trade as the predominant economic driver of the region.

With the Cadotte family as my focus, I hope this volume will provide readers with some insight into the importance of that trade as well as into how critical French Canadians and those of mixed French and Ojibwe heritage were in the history of this region, how their significance was intentionally diminished by those who arrived near the end of the fur trade's heyday, and how these people not only survived but in many instances thrived to play important roles in communities of the region.

—⊣⊢—

The Ojibwe, an Algonquin-speaking group of Indigenous people living mainly in Michigan, Wisconsin, Minnesota, North Dakota, and Ontario, have been known by a number of names over the centuries, with the name often changing depending on the group and the time period. In referring to themselves, the Ojibwe often use the name "Anishinaabe" or the plural term "Anishinaabeg," which has been translated as "person" or "human."[2] The terms can also be used to denote a broader group of Native people that included Odawa, Potawatomie, Cree, and others, as well as the Ojibwe. The first Europeans to encounter the Ojibwe were the French, who initially met them at Sault Ste. Marie and consequently called them "Saulteurs," "Sauteurs," or "Saulteaux" for many years.[3] It's not clear who first began calling them "Ojibwe," but early authors such as William Warren and Henry Rowe Schoolcraft claimed the word meant some version of "puckered up" and could have referred to the way their lips moved while speaking or the form of their moccasins. I have found no modern translation of the term, other than that it refers to a member of an Ojibwe band.

In October 1753, George Washington, then a major with the British army, wrote that the "Chippoways" were among the Indian nations then fighting against the English as allies of the French.[4] "Chippewa" and "Chippoway" were Anglicized and abbreviated versions of "Ojibwe." Even in Washington's time, however, some Europeans understood that the word "Chippewa" and its various derivatives were incorrect terms. Writing about his visit to Lake Superior in 1765, explorer and trader Alexander Henry said the Chequamegon Bay region surrounding Madeline Island was "the metropolis of the Chipeways, of whom the true name is O'chibbuoy."[5]

English speakers soon corrupted "Ojibwe" and turned it into "Chippeway" and later shortened that to "Chippewa." US treaties with the Ojibwe all used the term "Chippewa," and various bands of Ojibwe in Wisconsin and Michigan are still officially known as the Lake Superior Chippewa. Except when quoting or paraphrasing someone else, I use "Ojibwe" with an -e rather than an -ay throughout this book because it is the most common spelling. I have also relied on *The Ojibwe People's Dictionary*, a project headed by students and faculty at the University of Minnesota's Department of American Indian Studies, when I had questions about spelling or definitions of Ojibwe terms.

CHAPTER 1

MADELINE ISLAND AND LAKE SUPERIOR

In the midmorning sun, the shimmering waters of Lake Superior can be glimpsed through a copse of evergreen trees where Michel and Equaysayway Cadotte made their home two hundred years ago. A visitor can both see and feel the lake's presence and hear waves lapping at rocks a quarter mile away. When the wind is up, it brings cool air from the lake, even on a hot summer's day.

The Cadottes' home, their small farm, and their fur-trading post were near Grant's Point, the southern tip of what is now called Madeline Island. Many different names have been applied to the island over the centuries, but in the late nineteenth century, "Madeline" became the preferred appellation. It was named after Equaysayway, a corruption of her European name, "Magdelaine." The island, the largest of the string known as the Apostle Islands, is approximately fourteen miles long and three miles wide.

The location of the Cadotte compound today is a shady spot situated among young evergreen trees, isolated even in the twenty-first century. Although it is just a few miles from La Pointe—the main community on Madeline Island—it seems very distant from the souvenir shops, second homes, restaurants, and boat docks that, these days, generate most of the activity on the island. It's difficult to imagine that this peaceful, remote site was once the center of activity, not only for Madeline Island but for much of western Lake Superior.

A short walk from the copse of trees where the Cadotte enterprise once operated takes a visitor to the small beach on the lake shore, just north of the southeast point of Madeline Island. Here, canoes bringing supplies and furs to the Cadotte trading post beached two centuries ago. Other canoes

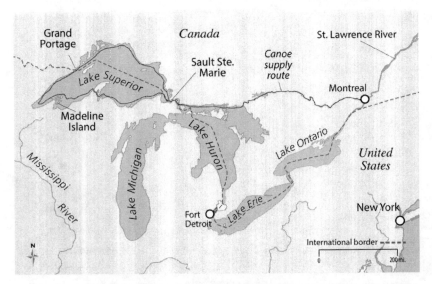

The primary canoe routes used by traders, voyageurs, and Native people heading from Montreal to the west end of Lake Superior. ROBERT GARCIA

launched from here, bound for the mainland to ferry goods to the Cadotte trading posts in northern Wisconsin or to carry furs to Montreal. Here, as well, is where the earliest French traders may have beached their canoes more than one hundred years before the Cadottes settled on the island.[1]

From this small beach, Superior stretches more than four hundred miles eastward. The nearest portion of the lake's North Shore, along the Minnesota coastline, is more than seventy miles away and hidden from sight. The closest point on Canada's mainland is more than one hundred miles distant across open water. To the southeast, you can see parts of Long Island, reaching toward Madeline Island from the southeast end of Chequamegon Bay. In the evening, the lights of communities to the south and southeast may be visible. But apart from that, any shoreline you can see is dark and tree-lined, appearing much as it must have looked when the Cadottes resided here.

Along the shores of Lake Superior are rocky cliffs, in some places more than one hundred feet high at the water's edge. Wolves, moose, bear, deer, caribou, and a multitude of other wild creatures live near the shore or on places like Isle Royale, the largest island in Lake Superior, 115 miles northeast of Madeline Island. Although shipping centers such as Duluth,

Minnesota, at the west end of the lake, and Sault Ste. Marie, Michigan, at the eastern entrance bustle with human activity, large parts of the lake and its surroundings seem as wild today as they must have in the eighteenth and early nineteenth centuries.

Standing on that remote beach where canoes once landed, or at the site of the Cadotte compound a short distance inland, one can't help wondering why the couple chose this particular spot on the isolated island as their home for so many years. Was it because of its defensible nature? Madeline Island is about three miles east of the mainland, where the town of Bayfield now sits. Long before the Cadottes took up residence here, Ojibwe reportedly moved to the island as a defensive measure to protect themselves from Fox, Dakota, and other nations.[2] During the early days of the Cadottes' residence there, it was accessible only by canoe in warmer months or by hiking across wide expanses of ice in the winter. In either case, there was little chance of concealment. Would-be attackers could not easily surprise anyone on the island.

Was it simple economics? Perhaps the island was just a good place to locate a fur-trading post when one's trading territory included much of the north woods of current-day Wisconsin, and when good lake access was necessary to get furs to market and provisions to the interior. Although some earlier traders, who dealt with the same economic concerns, such as Alexander Henry, situated their trading posts on the mainland surrounding Chequamegon Bay, others, such as John Johnston and unnamed French traders he encountered in 1791, located trading posts near the south end of the island.[3]

Maybe it was a familial tie. After all, Equaysayway was a daughter of La Grue ("The Crane"), also known as Waubujejack, the hereditary chief of the Ojibwe on Madeline Island and the immediate vicinity. Her family eventually deeded the land for the Cadotte compound to Equaysayway and Michel. Additionally, Michel's cousin the Ojibwe chief Great Buffalo made his home on the island, although it's not clear whether or not he lived there before the Cadottes opened their trading post on the island.

It's possible that Madeline Island was simply the most attractive place to live in the region. David Dale Owen, a geologist working for the US government in the mid-nineteenth century, noted that the island held several advantages over the nearby mainland. La Pointe, the town on Madeline

Island and the area around it, was perfect for a resort site, both for health and recreation, the geologist said, adding that it "offers advantages beyond any portion of the mainland in Wisconsin." He claimed, incorrectly, that the climate of the island was milder than that in any other part of Wisconsin, including the mainland around Lake Superior or inland areas much farther south along the Mississippi River. Because of the climate and the lake winds that swept across the island, then, "Madeline Island is probably not surpassed, in point of health, by any locality throughout the entire Western country." The geologist may have overstated the island's attributes, but it has long attracted people for a variety of reasons. Even in the twenty-first century, it remains an attractive place for summer visitors and a number of hardy year-round residents. [4]

Perhaps Michel and Equaysayway were simply enamored by the immense lake and wanted to live on it. They certainly wouldn't have been the first to be inspired by it. For instance, Pierre-Esprit Radisson, upon reaching Lake Superior around 1659, remarked, "We embarked ourselves on the delightfullest lake of the world." Radisson had traveled a great deal in western Europe, including parts of Italy. Yet he concluded that the lake and its surroundings were better than any of those lands. [5] More than a century later, North West Company partner and explorer Alexander Mackenzie, who had traveled overland to the Pacific and Arctic Oceans and seen many of Canada's large lakes, described Lake Superior as "the largest and most magnificent body of fresh water in the world." [6] Other visitors were equally captivated by the beauty of the lake, its wild surroundings, and the picturesque rock formations. John Bigsby, who stood at its eastern end near Sault Ste. Marie in 1824, marveled at its grandeur, describing the prospect of sailing on the lake as "beautifully wild." [7]

The island's ability to evoke awe hasn't diminished in the twenty-first century. Take a kayak trip to the sea caves on the shores of Lake Superior west of the Bayfield Peninsula, as my wife, Judy, and I did in 2013, and you'll be enchanted by the dozens of low sandstone arches through which you can paddle a kayak or small canoe. When the winter is cold enough, thousands of people visit the caves on foot. Similar caverns adorn the eastern shore of Madeline Island and the fringes of other Apostle Islands. The Cadottes often paddled past these caves in their travels. And the caves are just one of the impressive sights to be found along nearly every mile of

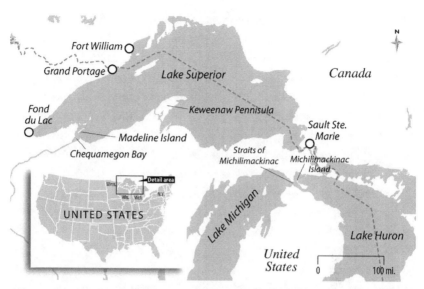

It required a canoe trip of roughly 400 miles to travel from Sault Ste. Marie at the east end of Lake Superior, to Grand Portage, Fort William, Fond du Lac, or Madeline Island at the west end. ROBERT GARCIA

Lake Superior's shoreline.

The French named this giant body of water *le lac supérieur*, not because it was so large, but because according to one hypothesis, it was the lake farthest upstream in the string of Great Lakes they had begun exploring late in the sixteenth century. It was the uppermost lake, hence the *superior* one.[8] Another hypothesis suggests that it may have been the French speakers' attempt to literally translate the Ojibwe word for the lake.[9] The Ojibwe who made their home around its shoreline, fished its waters, harvested its wild rice, and rode its waves in birch-bark canoes called it *gichigami*, or "large lake."[10] Henry Wadsworth Longfellow turned that name into "Gitche Gumee" for his famous poem, "The Song of Hiawatha."

Whatever one called the lake, and however much one was inspired by its beauty, all who spent much time around Lake Superior quickly understood how dangerous it could be. Bigsby wrote of pausing in his journey to eat breakfast on one of the Maple Islands, along the northeast shore of the lake, where everything appeared peaceful and serene. Yet it was at this very site a decade earlier, he noted, that two North West Company canoes were driven onto the rocky shore in a storm and nine people drowned.[11]

Two years after Bigsby's trip, Thomas McKenney, then Superintendent of Indian Affairs for the US government, traversed Lake Superior westward to what was then called Fond du Lac, the present site of Duluth, Minnesota, to negotiate a treaty with the Ojibwe. He remarked frequently about the fickle nature of weather on the lake. A cloudy and damp morning was replaced by sunshine on July 12, 1826, he wrote. But a sudden storm swamped the clear weather in the afternoon and forced McKenney's group to take shelter on shore. Finally, the sun came out again, but the temperature plummeted and McKenney was forced to don his overcoat.[12]

Later that day, he described watching a flat-bottomed freight boat carrying members of his party as it attempted to reach the mouth of a river where he and his canoe had already landed. The wind blew against the boat, and waves crashed with such ferocity that it was difficult for people to hear each other speak. The crew of the flat boat worked unsuccessfully for half an hour, straining on the oars as they tried to reach shore. Then, in the blink of an eye, the waves surged and the vessel was driven onto a nearby beach. All the passengers were safe but soaked, as were all the provisions in the boat.[13]

Despite the danger and inconvenience, McKenney was clearly wonderstruck by the moodiness of the lake. "By sun-down the lake was literally a sea of billows. The sight is grand and awful!" he wrote.[14] McKenney also hinted at one of the dangerous peculiarities of the lake that several early visitors to Superior noted: storms and large swells occurred with little warning and often in the absence of wind. Alexander Mackenzie discussed the phenomenon, noting that he had observed frequently large waves that rose up and subsided "without any subsequent wind."[15]

David Thompson, who circumnavigated the lake twice as a surveyor and crossed its length many times, was known for his careful scientific observations. But he was clearly amazed when he witnessed a natural phenomenon on the lake in 1822. He was about fifty miles east of Fond du Lac, but west of Chequamegon Bay, when he and his party put ashore to eat lunch. The surface of the lake was perfectly calm, he said, when suddenly a large wave appeared about a mile offshore from which materialized waterspouts over ten feet high. Next, a series of waves began to crash against the shore, forcing the small party to quickly secure their canoes. They were unable to launch their vessels onto the lake for three hours. Yet, during the entire time—in fact for the whole day—the wind remained calm.[16]

In the twenty-first century, Lake Superior still demands respect. On a clear day in 2012, the commercial tour boat on which my wife, Judy, and I were passengers was unable to dock at Raspberry Island, one of the smaller of the Apostle Islands, because large waves had developed in the hour since we had embarked. The tour operators and representatives of the National Park Service, which manages the Apostle Islands National Lakeshore, deemed it too dangerous to dock at the small pier on the island.

Recreational and commercial vessels that travel the lake in the summer, and people who drive on the ice near its shorelines during the winter, are always advised to be wary of the rapidly changing conditions on the lake. It's no great surprise that Lake Superior still claims several lives each year.

During a period of at least four decades beginning near the end of the eighteenth century, Michel and Equaysayway Cadotte accepted the dangers and swiftly changing moods of Lake Superior in order to live and work on Madeline Island. They could have resided on the mainland, or, after retiring from the fur trade, they might have moved to some inland location far removed from the lake and its tantrums. Yet they remained on Madeline Island with several of their children, their grandchildren, and their Ojibwe relatives.

During most of the time they lived on Madeline Island, the site was a critical location for the fur trade at the western end of Lake Superior. It had occupied a similar importance a century earlier, when the French controlled the Upper Great Lakes and the region's fur trade. For the Ojibwe, who arrived at Chequamegon Bay from the east long before Michel and Equaysayway Cadotte made their home there, the island still has important cultural and spiritual significance.

As for Lake Superior itself, its importance to the fur trade cannot be overstated, whether during the years of French control, under the British regime, or later when the United States governed the southern shore. It was the key link in the aquatic highway that brought traders and their supplies to the backcountry and carried furs back to Montreal. Along its shores were some of the most significant trading posts and resupply depots of the era, providing access to the fur-bearing territories to the south, west, and northwest. Its minerals—particularly copper—enticed Europeans for centuries and were sought by Native peoples long before

Europeans arrived. The lake offered opportunities not only to acquire furs but to obtain food such as whitefish, wild rice, and maple sugar. It was viewed as militarily important by early Native people as well as by all of the Europeans and Americans who arrived later.

And the compound where Michel and Equaysayway Cadotte lived, traded, and raised a family? The place that today is just an isolated copse of trees? It was something much more in the early nineteenth century: "like a fairy scene, and everything about it is enchantment," McKenney wrote after visiting the Cadottes in 1826. It provoked thoughts of more cultured localities in a region that, to McKenney, was wild, uncomfortable, and more than a little frightening. As they neared the Cadotte compound, he reported, "[I]t looked green and had the evidences of civilized life, in houses, horses, and cattle, and fences," which McKenney had not seen since his party left Sault Ste. Marie several weeks earlier. Why, the log houses in the Cadotte compound even had lathe-and-plaster interiors, he reported with amazement.[17]

Lake Superior, which has the largest surface area of any body of fresh water in the world, and Madeline Island, forty-two square miles of wooded land near the western end of the lake, may seem like outliers to most Americans today, but they were the landscape, the source of livelihood, and the home locations for generations of Cadottes, their Ojibwe relatives, French Canadian colleagues, and competitors. They are natural characters that have a substantial role in this narrative.

CHAPTER 2

BEAVER HATS AND STEEL TRAPS

The merchant who joined the other pilgrims in Geoffrey Chaucer's *Canterbury Tales* was a bit of a dandy. He wore a then-fashionable forked beard, a multicolored cloak, and "upon his heed a Flaundryssh bevere hat."[1]

This reference to a stylish man of the late 1300s wearing a Flemish beaver hat is the first known written account suggesting not only that men at the time wore hats made of beaver pelts, but that beaver hats were fashionable.[2] That headwear trend would drive the fur trade for nearly five hundred years, although hat fashions would change repeatedly. The Native people of North America had been hunting and killing beaver long before Europeans began making beaver hats *haute couture*. While beaver skins were used to make blankets and clothing items, beaver pelts were especially prized for hat-making because the tiny barbs on the short underfur of the animal make the fur interlock, creating a felt that holds together better than that of most furs and is nearly waterproof, flexible, and durable.[3] Before Europeans arrived, Native people used a variety of methods to capture beaver, including placing nets under the ice and setting snares and deadfall systems.[4]

Fur trader and explorer David Thompson described Indians of the north country using spears, bows and arrows, and snares to capture beaver and other animals before the arrival of Europeans. But he claimed that they had limited success with such weapons: "Without Iron, Man is weak, very weak, but armed with Iron, he becomes the Lord of the Earth. . . . Thus armed, the houses of the Beavers were pierced through, the Dams cut through, and the water of the Ponds lowered . . . by which means [beaver] became an easy prey to the Hunter."[5]

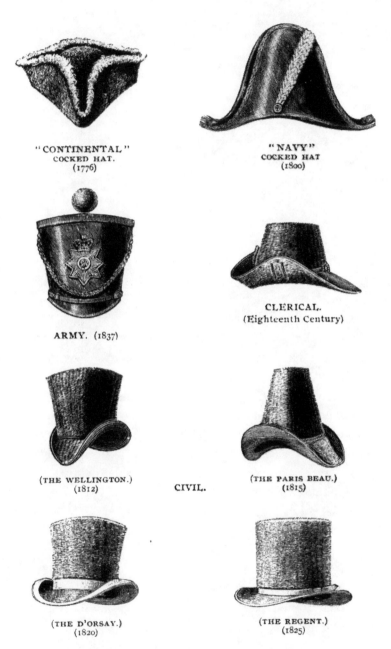

"CONTINENTAL"
COCKED HAT.
(1776)

"NAVY"
COCKED HAT
(1800)

ARMY. (1837)

CLERICAL.
(Eighteenth Century)

(THE WELLINGTON.)
(1812)

CIVIL.

(THE PARIS BEAU.)
(1815)

(THE D'ORSAY.)
(1820)

(THE REGENT.)
(1825)

MODIFICATIONS OF THE BEAVER HAT.

Beaver hat styles through the centuries. *CASTOROLOGIA, OR, THE HISTORY AND TRADITIONS OF THE CANADIAN BEAVER* BY HORACE T. MARTIN, 1892.

Beavers building a dam. WHI IMAGE ID 35065, GEORGE CATLIN DRAWING, 1859

From the very beginning, the fur trade was important to European settlers in much of North America, even among the Pilgrims who settled at Plymouth Rock. Through the 1620s and 1630s, much of the Plymouth economy was based on trapping or trading for furs and sending them to Europe. Furs were also important to Dutch settlers and independent English colonists from Massachusetts to Maine.[6] Nonetheless, areas around those settlements were soon cleared of beaver and other valuable fur-bearing animals. Consequently, the bulk of the fur trade soon was being conducted around the Great Lakes by the French, who called beaver "castors," and by the British from around Hudson Bay. Importantly, just after they arrived, the Europeans introduced a mechanism that revolutionized the fur trade: metal, spring-operated, leg-hold traps. When an animal stepped on the trap's steel plate, it released the spring, and the metal jaws snapped shut, catching the animal's foot or leg. Because the trap was staked to the ground (or underwater), the animal was usually held by the trap until the trapper arrived, who then shot or bludgeoned the animal to death.

Those metal traps were based on an ancient design, long used in Europe, Asia, and Africa, that employed wood, plant fibers, and animal sinews.

The first metal versions came into use around 1300, just a few decades be-fore Chaucer wrote his *Canterbury Tales*.[7] Metal leg-hold traps arrived in North America soon after the first Europeans, probably by the early 1600s. They were initially used by colonists to trap wolves that preyed on their livestock. Gradually, though, they began to be used to trap animals for precious furs as well.[8] By the eighteenth century, metal traps were simply a part of the merchandise associated with the fur trade. Many pages in the Cadotte family account book list traps among the goods purchased to be sent to backcountry posts.[9]

I have been an occasional hunter since I was a teenager, shooting squir-rels in the woods of our Wisconsin farm, then later pheasants, rabbit, and larger game. My only successful trapping experience, however, involved using a live trap to catch a feral kitten that had found its way into our ga-rage. I have no experience with conventional trapping techniques using leg-hold traps, so I sought out Erik Vosteen of Noble County, Indiana, who has been trapping since he was eight years old, initially using home-made traps of various types. He first used modern steel traps when he was fourteen. Vosteen has been a professional, state-licensed nuisance wildlife trapper in Indiana since 2012 and also the assistant director of the Great Lakes Traditional Arts Gathering on Drummond Island in Lake Huron, a backcountry clinic that examines how Native people traditionally hunted, gathered food, cooked, and constructed the necessities for their lives, in-cluding canoes and pre-European weapons.

Vosteen has described his own evolution as a trapper: "I have been in-terested in hand-made traps from natural materials since childhood, and learned to make several when I was quite young, and managed to catch animals ranging from mice to raccoons in them. As for snares, I use them every day. They are my favorite beaver restraint. They have many advan-tages—they are no danger to humans, they have no "snap" action to scare animals if they miss, and they can be very selective to reduce nontarget catches."[10]

Still, "leg-hold traps," which Vosteen says should properly be called "foot-hold traps," have many advantages over other means of capturing animals. "Versatility is the most attractive attribute. They are adaptable to many situations," Vosteen explains. They are also more easily concealed than other styles of traps. Additionally, they can be prepared quickly and set on site. This kind of trap can be used to hold animals unharmed and alive, so that the animal can be released if need be. "I released a Canada Goose from a large beaver foothold trap a few days ago, completely un-harmed," he says. "It quickly rejoined its flock in the middle of the lake and flew away with them minutes later."

Vosteen rejects the notion that foot-hold or leg-hold traps are inher-ently inhumane: "Seventy percent of the animals I find alive in traps are calm and relaxed, often even sleeping. The other 30 percent are just pac-ing. They get excited when I approach, but that is the worst of it." Some organizations, however, argue that such traps are cruel. For instance, the American Humane Society calls the trap "so inhumane that it has been banned in 65 countries but not in the United States."[11]

By the mid-1840s, the massive international market for men's beaver hats had largely evaporated as fashion trends changed. But that doesn't mean beaver hats have disappeared entirely. One can still find many cowboy hats and fedoras that are advertised as "beaver felt." Many of the cheaper hats are actually rabbit or some blend of rabbit and beaver.

To obtain the pelts for those hats, trapping remains a major activity in much of the United States and Canada. And, although most of the mink used in fur coats today are raised on farms, beaver are still caught by trap-ping, as are many other animals, including muskrats, raccoons, foxes, and coyotes. North American Fur Auctions, a Toronto organization that traces its roots back to the Hudson's Bay Company, holds fur auctions three or four times each year.[12]

Beaver hats were clearly worn in Chaucer's time, but they weren't the dominant form of male headwear. The same is true today. However, beaver-felt hats are still around, and demand for them continues to drive a significant amount of trapping.

CHAPTER 3

THE OJIBWE AND THE CADOTTES

Unlike some of the Native people that Europeans met to the east, such as the Huron and members of the Iroquois Confederacy, who often lived in semi-permanent villages, the Ojibwe, Odawa, Cree, and others who were considered Anishinaabe moved seasonally and regularly divided into small family bands to hunt, trap for furs, make maple sugar, and collect wild rice. What's more, even those family bands could change with different situations.

As Anishinaabe author and historian Michael Witgen explains, "It's not that the Anishinaabe had no sense of themselves as a people, but rather that to be Anishinaabe could mean different things in different places . . . Anishinaabe bands accepted the need to transform their collective identity to fit the circumstances on the ground." That could mean joining relatives at Sault Ste. Marie to harvest whitefish in the St. Mary's River; heading to Chequamegon Bay to trade at this "vital crossroads village that connected a transcontinental trading system;" or traveling farther north and west to visit, hunt, and trade with Native people living near such places as Rainy Lake or Lake Winnipeg.[1]

Exactly when the Ojibwe first arrived at the western end of Lake Superior and made Madeline Island their seasonal home has been a matter of debate among scholars and historians for some time. However, there is little question that the island has special significance for the Ojibwe. According to Anishinaabe author Thomas Peacock, Madeline Island "is the great homeland of the Ojibwe. Most of our Ojibwe ancestors originally came from Madeline Island."[2] In 1831, Henry Rowe Schoolcraft, who lived among the Ojibwe and married an Ojibwe-Irish woman, recognized Madeline Island as "the focus from which, as radii from a centre, the ancient population emigrated; and the interior bands consequently look back to it with something of the feelings of parental relations."[3]

A large encampment existed on and around the island in 1665 when Jesuit priest Claude Allouez first visited Chequamegon Bay to establish a mission at the western end of Lake Superior. He wrote that "this part of the Lake where we have halted is between two large villages and forms a kind of center for all the nations of these regions," and also that there were some two thousand people living in forty-five to fifty large dwellings, with several smaller villages farther inland. Allouez also noted that people moved continuously among the different sites for various activities. A few years later, Jesuits described a multitude of people from different Native groups gathered around Chequamegon,[4] but none of these was a permanent encampment. Most of the people involved, including the Ojibwe, would leave in small family or clan groups in the winter to hunt, trade, and gather furs.[5]

While it's impossible to pinpoint a specific year when the Ojibwe first arrived, historians like William Warren, Michel and Equaysayway's grandson, have tried to settle on a general time period. In the late 1840s, Warren interviewed Ojibwe elders in Leech Lake, Minnesota, and at La Pointe on Madeline Island, including his grandmother; his uncle, Michel Cadotte Jr.; and his great uncle, Great Buffalo.[6] In his seminal book on the Ojibwe, *History of the Ojibway People*, Warren put the group's arrival at Lake Superior and the Chequamegon region in the late 1400s, based on what the Ojibwe elders told him during interviews. The stories recounted to him told of a large group of Algonquin-speaking Indians leaving their home near the mouth of the St. Lawrence River and the shores of the Atlantic Ocean. Led by a great seashell—or Megis—that appeared, disappeared, and then reappeared years or even generations later, the Indians were led steadily westward to locations that would become their homes.[7]

In Warren's telling, the three groups of Algonquin or Anishinaabe people separated near the Straits of Michilimackinac, between Lake Michigan and Lake Huron, with the Odawa remaining in the area between Montreal and Michilimackinac, and the Potawatomi heading south to the lands we now know as Michigan and Illinois. Only the Ojibwe continued northwest to Sault Ste. Marie and Lake Superior, he said. At the Sault, they split again, with several bands heading west along the north shore of Lake Superior

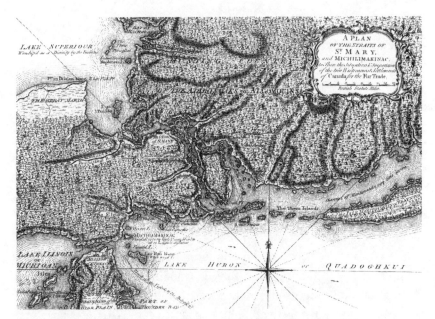

A map of the plan for the Straits of St. Mary and Michilimackinac from 1761. WHI IMAGE ID 43947

to become ancestors of what are now the Canadian Ojibwe bands. Others remained at the Sault and established a sizeable seasonal camp. They were present when the first Frenchmen arrived, who therefore called them "Saulteurs."[8] However, another sizeable group of Ojibwe continued westward along Lake Superior's southern shore, still guided by the Megis, until the symbol settled on Madeline Island.

Canadian Anishinaabe author and historian Basil Johnston, writing in the late twentieth century, offered a similar, though abbreviated, description of the Ojibwe/Anishinaabe migration: "Led ever westward by the sea shell, the prodigal Anishnabeg [Anishinaabeg] after many months at last arrived in their own land . . . Some say that the Anishnabeg settled at Boweting (Sault St. Marie); others said that the Anishnabeg went further west establishing their homes at Moningwakauning (now La Pointe in Wisconsin)." To honor this migration, a small sea shell is used in the important Anishinaabeg spiritual ceremony known as the Midewiwin. Johnston wrote: "[T]he little shell symbolized the return to the true path to find fulfilment [sic] and to resume purpose."[9]

Peacock and Johnston both explain that Ojibwe oral history tells of a time when the Anishinaabe lived at some unknown location in the west and traveled eastward to the Atlantic Ocean, where they dispersed, became different people, and took on new names. That journey, by a people known as the Lenni Lenape, is recorded on bark tablets and song sticks and is known as the Wallum Olum, according to Peacock. The record of the journey on bark tablets is one of the oldest written records in North America, "dating back before 1600 b.c."[10]

Warren wrote that in 1842 he was shown "a curious family register" by Ojibwe Chief Tugwaugaunay, his great uncle and Equaysayway's brother. It was created on a copper plate and used deep indentations to mark the eight generations that had passed since the Ojibwe arrived in the Chequamegon region. The symbol of a man with a hat on his head, drawn near one of the indentations, indicated when the first Europeans arrived. As Warren wrote: "This mark occurred in the third generation, leaving five generations which had passed" since the first contact with the French.[11] Warren calculated the average length of an Ojibwe generation at forty years, and based on this calculation, he wrote in the early 1850s that it had been 360 years since the Ojibwe settled on Madeline Island—about 1490—and 240 years since their first contact with Europeans.

For many contemporary Ojibwe writers, larger time spans are more useful than exact dates for the arrival of their ancestors at Lake Superior and nearby regions. According to Anton Treuer, "For hundreds of years, the Ojibwe people had been slowly migrating westward. Even before the arrival of Euroamericans, spiritual and economic incentives had propelled the Ojibwe and their close allies the Odaawaa (Ottawa) and Boodawaadamii (Potawatomi) to push westward through the Great Lakes into present-day Wisconsin, Minnesota and Ontario."[12]

In a six-volume text for the US Bureau of Indian Affairs published in 1851, Schoolcraft wrote that the Algonquin—a linguistic group that includes the Ojibwe, Odawa, and Potawatomi—arrived at the Great Lakes after having been forced out of their previous homes around the mouth of the St. Lawrence River by the Iroquois. "It is not known when they first reached these lakes," Schoolcraft said, but he estimated that they arrived at Lakes Huron and Michigan early in the sixteenth century.[13] The same document reported that by 1653, the Ojibwe lived at Sault Ste. Marie "and on the shores of Lake Superior."[14]

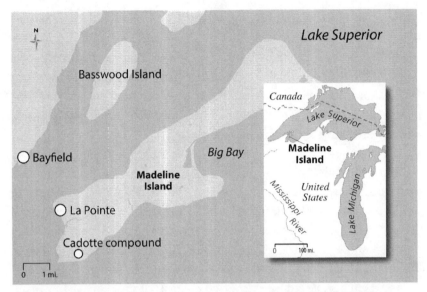

The Cadotte compound was located near the southeast corner of Madeline Island, while the modern village of La Pointe, established in the 1830s, was to the northwest.
ROBERT GARCIA

Regardless of when they first arrived at the western end of Lake Superior, the Ojibwe prospered on and around their Madeline Island homeland for many generations, engaging in fishing, hunting, and some limited agriculture, making sugar, and gathering rice in areas south of Chequamegon Bay. In Ojibwe oral tradition, there was "an extensive and dominant Ojibwe village reaching back into prehistory."[15] Long after the island village had been abandoned by most Ojibwe sometime in the late seventeenth century, according to Warren, signs of that large village were reportedly still present. As Warren noted, "When my maternal grandfather, Michel Cadotte, first located a trading post on this island" around 1800, "these different signs and vestiges were still discernible."[16] Other authors point out that Madeline Island has for generations been a center of Ojibwe spiritual practices.[17] The island, therefore, is critical to understanding the concept of an Ojibwe homeland.[18]

For much of the year, the Ojibwe formed in small bands based on family or clan connections and migrated to different locations to hunt and trade, make maple sugar, and gather wild rice. Seasonal rounds were a way to survive in the harsh northern climate. However, their seasonal movements, according to historian Michael Witgen, "did not follow a set pattern, but reflected strategic decisions designed to allow the maximum harvest of seasonal resources within a given territory." As he goes on to explain, "The migration patterns of the Anishinaabe peoples actually required a sophisticated understanding of the seasonal availability of resources and carrying capacity of the land. The movement of nomadic peoples in North America was not random, nor was this life a result of the lack of social development," even though European and American observers, from the earliest contact into the twenty-first century, often viewed seasonal migration patterns as evidence the Native people were "politically unformed and culturally primitive."[19]

The Jesuits who arrived in the region in the seventeenth century preferred to deal with large communities of Native people, such as those they found at Chequamegon and at Sault Ste. Marie during the summer and autumn months, according to anthropologist Howard Paap, because such concentrated sites made it easier for priests to reach a large number of potential Catholic converts than if they had to travel to small, outlying sites. Also, the Jesuits didn't really comprehend the importance of the small groups that migrated with the resources they needed.[20] As Anishinaabe author Erik M. Redix notes, "even during the summer months, village sites could be devoid of people due to labor activities such as gathering berries or social events in other communities." He pointed out that in July of 1831, Schoolcraft passed through a village on the Namekagon River in northwestern Wisconsin and reported, "We found it completely deserted, according to the custom of the Indians, who after planting gardens, leave them to go on summer hunts, gather berries, etc." Additionally, Redix has said that nineteenth-century reports of one seasonal village at Long Lake, also in northwestern Wisconsin, gave different locations for that village: "It's likely the community occupied two different sites on Long Lake over the course of the nineteenth century due to exhausting firewood."[21] When French explorers and religious leaders first encountered the Ojibwe and their allies in the early seventeenth century, they were surprised to discover the Native people were so mobile and their band organizations continually changing. "[T]hey continually divide themselves up" to fish and hunt in the surrounding forests and lakes, complained Jesuit missionary Jerome Lalemont in 1642 about the Anishinaabeg he found around Lake Nipissing.[22]

It was an issue that would reoccur, not just with the French, but also with the British and Americans who arrived in Anishinaabewaki, the homeland of the Anishinaabe people. The French and later British and American authorities sought relentlessly to attach collective identities to these groups of people, to establish a European idea of nation to the groups. But, while these people identified themselves generally as Anishinaabe, or Ojibwe for many of those living around Lake Superior, they more closely identified with their family bands and clan designation. The attempts to attach fixed identities to these people as members of the Odawa, Ojibwe, Cree, or other nations were, Witgen has written, "bound to create invented and unreliable social and political categories."[23] Still, over time, the largest group of Native people living around Lake Superior, from Sault Ste. Marie on the east to Fond du Lac at the west end and north into Canada, came to be identified as Ojibwe, though the French called them Saulteurs, Sauteurs, or Sauteaux.

The Ojibwe were among many Indian nations that participated in the fur trade around the Great Lakes and in Canada. In the Lake Superior region, including what is now known as northern Wisconsin, northern Minnesota, and Michigan's Upper Peninsula, the Ojibwe were the most important and most prominent nation in that trade. The Cadotte family was closely linked to these Ojibwe, both by commerce and by kinship. For example, Athanasie, the wife of Jean-Baptiste Cadot Sr., was a close relative of Madjeckewiss, the Ojibwe leader who led an attack on English forces at Michilimackinac in 1763 but later became an ally of the British. Athanasie's Ojibwe name was Equawaice—not to be confused with Equaysayway, who was married to Michel Cadotte. She was born in the Lake Nipissing region northwest of Lake Huron.[24] Through Athanasie, Michel and Jean-Baptiste Jr. were first cousins of Nodin, a chief at Snake River in northern Wisconsin, and of Nodin's brother Le Trappe, a warrior. They were also second cousins of Great Marten, chief of the area around the Wisconsin River, as well as Great Buffalo of Madeline Island.[25]

In addition to those connections, Equaysayway was a member of the important Crane clan on Madeline Island. The clan system was critical in tribal organizations. Clans were groups of people related through their fathers' bloodlines. Animal names, or totems, a corruption of the Anishinaabe word *doodem*, were used to distinguish one clan from another.

As historian Edmund Jefferson Danziger Jr. has explained, "Chippewa families, whether in villages or on the move, shared . . . a tribal-wide network of totemic clans."[26] Anishinaabe historian Patty Loew explains that there were originally seven clans: Crane, Loon, Fish, Bear, Marten, Deer, and Bird.[27] However, Warren listed as many as twenty-one different clan designations in his *History of the Ojibway People*.[28]

Tribal leaders usually came from the Crane and Loon clans, "and their shared leadership provided important checks and balances," according to Loew.[29] Intellectuals and mediators came from the Fish Clan, while the Marten Clan provided warriors. The Deer Clan members were poets, and the Bird Clan provided spiritual leaders. Bear Clan members could be village protectors and healers. Ojibwe were prohibited from marrying within their own clan. Another Anishinaabe author, Anton Treuer, put it this way: "Among the Ojibwe, clans defined the core of one's spiritual essence. Just as *odé* [heart] was the heart of one's physical being, *doodem* was the heart of one's metaphysical being. Originally, only Ojibwe people from certain families of the *maang doodem* (loon clan) and *ajijaak doodem* (crane clan) could be chiefs."[30]

Treuer also explains that there were several different types of leaders among the Ojibwe. Civil or political leadership positions "were almost invariably held by men. The authority to assume civil leadership most often was inherited through the father's line." Religious leaders, although they didn't hold hereditary posts, "received the highest esteem and respect, and it usually took many years of hard work to achieve this high status." Moreover, both women and men could become religious leaders, "and many ceremonies required the guidance of both a male and a female leader." Finally, there was military leadership, almost entirely male, which was "more fluid and more easily attained than religious or political leadership." War chiefs were respected but were not as important as civil and religious leaders.[31]

By the mid-nineteenth century, the importance of the clan system in Ojibwe leadership had begun to diminish, and a new leadership system based on charismatic and politically powerful chieftains was starting to replace it.[32] Even so, clan connections were still important and honored by most Ojibwe, and they have continued to shape both spirituality and kinship connections to this day. These connections to the Ojibwe who lived along the southern shore of Lake Superior and in northern Wisconsin, Michigan, and Minnesota were critical to the Cadotte family's ability to operate successfully in the Ojibwe world.

These interior sites, with their access to abundant wild rice, fish, wildlife, and other resources, were key locations for several bands of Ojibwe and others who likely visited them occasionally. But Madeline Island and the village of La Pointe remained important to the Ojibwe—beyond their spiritual and ancestral connections to the island—into the late 1800s. One reason was that that's where annuities paid to most Wisconsin Ojibwe bands under a variety of treaties were dispersed for many decades. Also, a number of treaties between the US government and the Ojibwe as well as several other Native nations were negotiated on the island, usually when large numbers of Native people had gathered there as part of their seasonal migration pattern. When American authorities began pushing those treaties, demanding land and resource concessions from the Ojibwe, those seasonal migration patterns were among the factors that made negotiating treaties difficult for the Americans.[33] Treaty officials had to hold multiple negotiating sessions in different locations or delay sessions for many days to try to get important leaders from different bands together. Additionally, whether intentionally or accidentally, they often misconstrued the nature of Ojibwe affiliations, attempting to combine all Ojibwe groups as a single nation rather than a conglomeration of small bands and family and clan associations.

Today, the Ojibwe are one of the largest groups of Indigenous people north of Mexico, with different bands and tribal villages stretching from Ontario in Canada to Montana in the United States. The largest concentrations of Ojibwe are in Michigan, Wisconsin, and Minnesota. Currently, nineteen bands reside on the south shores of Lake Superior in Wisconsin, as well as in northern Minnesota and Michigan.[34]

No matter when in the distant past the Ojibwe arrived at the western end of Lake Superior or when they took up seasonal residence on and around Madeline Island along with other Native people, they were there when the first Europeans arrived in the form of French explorers, unlicensed traders, and Jesuit priests.

CHAPTER 4

SNOWSHOES ON THE TRAIL

On a brisk morning in February, my son, Derek, and I set off on snowshoes on the North Country Trail along Lake Owen in the Chequamegon National Forest of northwestern Wisconsin. Part of the trail parallels an ancient fur-trade route.[1]

This old trail was probably used more than two centuries ago by traders like Michel and Equaysayway and Michel's brother, Jean-Baptiste Jr. The trail in question leads from the southern end of Chequamegon Bay southwest toward territory where the Cadottes and others spent winters trading and trapping.

We were roughly following a trail included on a map in Hamilton Nelson Ross's 1960 book, *La Pointe: Village Outpost on Madeline Island*, as well as an 1884 map showing early railroads, wagon roads, and trails south of Chequamegon Bay.[2] Both indicate trails or roads near Lake Owen. In the legend accompanying his map, Ross wrote that the trail from Lake Superior past Lake Owen, and another trail to Lac du Flambeau, were "probably used by the French in the eighteenth century and by Indians before that time."[3] There is a good possibility, though no firm proof exists, that Michel and Equaysayway used portions of this trail as they set out to establish winter quarters not far from Dakota Territory in the autumn of 1788.

Our trek occurred on a sparklingly clear day. It was relatively warm for early February in the southern Lake Superior region, with temperatures in the mid-teens and almost no wind. We were fortunate in our timing. A week later, the temperature dropped below zero and remained there for nearly ten days.

We saw little wildlife as we snowshoed, although there were plenty of deer, rabbit, and squirrel tracks. We startled a grouse into flight at one point along the trail. Nonetheless, we snowshoed only a small portion of the trail—approximately five miles—which took us just over three hours. Rather than attempt to retrace the fur traders' entire route, we hoped to gain a bit of insight into the territory they traversed and the work they endured while traveling in the winter.

We hiked through a variegated landscape of black lines—shadows cast by trees—and bright snow. Lake Owen was visible occasionally to our right—first beside us, then hidden behind trees or low hills as the trail meandered near its shore. The snow muffled all sound as the trail wound among slender birch trees, balsam fir, and towering pines, as well as large oaks.

My son and I were equipped with modern aluminum-and-nylon snowshoes for our trip, which are much lighter and more maneuverable than the old, traditional snowshoes with wooden frames and rawhide webbing. I own a pair of the old-style shoes that I have used infrequently over the years. Because of their length—55 inches—they actually work better in deep, unpacked snow than the 30-inch modern shoes. The traditional snowshoes had the added advantage that they could be manufactured and repaired on the trail with materials readily available to fur traders and Native Americans.

The French called these snowshoes *raquettes* or *raquettes de neige* because they reminded them of the tennis racquets that had first appeared in France in the late 1400s. In 1603, French explorer Samuel de Champlain made one of the first documented references to snowshoes in the New World, explaining their importance: "In the winter when the snows come heavy, [the Indians] make a kind of raquette which is two to three times larger than those in France. Using them they travel on the snow without plunging through; otherwise they could not hunt, nor many places go at all."[4] Pierre-Esprit Radisson also mentioned snowshoes in a journal of his trip that he wrote in English for King Charles II of England. He was discussing the situation as spring approached on Chequamegon Bay, where he and his brother-in-law spent the winter: "In the morning it was a pleasure to walke [sic], because we could go without racketts." Cold temperatures from the previous night made the snow temporarily hard enough to walk upon in conventional boots. But as temperatures warmed throughout the day,

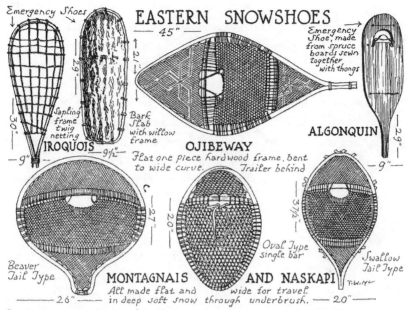

Emergency Shoes

EASTERN SNOWSHOES
— 45" —

Emergency Shoe, made from spruce boards sewn together with thongs

Sapling frame twig netting

Bark Slab with willow frame

IROQUOIS — 9½" —

OJIBEWAY
Flat one piece hardwood frame, bent to wide curve. Trailer behind

ALGONQUIN

Beaver Jail Type

Oval Type single bar

Swallow Jail Type

MONTAGNAIS — 26" — All made flat and in deep soft snow

AND NASKAPI — 20" — wide for travel through underbrush.

From The Canadian Snowshoe, by J. Drummond. Transactions Royal Society of Canada, 1916.

The Ojibwe style of snowshoe, highlighted in this drawing, was probably the most prominent style in use in the region. LIBRARY AND ARCHIVES CANADA/CHARLES WILLIAM JEFFERYS FONDS/ACC. NO. 1972-26-229

snowshoes became a necessity. And when it grew really warm, Radisson discovered that attempting to use snowshoes when the snow was wet and melting significantly increased the hardship. He estimated the slush added thirty pounds to the snowshoes.[5]

The snow was not deep on the February day we snowshoed near Lake Owen, so the light modern shoes worked fine. Even so, it was hard work. My son was thirty-six at the time, and I was sixty-two. Both of us were in reasonably good physical condition, and I had snowshoed in the mountains near my home in Colorado that winter to prepare for the Wisconsin trip. Still, at the end of three hours, my hips, knees, and ankles were sore, and I was exhausted. But at least I had not suffered any of the severe problems that often struck early travelers.

Alexander Henry, who traveled to Lake Superior in the 1760s and became a friend and partner of Jean-Baptiste Cadot Sr., noted one such problem in his description of a trek he made in March of 1763 to get from

Michilimackinac to Sault Ste. Marie, taking an overland shortcut. The two-day journey through the woods was not difficult, but he arrived at his destination "troubled with a disorder known as the snow-shoe evil." It was caused by strain on the tendons of the leg created by the weight of the snowshoes, and it resulted in severe inflammation of the lower leg and ankle. However, Henry said he declined to be treated with a backcountry remedy that involved placing a hot ember on the leg "and leaving it there till the flesh is burnt to the nerve."[6] Winter travelers "often suffered from *mal de racquet*," a kind of "painful inflammation at the ankle, [specifically] of the tendon that flexes the great toe."[7] Newcomers to the country nearly always suffered from the malady after their first lengthy trek on snow-shoes, for which the only true remedy was rest.

Even when they didn't cause lameness, snowshoes were troublesome. David Thompson, who spent nearly thirty years in the fur trade, work-ing first for the Hudson's Bay Company and later as a partner with the North West Company, described winter travel in this fashion when he was at Hudson Bay: "From the end of October to the end of April every step we walk is in Snow Shoes." Although the Native people who visited the trading center maneuvered easily on the snowshoes, Thompson reported that some of the traders and other workers at the post viewed them as "a sad encumbrance." They suffered sore feet, sprained ankles, and "many a tumble in the snow" trying to use the awkward foot gear.[8]

George Nelson, who began working as a trader in northwestern Wis-consin in the early nineteenth century, wrote of his experience with snow-shoes in 1804, while trading at his post on the Yellow River. Like Radisson, he found them especially awkward when melting began and water formed under the surface of the snow or upon the ice.[9] However, Nelson also noted indirectly the importance of snowshoes in the rugged country. Before starting on a journey, he hired the Native American wife of one of his French Canadian *voyageurs* (those who transported goods to trading posts but did no trading of their own) to make a pair of snowshoes for another member of his party who had none and therefore couldn't travel across the snow-covered terrain.[10]

Our snowshoe trip south of Lake Superior on a sunny day in the twenty-first century was a far cry from the long-distance travel, in brutal cold with life-threatening consequences, that the Cadottes and their Indian partners often engaged in during the winter. Still, our jaunt took us along a portion of a route likely used by the Cadottes and other fur traders, by Indians, missionaries, and explorers. It gave us an appreciation of the difficult journeys Michel and Equasayway and their Ojibwe friends and family members regularly undertook during many years in the forests of northern Wisconsin and in the Lake Superior region.

CHAPTER 5

THE FRENCH ARRIVE

Exactly when the first Frenchman paddled a vessel on the waters of Lake Superior or trod along its tree-lined shores is unknown. Étienne Brûlé, among the first European explorers known to have traveled beyond the St. Lawrence River into modern-day Canada, probably visited the lake sometime early in the seventeenth century, perhaps as early as 1621 or 1623. But Brûlé left little record of his explorations, and we know about them mostly from others.[1]

Pierre-Esprit Radisson and his brother-in-law Médard Chouart, Sieur des Groseilliers explored the lake in 1659–1660. The two men spent several months along the shores of Chequamegon Bay and reportedly built a small wooden cabin and stockade there before heading inland and spending time with several Native nations, including Ojibwe, possibly at Lac Courte Oreilles. The two Frenchmen returned to Québec, where they had started their journey, late in 1660.

Later, Radisson wrote a journal of their adventures, providing one of the earliest accounts of a European's visit to the region. But he also made it clear that he and his brother-in-law weren't the first French people in the area. When they arrived in the region of the big lake and "the nation of the Sault," or Ojibwe, Radisson wrote, "We found some french men that came up with us, who thanked us kindly for to come and visit them."[2] That cryptic note is one indication that numerous other adventurers and *coureurs de bois* also traveled through the region and traded with Natives for furs. But no records of their travels have survived.[3]

One such adventurer was Mathurin Cadot, whose surname was sometimes spelled "Cadeau," although he didn't arrive on the shores of Lake

Superior until at least a decade after Radisson and Groseilliers. The grandfather of Jean-Baptiste Cadot Sr. and great-grandfather of Michel and Jean-Baptiste Jr., Mathurin Cadot was born in France in 1649 and became the founder of the Cadotte clan in North America. It's not known when he arrived in New France—which would later become Canada—but official records show he was married in Montreal in 1688 to Marie-Catherine Durand.[4] He is believed to have operated as an unlicensed coureur de bois during the 1670s and early 1680s. In 1686, he obtained a *congé*, or official license, to legally trade with Indians in the backcountry. Trading mainly with the Odawa, Cadot continued to work in the fur trade until 1690. Then he turned his business over to his wife's half-brother and retired to an agricultural life near Montreal. He and Catherine had a daughter and four sons, including Jean-Francois, the father of Jean-Baptiste Cadot Sr. Mathurin lived to the age of eighty, dying at Bastican, about 110 miles northeast of Montreal.[5]

For most of the period in which the French were exploring steadily westward—to the far shores of Lake Superior and beyond—English colonists were settling the Atlantic Coast of North America south of New France. But with few exceptions, they didn't extend their domain as far to the west as the French did during the seventeenth and early eighteenth centuries. It's reasonable to wonder: Why not?

Landscape. That's what Wisconsin historian Reuben Thwaites argued in 1890: "The central geographical fact to be remembered in connection with the history of New France is that the St. Lawrence [River] and the chain of Great Lakes which serve as its feeders furnish a natural highway to the heart of the continent."[6] A map of North America confirms Thwaites's reasoning. The St. Lawrence River to Montreal, then the Ottawa River and its tributaries provide a direct water route, albeit one with multiple portages, from the Atlantic Ocean to Lake Superior. Farther south, in what would become the United States, no such direct east-west water route existed until the 1830s, when the Erie Canal, then later the Ohio and Erie Canal, connected the lower Great Lakes and the Ohio River Valley to water traffic from the Hudson River and the Atlantic.

And heading west by ground transportation, the preferred method for many emigrants in early-nineteenth-century America, was difficult. As historian Susan Sleeper-Smith explains, "The rivers that transported

Lithograph of voyageurs making a portage, 1879. WHI IMAGE ID 7009

the French to the western Great Lakes [to southern Michigan and Indiana] became formidable obstacles to the overland westward movement . . . Even the most determined Americans were thwarted by seasonal rains and floods the transformed swamplands and rivers into insurmountable barriers."[7] Where it wasn't blocked by flooding rivers and swamplands, the route west for British colonists and later American settlers was thwarted by mountain ranges and extreme distances between major river drainages.[8]

The landscape wasn't the only obstacle for the English colonists. Initially they had fewer contacts with various Native people around Lake Superior and the interior northwest of the lake because they hadn't spent much time there. That began to change after the formation of the Hudson's Bay Company by royal charter of English King Charles II in 1670. Soon, English trading posts on the western side of the bay began attracting different Native people from the interior west and the northern shores of Lake Superior and began to pose significant competition to the French fur trade.[9]

Both the French and English faced opposition from the region's Native people, especially the Iroquois Confederacy, throughout much of the seventeenth and early eighteenth centuries, but the French were able to utilize a more northerly route through the Great Lakes—at least Lakes Huron, Michigan, and Superior—that avoided the heart of Iroquois country.[10] However, the English, and Dutch colonists in New York, eventually allied themselves with the Iroquois nations, creating still more problems for the French regime.[11]

The Native people of the Lake Superior region, including the Ojibwe, knew of the Europeans and took economic advantage of their presence even before they met their first Frenchmen. Through the Huron, Odawa, and other nations, the Ojibwe learned of the newcomers and engaged in third-party trading that allowed them to acquire valuable French goods, including wool and cotton fabrics, pots, knives, and guns. They also traded with nations farther to the west, notably their sometime enemies, the Dakota, for additional furs to send to the French.[12] Sometime after 1642, the Ojibwe became more directly involved in the fur trade, traveling annually to Montreal to sell furs directly to the French and to obtain trade goods from them.[13]

Even so, Ojibwe trading trips east did not last long. Violent fighting between the Iroquois on one side, and the Huron and their allies on the other, made travel on the eastern Great Lakes and lower St. Lawrence River dangerous. In fact, the French fur trade became a trickle in the middle of the seventeenth century as the Iroquois wiped out villages of Indians allied with the French. In 1648 and 1649, elements of the Iroquois Confederacy destroyed several Huron villages in what's now Ontario, including St. Joseph and St. Ignace. The nearby Jesuit headquarters at Ste. Marie, in Ontario, was burned by the priests in 1649, who preferred that over its potential desecration. As a result of these repeated attacks, most of the Huron moved south and west, to the Green Bay region and the southern shores of Lake Superior.[14]

Things began to change, however, when adventurous and enterprising French Canadians began to take the trade to the Indians.[15] Some of those entrepreneurs may have been the unnamed Frenchmen that Radisson reported encountering near Lake Superior in 1659 and 1660. As a result of their trading, Lake Superior became a key part of the French commercial enterprise by the 1670s and 1680s. Native people along the big lake's shores eventually formed alliances with the French government. French explorers mapped rivers of the region, as well as the lake itself, and they established trading posts throughout the area. French priests followed the unauthorized traders, building missions and seeking religious converts.[16]

However, as they did throughout the Western Hemisphere, the Europeans brought something else to the Native people: diseases for which the Indians had no immunity. During the mid-1630s, the first epidemics of European disease are believed to have wreaked havoc on the Natives of the Great Lakes region. One estimate is that 60 to 70 percent of all of the Indians there died within several decades.[17]

Direct contact with Europeans wasn't required for disease to decimate Indian populations. In many cases, epidemics of European diseases probably preceded the arrival of white men to the backcountry. Native people themselves likely transported the viruses from coastal areas to other nations who lived far removed from Europeans. As author Charles Mann explains in his book, *1491: New Revelations of the Americas before Columbus*, Inca villages in South America, Aztec communities in Mexico, and Native communities in other parts of the Western Hemisphere all likely experienced devastating smallpox epidemics even though the residents of these areas "had never seen a white man."[18]

Despite such catastrophes, the fur trade continued, albeit in fits and starts. That was due in part to conflicts with warring nations. But it was also caused by the policies of the French government. French kings and their allies granted commercial fur-trade licenses to those whom the aristocracy favored, and they gave autocratic control to colonial governors. They viewed unlicensed traders, the coureurs de bois, as smugglers and adopted strict measures to try to curtail their activities. King Louis XIV and his ministers had a penchant for interfering in the fur trade and sought to repress all commercial activities that didn't involve merchants in their privileged circles. New France continually experienced royal micromanagement even in relatively insignificant affairs.[19]

Perhaps the greatest mistake committed by the government was the decision not to reward Radisson and Groseilliers for the discoveries they made in the mid-1600s and the rich cache of furs they brought back to Montreal. Instead, the French Crown rejected their advice for establishing a new route to reach the fur-bearing lands and punished them for violating the royal decrees against backcountry trading. The government also assessed excessive taxes on them and seized most of the goods they had collected on their voyage.

Dismayed at this treatment, the two explorers, with the aid of New England merchants, took their idea for expanding the fur trade through Hudson Bay to King Charles II of England. After some negotiations and interruptions, Charles approved the dispatch of two small ships to explore Hudson Bay, and in 1670, he approved a charter for a new company that was granted rights to a third of what is now Canada. Thus was the Hudson's Bay Company formed. It soon became one of the largest commercial enterprises in the world, and it remains the oldest continuously operating company in North America.[20] A decade after its founding, Radisson and Groseilliers abandoned the Hudson's Bay Company and returned to the service of the French government in order to open a trading post near the Nelson River west of Hudson Bay, after the English company refused to consider the project. Then, a few years after that, Radisson reverted his loyalty to the English.[21]

The Hudson's Bay Company began in territory that was nominally claimed by France but that the French were unable to control militarily. By 1713, with the Treaty of Utrecht, France officially relinquished its claim to Hudson Bay and its drainages, allowing the British to use those territories.[22] Even before that agreement, however, the Hudson's Bay Company made immense profits off resources that were claimed by France.[23]

For more than one hundred years after it was created, the Hudson's Bay Company refused to open trading posts in the interior of Canada. Instead, company officials expected Indians of various nations to come to York Factory, and later Churchill Factory, to trade on the shores of the bay. The system worked reasonably well, and the company became an economic force due to its trade, but this system also left the door open for independent French traders, some with royal licenses but most working outside the law, to travel into the interior and establish trade directly with Indians. According to Thwaites, corruption was rampant among those in power, with officials at many levels all "consider[ing] the public treasury and the resources of the colony as a source of individual profit."[24]

Then there was the *seigneurial* system, which granted large blocks of property to favorites of the king—be they nobles or commoners—who were supposed to put the land into production by leasing it to small farmers or *habitants*. It was essentially a feudal system that promoted class and economic divisions, but it did encourage the development of small farms.[25]

When Mathurin Cadot retired to a farm north of Montreal, he was considered a *habitant*, although he may have used money from his fur-trade years to purchase land rather than lease it. Three of his sons, led by the eldest, Jean-Francois, briefly engaged in the fur trade. Jean-Francois is known to have made only one trip to Michilimackinac, in 1712. His brothers René and Charles made a number of excursions to Michilimackinac in the early eighteenth century. They used proceeds from the fur business to acquire lands in the St. Lawrence region, which they turned into farms and homes where they raised their families.[26]

In the late 1700s, Alexander Mackenzie noted problems that French governance of the fur trade had created more than a century earlier. According to him, the independent traders, or coureurs de bois, with their propensity for using liquor to effect trades with the Indians and their own dissolute lifestyle, eventually ran afoul of the Jesuit priests who were attempting to establish missions and win Indian converts to Catholicism. The priests used their influence with the government to attempt to block the activities of these coureurs de bois, and soon no Frenchman could legally go into the backcountry to trade with the Indians unless he had a government license.[27]

However, Mackenzie added, the license system proved unsuccessful, largely because licenses were allotted based on who was in favor with the king or the governor of New France. Furthermore, few of those favored licensees wanted to travel into the backcountry themselves. So the license recipients were allowed to sell their permits to merchants, who contracted with the coureurs de bois to conduct the trading, and the same old problems returned. "[T]he remedy proved, in fact, worse than the disease," Mackenzie wrote.[28]

It wasn't the coureurs de bois who were to blame for the problems so much as the system that encouraged their illegal trading. Authorities in the Old Country were eager to get settlers in New France to take advantage of the area's resources—from timber to minerals to agriculture, as well as furs. Consequently, thousands of people emigrated from France to New France to join the labor force for the government's planned commercial activities.[29]

And yet, large numbers of the new emigrants deserted the settlements for the backcountry and the chance to join the fur trade, Mathurin Cadot among them. They could generally make more money in the fur trade than in farming and other endeavors, and they also had a greater chance of finding mates. There were so many more men than women in New France that, until roughly 1710, only about one out of seven men could expect to find a wife among the emigrant population. Mathurin Cadot, though, like many Frenchmen who took to the fur trade, found his spouse among those with Indian heritage. Marie-Catherine Durand Cadot had Huron ancestry.[30]

As Mackenzie noted, the *congé*, or license system, did little to control backcountry trade. Adventurous French Canadians were too impatient to wait for authorities to issue them a congé, especially when that might never occur if they hadn't curried favor with the governor. So they continued to leave the French settlements in large numbers to conduct their trade illegally.[31]

Despite the obstacles erected by the French government and opposition by some Native people to the fur traders' presence, the fur trade continued to grow under the French.[32] By the time the British defeated the French and assumed control of Canada in 1763, the French had established trading posts deep into the Saskatchewan River region, traveled to the Rocky Mountains, and learned about the Columbia River. They had also explored or established trading posts along all of the Great Lakes and their surrounding drainages, as well as the Mississippi and Ohio Rivers.[33]

Much of the credit for successful expansion of the trade is due to extraordinary men like Daniel Greysolon, Sieur du Lhut. His name is sometimes written as "Dulhut" or "du Luth," and he is the namesake of Duluth, Minnesota. In September 1678, he left Montreal secretly, en route to Lake Superior and farther west, to attempt to enact a peace treaty between the Dakota, Ojibwe, Fox, and others. He was partially successful. The Indians agreed to the peace he proposed, but they continued to engage in small-scale attacks on each other and on the French.[34]

Du Lhut was eventually forced to defend himself against charges that he violated the edict against going into the backcountry without permission to trade. He successfully argued that he had gone not to trade, but to negotiate a peace with the various nations, peace that would benefit New France.[35] Later, he established and operated the French fort at what would become Detroit, Michigan, and he helped raise a force of five hundred Indian warriors from among the western nations, including the Ojibwe, to support the French in fighting the Iroquois. He also engaged in the fur trade with his brother.[36]

Du Lhut wasn't the only important French explorer and adventurer who helped expand the fur trade. Nicholas Perrot spent nearly forty years traveling and living among the Indians of New France, fighting them at times, especially the Iroquois, but more often working toward peaceful solutions to disputes. He served as a hired guide and worker for the Jesuit missionaries, a coureur de bois, a licensed trader, and occasionally an agent for the government of New France. Jean Nicolet explored Lake Michigan and Green Bay in 1634, while trader Louis Joliet and Father Jacques Marquette followed a similar route beginning in 1673; unlike Nicolet, they reached the Mississippi River and traveled as far down the river as present-day St. Louis. Beginning in 1669, René-Robert Cavelier, Sieur de La Salle, traveled to lands farther south, including the Ohio River and the lower Mississippi.[37]

It wasn't just independent adventurers who helped extend the fur trade and make connections with the Native people, however. Despite all of its problems, the French government occasionally took action that helped its cause. One such event occurred in 1671, when Simon François Daumont, Sieur de Saint Lusson, acting on behalf of the king, gathered the leaders of multiple Indian nations at Sault Ste. Marie to claim the Lake Superior region and territory all the way west to the Pacific Ocean on behalf of the French Crown. He did so with much pomp and ceremony, but also in a manner that won support of the Indians gathered there.

A major factor in winning that support was the work of the interpreter, Father Claude Allouez. Although Saint Lusson offered a lengthy speech that declared the sovereignty and authority of the French king over the lands and peoples of the territory, the French priest spoke in a language more amenable to the Native people gathered there. Allouez "used Anishinaabe categories of identity, and relied upon Anishinaabe conceptions of power in order to tell a story," according to historian Michael Witgen. In Allouez's retelling, the ceremony "became less about the transfer of land and sovereignty, and more about the power of the French father and the mutual obligations of family."[38]

Nicholas Perrot agreed to serve on behalf of Saint Lusson, and he set out in the fall of 1670 to begin contacting various nations to inform them of the gathering set for the following spring. Using canoe and sled, he traveled extensively and sent Indian messengers to those he could not reach personally. "I notified these people to proceed to the Saulteur country [Sault Ste. Marie] in the springtime, as early as they could in order to hear the message from the king that Sieur Saint Lusson was carrying to them and to all the tribes," Perrot wrote. He arrived at the Sault on May 5, 1671, accompanied by representatives of four Indian nations. Others, including the Ojibwe, Kickapoo, Cree, and Miami, were already there when he arrived. Perrot reported that despite some fears among the groups about how they would treat one another, they all remained peaceful for the French presentation.[39]

Saint Lusson had a large stake or pole bearing the French flag and royal coat of arms, which he raised during the ceremony with the unanimous approval of the Indian leaders, according to Perrot. The Indian representatives "gave presents for their signatures, affirming thus that they placed themselves under the protection of the king, and in subjection to him."[40] The ceremony was not just an immediate success. As Perrot noted, it prompted long-lasting goodwill: "After that, all those people returned to their respective abodes, and lived many years without any trouble in any quarter."[41]

A century and a half after Perrot wrote his account of the occasion, William Warren afforded the ceremony even more importance, at least so far as Ojibwe of the Chequamegon Bay area were concerned. No event in the early days of European contact, Warren said, was more important in Ojibwe oral history than the grand council organized by Saint Lusson. Even in the 1840s, when Warren heard the stories, Ojibwe leaders at the western end of Lake Superior still talked of how their ancestors personally received an invitation to attend the ceremony when a messenger of the French king—possibly Perrot—visited the Ojibwe villages near Chequamegon Bay.[42]

The Ojibwe sent a large delegation to the Sault for the ceremony. "Keche-ne-zuh-yauh, head chief of the great Crane family, headed this party, and represented the nation of the Ojibways," Warren wrote.[43] During the ceremony, Saint Lusson asked for unhindered passage for French traders seeking to do business at Ojibwe villages. He also requested that "the fires of the French and Ojibway nations be made one, and everlasting."[43] Saint Lusson pledged that the French would protect the Ojibwe from their enemies, and he spoke pointedly to the Ojibwe leader from Chequamegon: "If you are in trouble, you, the Crane, must arise in the skies and cry with your 'far sounding' voice and I will hear you."[44]

At this grand ceremony, Warren said, the Ojibwe agreed to work in peace and mutual support with the French. They formally opened their homeland to French traders, although many Frenchmen had traded among them already. And they began to refer to the French king as their father.[45] Warren received his information from Ojibwe elders on Madeline Island and around Chequamegon Bay, so it's not surprising that he focused on the importance of the ceremony to those Ojibwe and that they were front-and-center in Saint Lusson's comments, as reported by Warren.

Warren also noted the presence of Mathurin Cadot at the grand gathering and said he received this information directly from his uncle Michel Cadotte Jr., Michel and Equaysayway's son. His uncle told him that Mathurin Cadot's inclusion as part of Saint Lusson's entourage in 1671 marked his first foray into the Ojibwe country.[46] Perrot, though, didn't mention Mathurin Cadot in his brief listing of the French people who attended the 1671 gathering and signed the official report. Those named signatories included Saint Lusson and several important French priests, as well as Perrot himself. But Perrot also noted that, in addition to these dignitaries, there were a number of unidentified "Frenchmen who were then trading in those quarters."[47]

The arrival of the French in the Lake Superior region, highlighted by the formal ceremony staged by Saint Lusson, led to more than a century of trading, social interaction, and intermarriage between the Ojibwe and the French, especially French Canadians from the St. Lawrence River Valley. Although there would be interruptions in that trade, the intermingling of cultures would continue. Madeline Island would grow in importance as a trade center, and the Cadotte family would begin to assume an important role in the trade.

CHAPTER 6

FRENCH FORTS ON MADELINE ISLAND

The same year (1671) that Saint Lusson gathered a variety of Native nations—including Ojibwe—at Sault Ste. Marie to declare the French king's sovereignty over the Lake Superior and Lake Huron regions and to win pledges of peace from the Indians, French priests abandoned Chequamegon Bay because they feared Dakota attacks.

It would be more than a century and a half before representatives of the Catholic Church returned with a permanent presence at Chequamegon Bay and the surrounding area. But French merchants and military officials weren't so reticent about returning. In fact, it's possible some of them never left at all. Unlicensed coureurs de bois likely continued to operate in the Chequamegon area even after Father Jacques Marquette left in 1671, becoming the last priest of the French era to serve the region.[1]

Soon afterward, Daniel Graysolon, Sieur du Lhut, visited the western end of Lake Superior. In 1678–1679, he built a fort at the present site of Thunder Bay, Ontario, and then explored what is now northern Wisconsin and Minnesota, as well as the Upper Mississippi River. More importantly, he negotiated a fragile truce among the Dakota, Ojibwe, Fox, and other nations.

With peace, the western end of Lake Superior became even more amenable to French traders. Even so, they remained fearful of a possible attack by the Dakota or other nations hostile to the French. Thus, they sought security at the western end of Lake Superior by locating a trading post at Chequamegon Point, the northern end of a narrow, shifting, sandy peninsula that extends from the eastern shore of Chequamegon Bay northwesterly toward Madeline Island. It provides a natural breaker protecting

View of La Pointe, 1842: the small village included the American Fur Company warehouses (upper left), the Catholic Church (standing alone on the right). WHI IMAGE ID 42457

Chequamegon Bay from Lake Superior. The French initially called that location "La Pointe," although the name would later be transferred to the trading site and village on Madeline Island. The French trading post at Chequamegon Point was probably built around 1690.[2]

Three years later, there arrived at Chequamegon Bay a coureur de bois named Pierre Le Sueur, who obtained an official commission to reopen trade with Native people at the west end of Lake Superior and to operate a trading post at Chequamegon.[3] Le Sueur quickly determined, however, that the existing trading post on the peninsula was not ideal, either for access or for defense. He decided to locate his trading post near the southernmost point of Madeline Island. The French referred to the island itself by various names at different times: St. Esprit, Isle Detour, La Pointe, La Ronde, St. Michael's, and Montreal Island. It was at about this time that the French also began referring to the group of islands north of Chequamegon Bay as the "Apostle Islands," probably because the French originally believed there were twelve such islands. (There are actually twenty-one.)

Le Sueur's fort was constructed near present-day Grant's Point on Madeline Island, a few hundred yards southeast of where Michel Cadotte located his trading post roughly a century later.[4] Le Sueur's important mission also included maintaining the peace that had recently been concluded between the Ojibwe and Dakota, thus keeping open a northern trade route. Fox and other nations had closed the southern trading route, which went through Green Bay to the Fox and Wisconsin Rivers, then on to the Mississippi. Consequently, the northern route across Lake Superior was then the only one available for transporting goods between Montreal and the western fur-trade regions.[5] The closing of the Green Bay route made La Pointe one of the most important centers during the French era. It became the assembly point for most furs heading east, much as Grand Portage would serve as the central collecting point for British fur traders a century later.[6]

Le Sueur also established a post in what is now northern Minnesota to trade with the Dakota and to serve as a buffer between the Dakota and the Ojibwe. To fulfill his assignment to maintain the peace between the two nations, he traveled to Montreal in July of 1695, accompanied by a party of Ojibwe and Teeoskahtay, the first Dakota leader ever to visit the French city.[7] The governor of New France, Louis de Buade de Frontenac, held an audience with the Indians, and the Ojibwe leader from Chequamegon, named Shingowahbay, was the first to speak. After paying his respects to the governor, Shingowahbay asked permission for the Ojibwe, with the Dakota as their allies, to exact revenge on the Fox and others who had recently attacked them.[8] Then he, as well as the Dakota leader, asked Frontenac to allow Le Sueur to serve both nations as their trader. "Le Sueur alone, who is acquainted with the language of the one and the other, can serve us," Shigowahbay said. "We ask that he return with us."[9]

Le Sueur apparently did return to the region, possibly after visiting France in 1697 and obtaining a royal license to explore for copper and lead in the upper Mississippi River drainage. But that license was withdrawn the following year at the urging of Le Sueur's enemies within the government of New France. For several years he continued to explore the region, sometimes with official sanction and sometimes without. Eventually, he relocated to the lower end of the Mississippi River in Louisiana.[10]

Meanwhile, in 1698, French officials halted fur trading at the western end of Lake Superior, including on Madeline Island, which may have been the result of the great success that Le Sueur and other traders in the far western part of the French empire had in gathering furs, thus creating a glut in the supply and driving prices down.[11] Or, just as likely, it was due to the growing conflict with the Fox and Sauk, who were waging war against the French traders and the Frenchmen's Ojibwe and Dakota allies.[12]

Some independent coureurs de bois probably remained in the west, but it would be twenty years before the French officially returned to the region. The threat from the Fox and other nations had not been eliminated then, but the English were beginning to make incursions into the region and the French feared losing their monopoly on the valuable fur trade there. They decided it was time to reestablish their presence in the western Great Lakes. In September 1718, Captain Jean-Paul Le Gardeur, Sieur de Repentigny (also known as Saint-Pierre), was sent with a small contingent of soldiers to reoccupy the post at La Pointe. Saint-Pierre remained at the post only until 1720. Accompanying him was Ensign René Godefroy, Sieur de Linctot de Tonnancour, who replaced Saint-Pierre and remained as commander at La Pointe until 1726.[13]

It was a relatively uneventful time for the French trading with the Ojibwe and Dakota at the western end of Lake Superior and into what is now northern Minnesota. But that wasn't true to the south, from Green Bay westward to the Mississippi River and beyond, where the Fox and Sauk continued to fight the French and their Indian allies. In 1728, French officials sent an army of 450 French soldiers and an estimated 1,200 Indian allies to attack Sauk and Fox villages and eliminate the obstacle to their trading interests. But leaders of those nations remained a step ahead of the large army, which succeeded in doing little but driving their enemies westward while burning their abandoned villages. Next, the French and their Ojibwe allies decided to attack and harass the Fox and Sauk. As a result, the Fox finally sought a formal peace with the French in 1729 and 1730, although they would continue to create headaches for the French traders and their allies for decades to come, primarily west of the Mississippi.[14] Fox warriors killed French traders in the Mississippi River Valley as late as 1741, which led to the governor of New France assembling an expedition of "some of the most experienced officers in the Indian Service" to again attack the Native group, which the French called the Renards. They engaged in a two-pronged attack on the major Fox village on the Fox River in Wisconsin, "and many were killed." Those who weren't retreated to a site near Prairie du Chien, where the French forces attacked again the following winter "and slew nearly the whole settlement."[15] The French war with the Fox lasted "a dreary half-century," according to historian Reuben Gold Thwaites, and "helped drain the treasury of New France."[16]

As the efforts to fight the Fox and Sauk and to reopen the Green Bay route to the west were underway, a new officer had been placed in charge of the small fort and trading post at La Pointe. In 1727, Louis Denis, Sieur de la Ronde, assumed control of the fort and managed to keep his post and his Indian allies out of the hostilities that were occurring to the south and southwest. La Ronde was a French military officer with a record of interacting with the Mi'Kmaq of Canada[17] and performing in battle, both on land and on sea. He proved particularly adept at working with the Ojibwe and maintaining peace around Chequamegon Bay, thus preserving the trade route to the pelt-rich Mississippi area through Lake Superior.[18]

But La Ronde was more than just a peacekeeper. He was "probably La Pointe's most active and famous commandant" under the French regime.[19] La Ronde served fourteen years at La Pointe, not only protecting and expanding the fur trade, but also conducting officially approved expeditions to search for copper and develop copper mines on the southern shores of Lake Superior. He succeeded in obtaining specimens of copper from the Ontonagon River, which flows into Lake Superior about seventy miles east of Chequamegon Bay.[20] La Ronde shipped his own ore samples to France to be assayed, where they stirred up enough excitement that royal authorities sent two experienced miners to advise La Ronde on the best places to mine.[21]

To handle the expected copper ore and to ferry supplies from Sault St. Marie to other parts of the lake, in 1731 La Ronde also built what is believed to be the first sailing vessel larger than a canoe on Lake Superior.[22] The mining ventures never entered production, however, and La Ronde fell in and out of favor with French authorities in Québec and Paris. Additionally, new hostilities developed between the Ojibwe and the Dakota, and he had to spend much of his time working to stem the animosity and maintain the fur trade. In 1741, he attempted to revive interest in his copper-mining proposal during a visit east, but he fell ill and died in Québec that year.[23]

For the two years after his death, command of the La Pointe post was given to La Ronde's son, Philippe La Ronde, though he left in 1743, apparently to join military efforts against the British. Upon his departure, command of La Pointe was officially turned over to Philippe La Ronde's mother—and Denis La Ronde's widow—Louise Chartier La Ronde.[24]

Madame La Ronde was the commander of the post on Madeline Island until 1748, when she retired to Montreal, although little has been recorded of her time at La Pointe. She apparently relished the position and the money it provided, and she made a trip to France in an attempt to extend her tenure there. In November 1747, the newly appointed governor of New France sent a letter to his superior back on the Continent on Madame La Ronde's behalf in which he said that Madame La Ronde was "going to France to ask you to let her Continue to have That post."[25] He also noted that the French minister to whom he addressed his letter had, in 1745, granted Madame La Ronde a three-year extension of her contract to operate the La Pointe post. That was done in part "out of consideration for her family, for her husband's services, and for the expense he had incurred in connection with The Working of the Copper Mines." However, the governor of New France also told the minister that renewed hostilities between the Ojibwe and the Dakota again threatened the fur trade in the region. He asked that Madame La Ronde's commission at La Pointe be extended for three more years, but only on the condition that peace could be restored between the warring nations.[26]

Whatever the cause, the commission was not extended, and Madame La Ronde left Chequamegon at the end of 1748, thus ending twenty-one years of La Ronde–family command of the post on Madeline Island. Following Madame La Ronde's tenure, a series of unremarkable French overseers commanded the post at La Pointe, culminating in 1758 with Luc de La Corne (also known as La Corne Saint-Luc). He paid the French government an estimated eight thousand francs for the right to trade at La Pointe, but it's not clear whether or not he enjoyed much success in the fur trade there. By the time he took over, the French were deeply embroiled in the Seven Years' War with the British. They would surrender most of New France to the English with the Treaty of Paris in 1763.[27]

Sometime during the years of French control, a murder occurred on Madeline Island: a Frenchman working at the La Pointe post killed the

French clerk, his wife, and one or more children. At least two versions of the event were recorded, and they both hint at the dangers of serving at a site as isolated as La Pointe.

William Warren said the crime occurred in 1722 when a clerk named Joseph was in charge of the La Pointe post. He lived there with his wife, two children, and a worker. The worker became obsessed with the wife and tried to seduce her while the clerk was out hunting. When she rejected his advances, he killed her, then lay in wait and murdered Joseph when he returned. Next he killed the couple's two children and buried the entire family in a rubbish heap near the trading post. Weeks later, a visiting French official arrived and saw signs of blood and suspected foul play. Probing the rubbish pile with his sword, the official discovered the corpses. He confronted the employee, who confessed to the crime. While he was being taken to Montreal to stand trial, however, the accused murderer escaped and joined a band of Huron. One night, when the warriors were recounting their heroic deeds in battle, the murderer stood up and bragged of his own killing spree, believing it would impress the Native men. "He was, however, mistaken, for before he had finished his tale of the bloody deed, an Indian warrior arose, and . . . buried a tomahawk deep into his brain."[28]

Another version of the story, published in the *Detroit Gazette* in 1822, came from trader William Morrison, who said the events transpired around 1760. A trader, his wife, their young son, and a servant had remained at the La Pointe trading post one winter while other workers were out trapping. The servant decided to rob his employer by first killing the trader and his wife and then, a few days later, murdering the son. Local Ojibwe, suspicious of the story the servant told them about how his employer and family had vanished, discovered the bodies. They immediately seized the servant and hauled him toward Montreal to seek justice for the clerk and his family. But their trip was interrupted by the ongoing war between the French and British, and the Ojibwe decided to return home. Stopping at Sault Ste. Marie on their way back, they held a dance, and the Ojibwe warriors each rose and told of their exploits in battle. The murderer stood up and bragged of killing the La Pointe trader and his family. The Ojibwe listened in silence. Then their chief said, "We boast of having killed our enemies—never our friends." Rather than take the murderer back to

La Pointe, they executed him.[29]

Shortly after the murder, according to Morrison's timeframe, the last trader officially approved by the French government, Saint-Luc, left La Pointe. That was in 1762, and the Ojibwe of the region, stalwart allies of the French, found themselves in a tenuous position. Mamongazida, a leader of the Ojibwe in the Chequamegon region and Equaysayway's great-great uncle, had led an Ojibwe war party as far east as Québec to fight on behalf of the French. His war party was present at the Battle of the Plains of Abraham in 1759, when Québec fell to the British.[30] Mamongazida, who was noted for his love for the French and his enmity toward the British, was keenly aware of the changing political situation. He was also an astute leader. Five years after the fall of Québec, when it was clear the British had won, and when Sir William Johnson, the head of the British government's Indian Department in the colonies of present-day Canada, conducted a large peace gathering with various Indian nations from the Great Lakes, Mamongazida "became a fast friend to the English."[31]

Soon the British would arrive at Chequamegon Bay in the person of adventurer and entrepreneur Alexander Henry, working in partnership with Jean-Baptiste Cadot Sr. And soon, too, the British would find themselves in another conflict that affected the Lake Superior trade. This time their enemies were not the French but their own colonists in what would later become the United States.

CHAPTER 7

COUREURS DE BOIS AND VOYAGEURS

Centuries before cowboys earned renown as the free-spirited laborers of the West, another group of hard-working, hard-drinking, independent-minded workers became known for their activities on the rivers and lakes of Canada and the northern United States. They were *voyageurs*—the cowboys of canoes. They dressed in flashy clothes, sang songs while they worked, and became famous for their almost superhuman strength and their skills with canoes, as well as for their eating and drinking capacity. Although largely forgotten in twenty-first-century America, they were once viewed with awe in the Great Lakes region.

Voyageurs were employees of fur traders and were mostly French Canadian men or those of mixed French Canadian and Native descent, who usually worked on contracts for the traders. They paddled canoes, packed goods over portages, helped in trapping and trading during the winter, and performed other work for their employers. In conducting their fur-trade business, the Cadottes—Jean-Baptiste Sr., Jean-Baptiste Jr., and Michel—all depended on voyageurs. However, except for brief periods early in their careers, these men weren't considered voyageurs themselves. Rather, they were traders, independent merchants, and later, contractors for the large fur-trade companies. Their ancestor, Mathurin Cadot, was likely an unlicensed coureur de bois, at least until he received an official *congé*. Unlike voyageurs, coureurs de bois were independent traders, men who during the French control of New France operated outside of the legally authorized system for trading with Native people.

Both voyageurs and coureurs de bois were critical to the development of the fur trade in the Lake Superior region. When the French government

in the mid-seventeenth century decreed that citizens of New France
could not independently go off to
trade with Indians, it's not surprising that large numbers of French
Canadians ignored the edict. After
all, there was good money to be
made in the fur trade and more
adventure than was to be found
on a small farm or in a tiny settlement. Equally important, it offered
freedom from the sometimes mys-
tifying and oppressive rules established by the French king and his
ministers, who were thousands of
miles from the realities of life in
New France.

A voyageur with a "tumpline" or a strap
attached at both ends to a load and used
to carry the object by placing the strap
over the top of the head. FREDERIC REMING-
TON, WHI IMAGE ID 30348

Explorer and trader Alexander
Mackenzie discussed these early
entrepreneurs in his journal, more
than one hundred years after they
proliferated. He found little to admire in the coureurs de bois. After a
year to fifteen months in the backcountry, he noted, they would return to
places such as Montreal in canoes filled with furs. Yet within a month, most
had spent the bulk of their earnings on liquor and extravagant purchases,
even as they flouted the laws enacted to halt their independent endeavors.[1]
Because coureurs de bois necessarily had to be circumspect about their
activities, they left few records of their lives. Modern researchers must
depend mostly on other observers, such as Mackenzie, for descriptions of
how they lived—including the reports of debauchery and licentiousness.

Decades before Mackenzie offered his observations, one self-acknowledged
coureur de bois was captured by the British at Hudson Bay. After being
shipped to England, then held under guard there, Joseph La France told a
remarkable tale to British authorities of his nearly twenty years as an independent, outlaw trader. He died aboard a guard ship in England in 1743
from "fever and ague" at the age of thirty-six.[2] Whether he was a man of

good reputation or someone who confirmed the low opinion that Mackenzie and others held for coureurs de bois, La France's story gives clues about these outlaw traders who worked from the mid-seventeenth to the mid-eighteenth centuries. They traveled extensively, mingled freely with the Native populations, maintained political loyalty only as long as it was economically expedient, and were discouraged in changing their ways by the policies of the French government.

La France was born at Michilimackinac in 1707, the son of a French Canadian father and Ojibwe mother. He visited Québec as a youngster but spent most of his childhood in the Michilimackinac region. He was fourteen when his father died and sixteen when he entered the fur trade, probably with the assistance of his Ojibwe relatives. Though he initially traded primarily along the north shore of Lake Superior, La France eventually traveled south as far as present-day St. Louis on the Mississippi River, west beyond Lake Winnipeg in Canada, and north to York Fort on Hudson Bay. He made it to Fort Detroit, to the southern end of Lake Erie and into upstate New York to trade with the British.[3]

Twice he tried to become a legal trader, seeking a *congé* from the government of New France. On the first occasion, La France paid the governor-general at Montreal "one thousand crowns and gave an additional present of a pack of valuable marten skins."[4] But the governor accused him of trading brandy to the Indians—which nearly all traders did—and threatened to arrest him if he attempted to regain any of the gifts he had given the governor. On his second attempt to become a legal trader, La France was seized as a runaway as he and his two Indian slaves made their way toward Montreal. He escaped before he could be imprisoned but lost all of his furs, canoes, and weapons. What happened to his Indian slaves is not known. After that, La France decided to turn his trading efforts toward the more accommodating British. He headed west across Lake Superior and the Grand Portage, then north and west to Lake of the Woods to trade for the winter, planning to sell his furs at Hudson Bay the following summer.

La France traveled voluntarily to York Fort in 1742, along with many Native people making their annual summer trading trip there. He led a large contingent of Indians and canoes during that journey. There, British military officials at the fort took him into custody, although it's not clear why. The authorities shipped La France across the Atlantic to England, where he met Sir Arthur Dobbs, an Irish nobleman eager to find the mythic Northwest Passage. He believed La France might help him in that regard, and he interviewed the coureur de bois about his life and travels.

La France was said by Dobbs's associates to have a solid reputation, and Dobbs believed his accounts were accurate. But the ship captain who ferried him to England said La France told him quite different stories than those he told Dobbs. And, the captain said, La France had showed up at York Fort only after killing his Indian "consort."[5] During his interviews with Dobbs, La France apparently didn't discuss events of excessive revelry or debauchery, or Dobbs edited them out of his report. But, based on the stories he told Dobbs, it's estimated he canoed more than seventeen thousand miles during his career and traveled overland at least five hundred miles.[6]

Not all coureurs de bois traveled so widely or had the kinds of adventures that La France did. There's no indication that Mathurin Cadot experienced the sorts of legal difficulties that La France suffered or that he lived as unrestrained a life as the traders described by Mackenzie, though he probably traded as a coureur de bois for a number of years prior to receiving a *congé* from the French government in 1686. And, unlike the traders described by Mackenzie, he didn't spend everything he made on liquor and wild parties. Instead, Cadot used the money he made in the fur trade to purchase land and raise a family. However, he undoubtedly faced many of the same obstacles and frustrations that La France did, at least until he received his *congé*.[7]

When traders—legal and illegal—headed into the western country to conduct business, they hired the men who eventually became known as voyageurs to paddle their canoes and carry their heavy packages over portages. The voyageurs' strength, indeed, was legendary. Thomas McKenney, Superintendent of Indian Affairs for the US government, was astonished by it when he visited Lake Superior in 1826. On his trip from Sault Ste. Marie to Fond du Lac, he described one incident in which a barge carrying some of his party was driven up on shore by large waves and all its contents soaked. "[O]ur voyageurs, seized the articles [and] shouldered what only a horse in our country would be expected to carry," McKenney reported. They hauled the heavy burdens to McKenney's encampment on a hill high above the beach.[8] Alexander Mackenzie also remarked on the legendary strength and endurance of the voyageurs, noting their particularly amazing efforts at Grand Portage, the 8.5-mile hike from the west end of Lake Superior, over hills and through marshes, then on to the Pigeon River.[9] Equally impressive was their skill with a canoe, as far as McKenney was concerned. He said it was impossible to adequately describe what it was like to witness a large canoe propelled by eight voyageurs glide smoothly upstream against a strong river current. Even more impressive was when they turned and paddled with the current and "the thing appeared to fly!"[10]

McKenney recalled one incident at the edge of the rapids of Sault Ste. Marie, as voyageurs were preparing to launch a canoe. One member of McKenney's American party asked loudly, "'I wonder if these fellows know how to paddle that canoe?'" At first, because they spoke little English, the voyageurs appeared not to understand the comment. But once they grasped the derogatory nature of the remark, they pushed their canoe into the current, began a chant, and made the vessel speed along the edge of the rapids. They zipped upstream and then down, into the rapids and out again. Finally, they beached their canoe with great speed and dexterity, right at the feet of the Americans, leaving little doubt that they believed they had more than satisfactorily answered the demeaning query.[11]

Not only were the voyageurs strong and long on endurance, but they could also survive on very little food. "[O]ften, notwithstanding every exertion, the men went supperless to bed," explorer and trader Alexander Henry wrote in his record of his travels in the Lake Superior region. He called the French Canadian voyageurs "the best men in the world" for handling such difficult situations without complaint.[12] Even so, voyageurs had legendary appetites. Although they subsisted much of the time while traveling on little but corn or pea meal and lard, when they had the opportunity to eat well, they relished it. Explorer David Thompson recalled chastising some voyageurs for gluttony after watching seven of them consume as much as *eight pounds* of fresh meat in a day. They responded cheerfully by telling Thompson "that their greatest enjoyment of life was Eating."[13]

Alexander Henry also reported on a darker side of the voyageurs' appetites. While spending the winter of 1767–1768 in northern Michigan, he decided to visit Sault Ste. Marie, where his friend Jean-Baptiste Cadot Sr. lived. He took with him three French Canadian voyageurs and a young

Engraving of what a group of voyageurs may have looked like as they gathered around their evening campfire, 1892. FREDERIC REMINGTON, WHI IMAGE ID 3776

Ojibwe woman who wanted to visit her relatives at the Sault. Because it was not a long trip and they expected to catch fish on the way, they took only a quart of corn meal apiece for provisions.

Their preparations proved inadequate when a violent storm blew in for three days, and the small company was unable to travel or tend to fishing nets. All the food was consumed in the first evening, and by the third day, a weakened Henry attempted to hunt but returned to camp with only two small birds. "On my arrival, one of my men informed me that the other two had proposed to kill and feed upon the young woman," Henry said. When he questioned the other two voyageurs, he discovered that they indeed looked upon the Indian woman as a food source rather than a fellow human being. They were highly indignant when Henry refused to go along with their plan. The woman's life was spared and cannibalism avoided when, the following day, Henry found a kind of lichen that the Ojibwe had told him could be used for food in an emergency. The woman who was to have been their victim prepared the life-sustaining meal for all of them. But Henry was appalled to learn that one of his men was no newcomer to eating human flesh.[14]

Being a voyageur meant facing not only rough work and danger, including the real possibility of starvation, but also taking pride in one's work and ability. Voyageurs were never reluctant to tout their abilities. They bragged about how much they could carry, about the quality of their canoes, and about their own skill in maneuvering those vessels. They boasted about the speed of their sled dogs and their singing ability. They eagerly told tall tales, along the lines of the Paul Bunyan stories that later became popular in the north woods. But there was a difference in their storytelling, according to historian Grace Lee Nute: "[T]he hero of every voyageur's yarn was himself."[15]

Voyageurs and coureurs de bois lived difficult lives, but ones largely of their own choosing, and most relished it. One retired voyageur who was over seventy years old told Minnesota pioneer and historian General James B. Baker in the late nineteenth century that he spent twenty-four years as a canoe man and forty-one years in the fur-trade: "I could carry, paddle, walk and sing with any man I ever saw. . . . No portage was ever too long for me. . . . I have saved the lives of ten voyageurs. Have had twelve wives and six running dogs. I spent all my money in pleasure. Were I young again, I should spend my life the same way over. There is no life so happy as a voyageur's life."[16]

CHAPTER 8

JEAN-BAPTISTE CADOT SR.

In 1780, at the height of the American Revolutionary War, the British grew concerned about American General George Rogers Clark's victories in the West and about Spanish holdings along the Mississippi River. The British, therefore, hatched a plan to launch a three-pronged attack against the small French community of St. Louis, which Spain had recently acquired. They also planned a simultaneous attack on the American community of Cahokia—on the east side of the Mississippi, across from St. Louis—hoping to lure Clark to the battle and decimate his army.[1] One prong of the British force was to trek north up the Mississippi River from the Gulf of Mexico, while another was to work its way from the English Fort Detroit to Cahokia. The third was to march from Lake Superior to the Mississippi River, then south to St. Louis.[2]

Few British troops were available on the western frontier, so all three forces were to be made up primarily of French Canadians loyal to the British and large numbers of the Crown's Indian allies. But the Indians couldn't be conscripted into service for the king; they had to be persuaded to join the effort. And on the southern shores of Lake Superior, British officials knew just the man to do the persuading: Jean-Baptiste Cadot Sr.

Cadot, who was viewed by British authorities as someone who had "great influence with the Indians," and who was himself of mixed French Canadian and Native descent, accepted the assignment to help recruit Native people for the attack on St. Louis.[3] But apparently he didn't join the attack itself, which was far from successful.

Born in 1723 in Batiscan, Québec, about one hundred miles northeast of Montreal on the St. Lawrence River, Cadot was the son of Jean-Francois

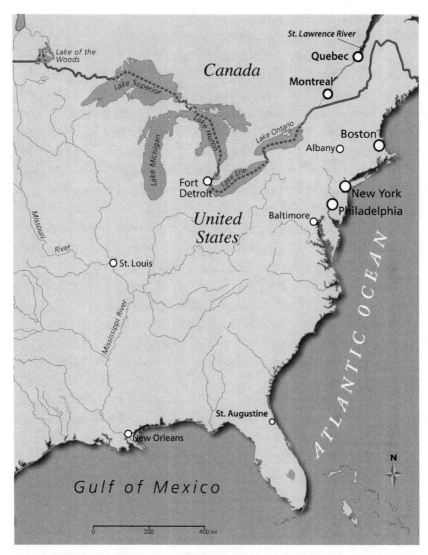

Eastern North America ca. 1790. The Ojibwe and other Native peoples recruited in 1780 by Jean-Baptiste Cadot Sr. to assist the British in attacking St. Louis had hundreds of miles to travel from Lake Superior to the small French and Spanish community.
ROBERT GARCIA

Cadot and Marie-Josephe Proteau and the grandson of Mathurin Cadot.[4] His father, two uncles, and four brothers engaged briefly in the fur trade and used the money they earned to settle on farms in Québec Province. But farming life had little appeal for Cadot, and at the age of eighteen, he

apprenticed himself as a voyageur with Jean-Baptiste-Nicolas Roch de
Ramezay for a period of three years. He was assigned to a post on Lake
Nipigon, north of Lake Superior.[5]

Sometime around 1750, Cadot moved to the important east entrance of
Lake Superior: Sault Ste. Marie.[6] It is a relatively narrow neck of land between
Lake Huron and Lake Superior, now famous for its locks that allow large ships
access to Superior. Yet even in the middle of the eighteenth century, it was
recognized for its importance to canoe traffic between Lake Superior and
key areas to the east. It provided a stopping point where fish were abundant
and there was plenty of open ground for camps. Canoes had to be portaged
around the falls of St. Mary, and crews often stopped briefly before heading
west across Lake Superior or east across Lake Huron and then on to Montreal.

Also in 1750, Captain Louis Legardeur de Repentigny and Captain Louis
de Bonne, officers in the French army, received a grant from the authorities of New France for roughly 260,000 acres surrounding the falls at
Sault Ste. Marie to establish a fort and small farm, which would provide
a resting place for French travelers and fur traders. They were also to use
this critical location, through which many Indians traveled, to dissuade the
Native people from trading with the British, who were a threat to French
dominance of the region.[7]

The French trusted Cadot to serve as their resident agent at Sault
Ste. Marie, the critical link between Lake Huron and Lake Superior. After
the British gained control of the region in the 1760s, Cadot turned his allegiance to them and quickly earned their trust. In addition to his military
assignments and business interactions, he served as an interpreter between
the British and Ojibwe. Equally important, Cadot had the respect of the
Lake Superior Ojibwe.

No portraits of Cadot are known to exist, but if he was built like most
French Canadian voyageurs, he would have been relatively short. The
typical voyageur was no more than five feet, eight inches tall, but prefer-
ably five-four to five-six in order to sit comfortably in small canoes and
still have the strong legs necessary for portaging. Voyageurs had powerful
shoulders for paddling and strong backs and legs to carry packs and heavy
canoes over portages.[8] Regardless of his physical stature, Cadot must have
had a commanding presence. Clearly, he won the respect of both French
and British authorities and was given important duties by both.

Even before the Revolutionary War, Cadot had established himself with the British as someone who could be trusted to assist them and work well with the Native people. In a 1771 letter to General Thomas Gage, George Turnbull, then the commander at Michilimackinac, described Cadot as having "universall [sic] good character amongst both Canadians and Indians." That same year, Sir William Johnson said he considered Cadot one of the "two Most faithful Men amongst the French."[9]

Cadot was probably illiterate. Several entries in the family account book say he signed with "his mark," though on a few occasions, he did sign his name.[10] In any event, he was an intelligent man who developed a successful fur-trade business at a time when there was abundant competition and few rules. He raised his children with Athanasie and then later with his second wife, Catherine. The children he had with Athanasie were sent to Montreal to attend school. Eventually, sons Jean-Baptiste Jr. and Michel joined their father's business. Daughter Marie-Renée remained in Montreal but was also involved in the family fur trade.[11]

It's not hard to envision Cadot as a buckskin-clad backwoodsman, furiously paddling a canoe or racing through the forest with his musket in one hand and a tomahawk in the other. There were likely scenes akin to that, especially when Cadot was young, although because he was a French Canadian voyageur as a young man, he probably wore colorful cotton and woolen clothing more frequently than buckskins. But such a picture also fails to do Cadot justice.

In actuality, Cadot operated a sprawling business in which he oversaw employees at a number of isolated trading posts. He interacted regularly with Ojibwe and other Native people to make transactions at one end of his business chain. At the other end, he dealt with Montreal merchants of both French Canadian and English lineage, and he had to understand the complicated global market for furs. Simultaneously, Cadot had to provide for his family and ensure their needs were met as they attended school in a city more than six hundred miles from the family home, over a route that was accessible only by canoe and portages.

In 1772, Cadot's young sons were living in Montreal with their older sister and their mother.[12] The account books for that year give some insight into Cadot's family life and expenses. One entry for 1772 was titled "Account of the provisions made to mme. Cadot for her and The Children by Sieur Cazeau." It lists a variety of personal goods and school supplies purchased on behalf of Athanasie and their children and demonstrates that meeting the needs of his growing family and seeing his children properly educated were important to Cadot even as he operated his fur-trade business. Items on the list included cotton, muslin, and "royal Swiss linen"; red calico kerchiefs; silk fringe; blue thread; and one hundred needles.[13]

Decades earlier, when Repentigny went to the Sault in late 1750 to begin work on the fort, he had found Cadot and Athanasie already living there. Cadot was then the only non-Indian residing at the Sault. Repentigny hired the couple to establish a farm, and they worked diligently to do so. "They have cleared it up and sowed it and without frost they will gather 30 to 35 sacks of corn," the governor of New France wrote to authorities in Paris in 1751.[14] Repentigny remained at the Sault until 1755. When he departed to resume his military duties for France, he left Cadot in charge of the fort and farm. Cadot was also to oversee fur trading for Repentigny and his partners.[15]

There is disagreement, however, about whether Cadot was merely left in charge of the fort and farm, or whether he actually owned the entire land grant that Repentigny and de Bonne had been given by the French government. More than a century later, in 1866, a case regarding the title of the land on the American side of the Sault came before the US Supreme Court, and heirs of Repentigny and others sought to assert a claim on it. In the preliminary findings related to that case, descendants of Cadot testified in lower court that when Repentigny left, Cadot obtained ownership of the entire property, based on statements Jean-Baptiste Cadot Sr. had made to his sons and a nephew.[16] Although a lower court ruled in favor of the Repentigny heirs' claim to the property, the Supreme Court rejected the claim. In its ruling, the high court ignored the statements of Cadot's descendants.[17]

There are other indications that Cadot had some claim to land at the Sault, however. His great-grandson, William Warren, wrote that he was told by Great Buffalo and other Ojibwe leaders that Cadot had been granted land at the Sault, including the present site of the city of Sault Ste. Marie. The grant came from Ojibwe leaders grateful for Cadot's efforts on their behalf with both the French and the British. Great Buffalo said he had seen a copy of a document—"a very old-looking paper, being much torn and patched up, and the writing upon it hardly discernible"—that recorded the grant to Cadot. The document had reportedly been held by Cadot's one-time partner, Alexander Henry. After Henry's death in Montreal in 1824, some unidentified person took the document to Lake Superior, consulted with Great Buffalo and others, asked about descendants of Cadot, and then returned to Montreal. And the document "has never been heard of since."[18]

A 1927 newspaper article published in Washburn, Wisconsin, recounted a similar version of Cadot receiving a grant to the Sault from Ojibwe leaders, saying it was "a fairly well substantiated tradition."[19] On his deathbed, Cadot told family members that he once had such a document proving his ownership for much of the Sault but added that it had disappeared or possibly been taken by others. He pleaded with family members to go to Montreal and search for a copy of that document. Some did, but it was never found.[20]

There is little record of what occurred between 1755, when Repentigny left, and 1763, when the English gained control of Canada. But there were important changes and additions to the Cadot family. In 1756, after the birth of daughter Marie-Renée, Cadot and Athanasie decided to formalize their relationship in the European sense. They traveled to Michilimackinac and were married on October 28. Daughter Charlotte arrived in 1759, son Jean-Baptiste Jr. in 1761, and Michel in 1764.[21]

It's clear that during this time, Cadot had established himself as a friend and power figure with the Ojibwe and other Indian nations in the region. That occurred in part through Athanasie and her familial connection to important leaders such as Madjeckewiss. But his own character no doubt played a role as well. The Ojibwe have a long tradition of valuing leaders who are not only powerful warriors or hunters but eloquent speakers.[22] That description fit Cadot. Patrick Sinclair, lieutenant governor and commander of Michilimackinac in 1780, wrote that Cadot was recognized by the Indians "as a great village orator."[23]

Cadot used that talent to good effect on several occasions. The first recorded example of it came in 1764, shortly after the British won control of Canada, but when many of the Indian nations in the region maintained a decided preference for the French. The Odawa chief Pontiac had led an uprising against the British beginning in the spring of 1763. Pontiac objected to British treatment of the Indians and the continuing encroachment of settlers into Indian territory.

English explorer and entrepreneur Alexander Henry was then in the region of Michilimackinac and Sault Ste. Marie, attempting to work his way into the fur trade. But he found himself desperately trying to avoid being killed by Ojibwe in the area who had joined Pontiac's War. Led by Madjeckewiss, a contingent of Ojibwe had killed most of the British soldiers and civilians at Michilimackinac after luring them outside of the walls of their small fort to watch a lacrosse match. Henry had narrowly escaped death, having been hidden during the massacre and then spirited away by a friendly Ojibwe man. Earlier, Henry had met Jean-Baptiste and Athanasie Cadot at Sault Ste. Marie, and he considered them his friends. He spent months after the Michilimackinac massacre attempting to reach the Cadots without being captured by hostile Ojibwe.[24]

By the spring of 1764, Henry had returned to Michilimackinac with his friend and protector, Wamatam, when another group of Indians arrived at the island. They had come from Detroit, where they had joined Pontiac in the siege of the fort there. They were looking for Ojibwe recruits and were eager to kill Henry, the only Englishman then in residence on the island. Henry asked Wamatam to again sneak him off the island and escort him to the Sault, where he knew the Cadots would protect him. The Ojibwe at Sault Ste. Marie considered Cadot their chief, Henry claimed: "It was by him that the Chippeways of Lake Superior were prevented from joining Pontiac."[25]

That trip from Michilimackinac to the Sault was a life-threatening adventure in its own right. Three days into the canoe trip of roughly eighty miles, Wamatam's wife fell ill and determined from a dream that it was unsafe for the family to proceed. It appeared that they were headed back once more to Michilimackinac and, Henry feared, his certain death. Then he spotted a vessel on the horizon, later writing that "I therefore indulged the hope that it might be a Canadian canoe [rather than an Indian one] on its voyage to Montreal; and that I might be able to prevail upon the crew to take me with them and thus release me from all my troubles." He was ecstatic when he discovered the canoe carried Athanasie Cadot on her way from Montreal to her home at the Sault, accompanied by three French Canadians. They soon set off for the Sault. Henry makes no mention of the fact that Athanasie was pregnant at the time, but it was May of 1764, as he recorded, and the couple's fourth child, Michel, was born in July of that year.[26]

Henry disguised himself in the outfit of a French Canadian voyageur in case the party encountered other Indians hostile to the English. And that's exactly what occurred the second day out, when twenty canoes of Ojibwe returning from Detroit came upon their single canoe. One of the Indians immediately accused the disguised Henry of being British, and others angrily took up the charge. Henry feigned ignorance of what they were saying, but Athanasie, whom the Ojibwe clearly respected, "assured them that I was a Canadian whom she had brought on his first voyage from Montreal." They were allowed to pass without further incident and arrived safely at the Sault the following day. There, Henry was greeted warmly by Jean-Baptiste Cadot.[27]

The danger to his life had not ended, however. Henry reported spending five peaceful days at the Sault with the Cadot family and about thirty Ojibwe warriors "who were restrained from joining the war" only by Cadot's influence. On the sixth day, however, another contingent of Ojibwe appeared, eager to join the war against the British and looking for Henry, making it clear they wanted to kill him. Leading this group was Madjeckewiss, who acknowledged both the intention to proceed east to join Pontiac and his desire to kill Henry. However, Madjeckewiss abandoned the idea of killing the Englishman when he learned it would displease Cadot. So, Henry's life was spared once again.[28]

Next, Cadot and the chief of the local Indian settlement made speeches in which they harangued Madjeckewiss and the Ojibwe who followed him, arguing that they should abandon the notion of trying to recruit Sault Ste. Marie Indians for the war against the British. While Madjeckewiss and his allies considered this demand, another canoe arrived, this one bringing a message from Sir William Johnson at Fort Niagara (north of Buffalo, New York, where the Niagara River meets Lake Ontario). Johnson had reached peace with the Six Nations of the Iroquois Confederacy, historic enemies of the Ojibwe. He urged all nations to send representatives to Niagara for a large gathering to discuss peace with the British or face possible attack and destruction from combined British and Six Nations forces. Within days, a contingent of Ojibwe and others, including Henry and Madjeckewiss, was on its way to Niagara.[29]

The following May, after the British had regained control of Michilimackinac, Captain William Howard met with Cadot and sent him back to Sault Ste. Marie with peace offerings. Cadot was instructed to tell the Ojibwe and any other Indians in the area about the peace arrangements Johnson had negotiated at Niagara. A month later, in June 1765, Cadot led eighty canoes of Lake Superior Indians to Michilimackinac to accept a peace treaty with the British.[30] That summer, Henry returned to Michilimackinac with what he said was "the exclusive right to the Lake Superior fur trade," given to him by the commander of Fort Michilimackinac. He left shortly thereafter for Sault Ste. Marie, where, he said, he took Cadot on as a partner.[31] That was a smart move on Henry's part because, in reality, it was Cadot whom the Ojibwe sought as their primary trading partner. Captain Howard, the man whom Henry claimed had issued him the permit for the Lake Superior fur trade, made it clear that the Ojibwe wanted to trade with Cadot when they arrived in 1765 to discuss the peace treaty.

For several years, because of the war between the French and British, there had been virtually no fur trade in the Lake Superior region. Consequently, the Ojibwe leaders, as Howard wrote to Sir William Johnson, "represented to me the miserable situation they had been in for want of trade and begged that I would send some Trader to them, and asked for Mr. Cadot." Howard suggested that Cadot reestablish a post in the Chequamegon Bay region, while English merchants would be assigned to other posts around Lake Superior and neighboring regions. "Mr. Cadot will be near the Center" of fur-trade activity in that region, Howard explained; therefore, he was convinced that "all the Indians will remain in our interest."[32]

The arrangement was approved, but Cadot opted to remain at the Sault. He allowed his new partner, Alexander Henry, to travel west and establish a fur-trading post at Chequamegon Bay, while Cadot handled the eastern end of the business. Despite Henry's self-aggrandizing statements about how he established the British fur trade in the region, it was Cadot's influence with the Ojibwe that made Henry's venture possible.

The following summer, Cadot was officially appointed interpreter between the English and the Ojibwe.[33] In 1767, his influence with the Ojibwe resulted in the Indians of the Sault removing the French flag they had long flown and replacing it with a British one.[34] For the next few years, Cadot's activities seem to have been primarily commercial and domestic—maintaining his fur business, engaging in a copper-mining venture with Henry and others, and raising a family.

The copper enterprise began with exploratory efforts in 1767 and lasted until 1773. It involved a distinguished group of investors led by New York native Henry Bostwick and included the Duke of Gloucester, who was the brother of the king; Sir William Johnson, the head of the British government's Indian Department in the northern colonies; and a Russian mining expert and the consul of the empress of Russia. But despite searching for copper deposits along the north and south shores of Lake Superior, Henry said, the enterprise made "no discovery of importance," and the partnership was disbanded. Efforts to mine Lake Superior's copper deposits didn't resume until the 1840s.[35]

In 1775, Cadot joined Henry and several other men who would become prominent in the fur trade on an exploratory trip to the Northwest—beyond Grand Portage to the Saskatchewan River and the Lake Athabasca region. American trader Peter Pond joined them as they reached Lake Winnipeg. Later, they encountered English brothers Thomas and Joseph Frobisher. The journey, sometimes called the "Pedlars' Expedition," lasted two years, with different groups heading in separate directions. It would mark the last business alliance between Cadot and Henry, although they remained friends.[36] The expedition was successful in obtaining furs, as well as critical information about trading in the country that had been visited by the French but by few British adventurers before that time. More importantly, the informal partnership of independent traders that developed during the expedition provided the basis for the later formation of the North West Company.[37]

In 1780, the year that Lieutenant Governor Patrick Sinclair dispatched Cadot to help recruit Indians for the attack on St. Louis, the family account book listed bills that the senior Cadot had sent to a Montreal merchant on behalf of people like Joseph Frobisher.[38] A year later, in May of 1781, the account books recorded a packet of merchandise being sent to a trader working for Cadot at L'Anse, on the southern shore of Lake Superior in what is now Michigan's Upper Peninsula. The list of goods sent out for trading offers a glimpse of what the Indians wanted and how the traders accommodated their desires:

2 packages of blue Cloth

15 packages of Braid

15 Blankets

1 little Dress

1 1/2 doz. large Knives

1 doz. fire steels

3 mirrors

4 combs

8 closing Knives

1 Barrel of powder

50# of shot and ball

6 barrels of rum[39]

In the spring of 1780, Sinclair, recently installed as the chief British authority at Michilimackinac, wrote to his superiors in Québec that he had engaged Cadot to recruit a war party of Ojibwe and other Indians, which was prepared to head south. In a separate correspondence, Sinclair offered more information about Cadot and why he was chosen to assist in the St. Louis battle plan. For one thing, Cadot was "much esteemed by Sir William Johnson," the head of Indian affairs in Britain's northern colonies. Additionally, Cadot had a solid reputation as both an interpreter and friend of the English. He had been an ally of the British for nearly twenty years, Patrick wrote.[40]

Cadot was therefore chosen to recruit Ojibwe and other Indians along the shores of Lake Superior.[41] He had an important ally in this effort: the relative of his late wife Athanasie, the Ojibwe chief Madjeckewiss, who would lead the Ojibwe and Odawa forces heading south from Lake Superior. The Indian allies of the British also notably included a large contingent of Dakota, led by a well-known leader named Washaba. Cadot, Madjeckewiss, Washaba, and British leaders all had a hand in convincing the Dakota and Ojibwe to set aside their frequent enmity to work together on behalf of the British. Sauk, Fox, and Ho-Chunk were also involved in what became known as the Battle of St. Louis—the westernmost confrontation of the Revolutionary War.[42]

There is no evidence that Cadot took part in the Battle of St. Louis. Neither Sinclair nor other sources mention him being present, even though they list many of the Indian and French Canadian leaders, including Madjeckewiss. But Cadot was in his late fifties at the time, and his good relationship with the Indians was valued greatly around Sault Ste. Marie and Michilimackinac because the British feared the Americans would attempt to turn the Natives to their side. In an effort to reassure British authorities at Québec that all was well near Michilimackinac, Sinclair wrote later in 1780 that the Indians at the east end of Lake Superior were "under the absolute control of Mr. Cadot, who is a very honest man."[43]

It's just as well that Cadot didn't join the expedition to St. Louis, since it was less than successful. Although the British allies killed some sixty-eight people and took thirty-eight prisoners, the tiny Spanish garrison at St. Louis, aided by the town's French citizens, held off the much larger pro-British force.[44] Worse, George Rogers Clark sent a party of soldiers and America's Indian allies in pursuit of Madjeckewiss and his retreating forces, chasing them all the way to the Chicago River. There were fears he would continue north, to Michilimackinac and the Sault, but Sinclair assured Québec that the Sault was safe with Cadot present there.[45]

Cadot's family life was also changing during the years of the American Revolution. Athanasie died in May 1776, which must have been devastating for Cadot and his young family. Sometime later, he married Catherine, an Ojibwe woman whose family may have been from the Sandy Lake area in present-day Minnesota. They were joined in the Ojibwe tradition, but unlike his marriage to Athanasie, he did not have his second marriage recognized by the Catholic Church. Jean-Baptiste and Catherine had four children together—Augustin, Charlotte, Joseph, and Marie.[46] Additionally, Cadot remained closely allied with the region's Indians, especially the Ojibwe, as well as with his fellow fur traders. Near the end of his career, in July of 1784, he was chosen by his fellow traders as one of eight men to govern Michigan's first Board of Trade.[47]

Even though the 1780 expedition to St. Louis was unsuccessful, the English continued to trust Cadot and his ability to work with Native peoples of the region. In 1783, Sinclair again sent Cadot on a mission with Madjeckewiss. This time, their assignment as they headed to the west end of Lake Superior was to attempt to halt a war already underway between the Ojibwe on one side and Fox and Dakota on the other.[48] That same year, the Cadot family ledger hinted at the changing of the guard that was occurring in the family business. The account book listed, separately from all the other furs acquired that season, one pack of furs obtained by Jean-Baptiste Cadotte Jr.[49]

By then, Cadot's partnership with Henry had ended, and his business partner was Jean-Baptiste Barthe. By 1786, Cadot had largely retired from the fur trade. The Cadot account books in that year and subsequent years refer to either the short-lived *Société générale de Michilimackinac*, a newly formed company that hired two of Cadot's sons as traders, or to the new family business, Messrs. Cadots & Company.[50] In 1796, Cadot turned over his property to his sons Jean-Baptiste Jr. and Michel, with their assurance that they would take care of him.[51]

Jean-Baptiste Cadot Sr. died in 1800 at his home at Sault Ste. Marie. He was seventy-seven.[52]

CHAPTER 9

SUPERIOR WOMEN

Although much of the written narrative about the fur trade in the Great Lakes involves men—the trappers, traders, warriors and financiers who made the business run—women, and especially Native women, were a critical part of the trade. Those women played what historian Susan Sleeper-Smith calls "a highly important role . . . in establishing the fur trade as an avenue of sociocultural change." Native women who married fur traders not only assisted in the exchange of furs for trade goods, they often "used their intermediary role and their access to trade goods to augment their own authority and that of their households."[1]

Equaysayway Cadotte and Athanasie Cadot were two such Native women who married fur traders. And, like other Native women involved in the fur trade around Lake Superior, they showed their bravery and fortitude in the face of danger and unknown terrain. They were hardy and heroic partners with their husbands in the fur trade, but they weren't unique. The fur trade itself, in Canada and the United States, was exceptional because it allowed such intermingling among European men (or men of mixed Native and European ancestry) and Indigenous women and because it rewarded strong female partners.

Among the Ojibwe, gender roles were "mutually supportive," while women's labor was valued and their legal rights under tribal rules were respected.[2] But that doesn't mean that the lot of Ojibwe women was easy. When Nicholas Perrot visited the area, beginning in 1665, he remarked on the many duties required of women, though he did not specify which nation he referred to, except to say it involved those living along the shores of Lake Superior. His first and last sentences point to important aspects of

A painting of Ojibwe women by Eastman Johnson, 1856-57. ST. LOUIS COUNTY HISTORICAL
SOCIETY

Indian women's power: they had absolute control over the family home,
and they could manufacture items to trade outside the family.

> The obligations of the women are to carry into the cabin (of which
> she is the mistress) the meat which the husband leaves at the door,
> and to dry it; to take charge of the cooking; to go to get the fish at
> the landing, and clean it; to make twine, in order to provide nets for
> the men; to furnish firewood; to raise and harvest the grain; not to
> fail in supplying shoes for the entire family, and to dry those of her
> husband and give them to him when he needs them. The women also
> are obliged to go to bring water, if they have no servants in the house;
> to make bags for holding the grain, and mats of rushes (either flat,

or round, or long) to serve as roofing for the cabins or as mattresses. Finally, it is for them to dress the skins of the animals which the husband kills in hunting, and to make robes of those which have fur. When they are traveling, the women carry the roofing for the cabin, if there is no canoe. They apply themselves to fashioning dishes of bark, and their husbands make the wooden dishes. They fabricate many curious little articles which are much in demand by our French people, and which they even send to France as rarities.[3]

Perrot's description of an Ojibwe woman's duties is similar to what ethnographer Frances Densmore recorded in the early twentieth century. Densmore interviewed many Ojibwe men and women for a series of papers and books about their lives. One woman, Nodinens, who was a member of the Mille Lacs Ojibwe band in Minnesota and seventy-four years old when she spoke with Densmore, recalled a typical year in the life of her family when she was a young girl. Her account meshes closely with that of Perrot's, but Nodinens added gardening duties for the women and girls. She said both male and female members of her family and the five other families that usually accompanied them on their seasonal travels "worked day and night and made the best use of the material we had."[4]

Erik M. Redix notes that the division of labor among the Ojibwe was unequal in many circumstances, from travel to maple sugar processing to wild rice gathering and processing, with the burden falling more heavily upon women. However, "Ojibwe women still experienced less oppression than women did in the United State and Europe" at the time. For instance, they could end their marriage and retain all of their property, while that was rarely the case for American and European women. Furthermore, Ojibwe couples were highly dependent on each other, Redix noted, "as it was extremely difficult for an adult of either gender to survive without a spouse."[5]

During most of the era of European colonization of the Americas, sexual contact between European men and Native women was either illicit or fell into the realm of conqueror controlling the conquered. However, in Canada and the Great Lakes region of the United States, marriages between Native women and European men, beginning with the French, were critical to creating social and commercial connections between Native nations and traders.[6]

Often, these arrangements were what was called "marriage *a la façon du pays*," or marriage in the custom of the country—that is, unions without typical European religious or legal ceremonies. They were widespread throughout the French era and remained a frequent practice even after the British took over.[7] Such arrangements were critical in establishing kinship ties among Native people and Europeans, which were at the heart of how many Native nations engaged in the trade. As Sleeper-Smith explains, "In the fur trade, the obligations entailed in kinship controlled both entrance into the trade and access to peltry," whether church-sanctioned or not, and "transformed French fur traders into friends, family and allies. Kinship transformed the impersonal exchange process characteristic of capitalism into a socially accountable process."[8]

The less formal approach to marriage fit well with Ojibwe traditions. Ojibwe marriages required little ceremony or official sanction; all that was needed was that the man and woman move in together after securing approval of the woman's parents. In fact, the Ojibwe verb that is translated in English as "to marry"—*wiidigem*—also means "to live with," and *wiidigemaagan*, the word for spouse, also can mean "cohabitant" or "partner."[9] There were rituals by which an Ojibwe male suitor secured the approval of his beloved's family, such as killing a deer or other large game and leaving it at her parents' lodge door to demonstrate his ability to support a wife.[10] Marriage *a la façon du pays* was a system accepted with enthusiasm by Native people as well as Europeans. In fact, the leaders of many Indigenous groups initially encouraged these alliances between Native women and European traders because they created a reciprocal social bond and strengthened economic relationships with the Europeans.[11]

As was the case with both Michel Cadotte and his father, Jean-Baptiste Cadot Sr., many successful traders in the Lake Superior region gained economic and social status by marrying women of prominent Ojibwe bands.[12] Furthermore, Ojibwe society valued women, for both their life-giving ability and their importance in the material well-being of the community. Within their marriages, Native women were responsible for producing necessary goods ranging from moccasins and snowshoes to hunting small game and preparing food. They also helped make and repair canoes, and they maintained control of important wild rice areas and maple sugar grounds, as well as the family lodge.[13]

It was hard work, and the burden imposed on Ojibwe women stunned some of the Europeans and Americans who witnessed it. Fur trader George Nelson, recalling his second year in the business in September 1803, remarked on the work that women did during a particularly difficult portage: "I never took notice 'till today of the surprising weight the women in this Country can & do carry upon their backs." They lugged all of their bags, kettles and other cooking utensils, and often a young child, as well, he added. "[I]t cannot be believed but by those who see it themselves the trouble and misery these poor wretches have, while their husband goes on with only his Gun, unless he takes a fancy to carry his medicine bag."[14] Nelson also told of the abuse many Ojibwe women suffered when their husbands were drunk, but the violence he described is little different than the abuse suffered by many non-Native women at the hands of their spouses or partners.[15]

Thomas McKenney, who visited Lake Superior two decades after Nelson's first experiences in the region, arrived at a similar conclusion about an Ojibwe woman's lot: "The women, in fact, are expected to labour at everything. From the building of a lodge, to the boiling of a kettle; and from the making of their husbands' moccasins, to the construction of their canoes, and to the gumming and sewing them when they require it, is an Indian woman's employment . . . Every species of drudgery is imposed upon her." McKenney compared Ojibwe women to packhorses, who often carried staggering loads upon their backs. Meanwhile, he said, their husbands accompanying them on their journeys usually carried little but their weapons, their pipes and pouches containing tobacco, and a few important personal items.[16] Such a division of labor was sometimes a defensive tactic, allowing the men to keep their hands free and their weapons ready in case of attack. However, the same division usually occurred even when there was little or no chance of danger.

US Army Lieutenant James Allen commented on the strength and endurance of Ojibwe women after hiring several Native men and women in 1831 to help his troops through the difficult portage between the St. Louis River and Sandy Lake in today's Minnesota: "The Indian women carry better than the men," he said. "I saw a small young Indian woman, at the close of the day, carry a keg of one thousand musket ball cartridges, for a distance of one mile, without resting," completing most of the trek through a swamp with water up to her knees.[17]

Henry Rowe Schoolcraft, who first visited the lake five years before McKenney, was equally appalled by what he saw when it came to Native women. But Schoolcraft went further, disparaging the women themselves, not just the conditions in which they lived: "Of the state of female society among the northern Indians, I shall say little, because on a review of it, I find very little to admire, either in their collective morality, or personal endowments."[18]

However, despite what Nelson and Schoolcraft witnessed and wrote, both ended up marrying women with Native heritage. Nelson married—in the backcountry sense—two Ojibwe women, one in northwestern Wisconsin and one at Lake Winnipeg in Canada. The first, whose name is unknown, he abandoned. The second, Mary Ann, remained with him after he retired from the fur trade, and the couple moved to a farm in eastern Canada.[19]

Meanwhile, Schoolcraft's dismissal of Native women didn't last long, since he married on Ojibwe-Irish woman named Jane, or Bamewawagezhikaquay, in 1823. Her father was John Johnston, a long-time fur trader who had once lived on Madeline Island, but at the time Schoolcraft met him, he and his family lived at Sault Ste. Marie. That's where Schoolcraft was posted as the government agent for Indians in the Lake Superior region. Jane's mother, Susan or Oshaguscodawaqua, was an Ojibwe and the daughter of an important clan leader at Chequamegon Bay. Thus Schoolcraft, like so many early Europeans involved with the Native people—including the Cadottes—enhanced his influence with the Ojibwe by marrying into an important family. Much of his later writing about the Ojibwe and their history was based on information he obtained through Jane and her family.[20]

Native women had a degree of independence and autonomy that surprised many Europeans when they first encountered them. Some fur traders were initially confounded by the fact that many Indigenous women they met had significant influence in a variety of areas. As one historian put it, "Within her own sphere, the Indian woman enjoyed an autonomy which was relatively greater than that of her European counterpart at the time."[21] Furthermore, as Perrot noted, Indian women were the clear masters of the family abode. Additionally, a woman could, at her discretion, trade or give away items that she made, such as cooking utensils, moccasins, and other clothing. Providing important trade goods and even

Although men controlled hunting, warfare, and much of the trade in traditional Ojibwe society, women were considered the absolute masters of the family's home. ARTIST UNKNOWN. "INDIAN TRIBES OF WISCONSIN," LOT 2575 (G). LIBRARY OF CONGRESS

more important services, such as interpreting and guiding, to fur traders and explorers allowed some women to obtain dominant positions during the fur-trade era.[22]

Women, explains Anton Treuer, "contributed significantly to civil and especially religious affairs . . . As wives, mothers, and grandmothers, women wielded power, and male leaders sought their advice and consent in many important matters."[23] Women could even take on warrior roles that were normally reserved for men. Perhaps the most famous female Ojibwe warrior was Aazhaweyaa, a member of the Lac Courte Oreilles band living near Rice Lake. She joined her father and other warriors in attacks against the Dakota in the mid-nineteenth century, killed several Dakota warriors, and, equally important for a warrior, was noted for her speed. In one instance, she reportedly ran more than one hundred miles in several days to arrive at her village ahead of all other warriors, bringing news of a successful attack on the Dakota.[24]

William Warren described at least one incident of an Ojibwe woman, in this case a grandmother, taking part in a battle in the eighteenth century. Both he and Redix list examples of women carrying weapons into battle, either to assist the male warriors or to frighten the enemy.[25] Treuer, however, said, "Female use of guns, spears and bow and arrows were prohibited by taboo." They were only allowed to use weapons such as clubs.[26] Ojibwe women participated in other traditionally male roles. Occasionally, women took on leadership roles in their communities. One Lac du Flambeau woman represented her community in 1827 treaty negotiations after her husband became ill. Other women were leaders in spiritual ceremonies.[27]

Participation in such traditionally male roles did not diminish a woman's status within her community. According to Theresa Smith, "Across North America, and specifically in the case of the Anishinaabeg, women who engaged in what were commonly seen as male pursuits were understood as extraordinary in many senses but not generally . . . as unwomanly."[28] Even so, Ojibwe society has long recognized men who chose to function as women and women who chose to function as men, according to Treuer. Their roles in Ojibwe society were "believed to be sacred, often because they assumed their roles based on spiritual dreams or visions."[29]

Yet, in the case of Aazhaweyaa, her prowess as a warrior did create one significant problem: she was unable to find an Ojibwe husband because "few Ojibwe men desire a woman who was a superior warrior." As a result, Aazhaweyaa ended up marrying two non-Native men and one of mixed ancestry. Although she had multiple children with them, all three men abandoned Aazhaweyaa or had other wives.[30]

McKenney reported one example of an exceptional Ojibwe woman when discussing Susan Johnston, Schoolcraft's mother-in-law. He described her as "tall and large, but uncommonly active and cheerful." He added, "As to influence, there is no chief in the Chippeway nation who exercises it, when it is necessary for her to do so, with equal success."[31] McKenney recounted one instance, during negotiations for the Treaty of Sault Ste. Marie in 1820, when Ojibwe leaders were on the verge of rejecting the treaty. At that critical moment, Susan Johnston sent word for some of the most important Ojibwe leaders to meet her at her house so that they could speak privately. She told them of the power of the United States and their mistaken views about the proceedings and the government's intent. This, McKenney said, "produced a change which resulted, on that same evening, in the conclusion of a treaty."[32]

It wasn't just influence with the Native leaders that women provided to explorers and fur traders. They also offered important backcountry assistance, ranging from knowledge of the terrain to experience in hunting and finding food to the ability to handle canoes. McKenney took note of the latter talent, saying, "The Indian women, and even the little girls, paddle these canoes with great skill."[33] Women made moccasins, constructed snowshoes, cured pemmican, dried fish, made sugar, and gathered and cured wild rice. But their importance and skills weren't limited to tasks that European and colonial societies considered to be women's work. They also were proficient at trapping, especially small game. Furthermore, it was not unusual for women to serve as interpreters, as guides on expeditions, and as diplomatic agents for the fur traders in their interactions with Indian nations.[34] One trader in northern Canada blamed the failure of a 1770s Hudson Bay expedition on the lack of women on the trip.[35] These important functions meant that the daughters of mixed marriages, including those of Michel and Equaysayway Cadotte, "who grew up in fur-trade society and had been instructed by their Ojibwe mother" were particularly well versed in the skills valued by fur traders.[36]

Evidence of how prevalent unions were between Europeans and Native people or between Europeans and those of mixed ancestry can be found in the baptismal records of the Catholic Church and mission at Michilimackinac, later simply called Mackinac. Records for more than a century—from 1695 to 1821—document the baptisms of hundreds of children of mixed marriages from the regions around Lake Superior and what would become northern Wisconsin and Michigan. Sometimes, the parents were listed as legally married, as when the children of Jean-Baptiste Cadot Sr. and Athanasie were baptized: "June 29, 1762, I solemnly baptized in the church of this mission, jean baptiste, legitimate son of jean Baptiste Cadot and of Athanasie his wife, born at Sault Ste. Marie on the 25th of October last." It was signed by "P. Du Jaunay, miss. of the society of Jesus."[37] A similar document was recorded for Michel Cadotte on August 13, 1764. Jean-Baptiste Cadot Sr. and Athanasie had been married in the same church in October 1756.[38] But for many other baptisms, the French Canadian father was listed by name, while the mother might be referred to only as "a savage woman" or by the nation to which she belonged. So it was that when Michel and Equaysayway Cadotte's first children were baptized at the same church on July 10, 1799, Michel Jr. and Margerite were listed as being "born of Michel Cadot and of a Sauteux [Saulteur, or Ojibwe] woman." Equaysayway didn't even warrant a mention by name in the baptismal record for her children.[39]

These backcountry marriages weren't exclusive to French Canadians and Native women. When English and Scottish traders began showing up after 1763, many of them also aligned themselves with Native women. The pattern continued after the British takeover of the Canadian fur trade, especially within the ranks of the North West Company, where everyone from wintering partners to voyageurs were allowed, even expected, to marry Native women.[40] There was a difference in this regard between the North West Company and the older Hudson's Bay Company, which discouraged such marriages. That difference was due largely to the fact that the North West Company's leaders were more in touch with actual conditions in the backcountry and on the lake, and because even the leading partners made annual trips to Grand Portage and other important backcountry locations.[41]

It should come as no surprise that, along with marriage *a la façon du pays* and marriages that were formalized in the European sense, prostitution involving Native women also existed during the fur-trade era.[42] Jesuit priests, who viewed marriage *a la façon du pays* as immoral, accused some Native women of utilizing their bodies "in lieu of merchandise."[43] However, prostitution didn't become a more prominent part of fur-trade society in the Great Lakes region because there were other critical factors, such as the importance of kinship connections, that helped stabilize relationships and promote lengthy unions.[44]

One other aspect of these European–Native marriages deserves mention. In the custom known as "turning off," a trader leaving the backcountry could arrange to have his Native spouse or his entire family placed under the protection of another trader who remained in the country.[45] George Nelson apparently engaged in an unspoken version of this process with his first Ojibwe wife in 1804, shortly before he was reassigned from what is now northern Wisconsin to a new post at Lake Winnipeg in Canada. When he determined to leave his wife, he did so by "continuing to send her away and refusing to sleep with her 'until at last an interpretor [sic] took her.'"[46] Thus "turning off" could be convenient for the fur-trading men, but it sometimes helped protect women and their children from simply being abandoned, though if an Ojibwe woman and her children were still close to her family, she could also move back in with them.

Not all traders treated their Native or mixed-ancestry wives so roughly, however. In 1799, David Thompson, who explored as far west as Pacific Ocean and as far north as the Arctic, married a half-Cree woman who was the daughter of another fur trader and a Cree mother. The Cree are an Algonquin-speaking people like the Ojibwe, many of whom lived north and west of Lake Superior during the fur-trade era in what are now the Canadian provinces of Manitoba and Saskatchewan. Thompson's wife, who was given the English name Charlotte, accompanied him on many of his expeditions and was of great assistance to him in dealing with various Native peoples. They had thirteen children together, and Charlotte moved to the Montreal area with Thompson when he retired. They remained married fifty-eight years, and Charlotte was still with Thompson when he died in 1857.[47]

Many traders viewed their marriages *a la façon du pays* as being just as legitimate as those sanctioned by churches. In the first case to be legally tested in Canada, the justice system agreed. In 1867, Canada's Chief Justice Coram Monk wondered if it was valid to consider a backcountry marriage the equivalent of concubinage—and to call the children "bastards"—when there was clear fidelity and devotion on both sides that had persisted for many years. "I think not," he wrote. "There would be no law, no justice, no sense, no morality in such a judgment."[48]

But nineteen years later, another Canadian chief justice determined that marriage *a la façon du pays* did not constitute a legal marriage. He said the court could not accept that "the cohabitation of a civilized man and a savage women, even for a long period of time, gives rise to the presumption that they consented to be married in our sense of marriage."[49] By the time he issued that ruling, however, the fur trade and marriage *a la façon du pays* had already been in decline for some time.

When European women arrived in fur-trade country, they often felt pressured to protect their social status by diminishing the status of Native women and women of mixed ancestry, against whom they might have to compete for husbands. As a result, the European women were often agents of racism against their fellow women.[50] Despite this, the power and status of Native women and those of mixed descent didn't disappear entirely. Ojibwe women's historic rights to important property such as lodges, maple sugar groves, and wild rice beds "assured them a constant measure of power and respect."[51] Additionally, marriages between Ojibwe women and Europeans, or between Native people and those of mixed descent, continued throughout the nineteenth and twentieth centuries, and they continue today. But, as successful as these modern unions may be, for the most part they don't carry the same import for business ventures, social and cultural connections, and even survival as they did in the days when Athanasie, Equaysayway, and other Ojibwe women married and partnered with European fur traders.

CHAPTER 10

VESSELS OF THE
LAKE SUPERIOR FUR TRADE

M ost people with even a passing interest in the fur trade of the north-ern United States and Canada understand that canoes were the critical waterborne vessel for carrying people and gear across lakes and up and down rivers. But they weren't the only watercraft used during the eighteenth and nineteenth centuries in the fur trade, before steam engines transformed water travel. Flat-bottomed freight boats and even a handful of small sailing ships were used on the big lakes, as were several differ-ent types of canoes: the large Montreal canoes that carried up to a dozen people, plus freight, from Montreal to the west end of Lake Superior; the smaller northern canoes used to carry a handful of men and their gear into the backcountry; and even smaller canoes, often used by Native paddlers, meant to carry just one or two people on short jaunts. But all of these ves-sels could face difficulties and danger when used on the rough waters of Lake Superior or the fast-flowing rivers in the region.

In their written accounts, early fur traders frequently mention disas-ters or near catastrophes that occurred in canoes on the lakes and rivers of the fur-trade regions. Most often, these are brief, matter-of-fact accounts that offer little detail about the wreck and minimal explanation of what went wrong. However, one vivid first-hand account of a canoe accident was provided by David Thompson, the legendary trader, explorer, and surveyor who worked first for the Hudson's Bay Company and later for the North West Company. It occurred in 1796 while he and his North West Company colleagues were navigating a difficult rapid on the Black River

Navigating canoes through river rapids was often a dangerous undertaking. PAINTING BY HOWARD SIVERTSON

near Lake Athabasca in what is now northwestern Saskatchewan.

Thompson was alone in a canoe but was connected by a rope to his companions on the shore, who were attempting to help the vessel slowly descend through a treacherous stretch of water. However, when the canoe was swept broadside into the main current of the river, Thompson sliced the rope with his knife so the canoe could run with the current rather than be swamped. As it plunged toward the rapid, Thompson was helpless to do anything but point the vessel's bow downstream. It hurtled a dozen feet over a small waterfall, and, according to Thompson, "was buried under the waves." Thompson came to the surface, but the tumbling canoe forced him beneath the swirling water once more. He pushed off the rocky river bottom with his feet and surfaced again near his canoe, this time grabbing it and hanging on as it surged downstream in the rushing river. Thompson and the canoe made it finally to slow water, where he was pulled to safety by two companions. There he laid on the rocks, "wounded bruised and exhausted by [his] exertions."[1]

I have some experience with the panic that occurs when one suddenly

Rounding the Hat Point. Hat Point marked the opening of the small bay at Grand Portage.
PAINTING BY HOWARD SIVERTSON

finds oneself underwater, with his canoe above him, though my experiences don't involve anything like the terrible rapids that capsized David Thompson's canoe. My wrecks have all occurred in much calmer waters. However, my brother, my sister, my brother-in-law, and a number of friends are all experienced and skillful canoeists. I have joined them on a variety of successful canoe trips, including in the Boundary Waters Canoe Area Wilderness in northeastern Minnesota, whose eastern border lies near the western end of the Grand Portage.

Although I've suffered some damp indignity paddling small canoes, I was impressed with the larger ones used by fur traders. The Montreal canoe, that giant freighter of the fur-trade era, is as stable as they come. While visiting Fort William Historical Park in Thunder Bay, Ontario, in 2014, my wife, Judy, and I enjoyed a ride in a birch-bark replica of the large Montreal canoes that once supplied the fur trade from Montreal through Lake Superior. The canoe, sometimes called the *canot du maître*, was long, broad, and incredibly stable, as such vessels had to be able to handle the waves of Lake Superior while carrying tons of cargo and human passengers. Averaging thirty-six feet long and six feet wide, it usually carried a crew of between eight and twelve voyageurs. Empty, it often weighed over six hundred pounds.[2]

The primary function of the Montreal canoes was to haul provisions and passengers approximately twelve hundred miles from Montreal to Grand Portage at the west end of Lake Superior. Later, the western destination would be Fort William at what is now Thunder Bay, Ontario, after the North West Company moved its Lake Superior headquarters there in 1803. Equally important, the Montreal canoes carried the valuable furs collected in the backcountry on the traders' return journey to Montreal.

Despite their size and the amount of freight they hauled, the Montreal canoes had to be carried over multiple portages on the trip from Montreal to Lake Superior. These large canoes traveled from Montreal, up the Ottawa and Mattawa Rivers, across Lake Nipissing, then down to Georgian Bay on Lake Huron. Next they traveled west on Lake Huron to Sault Ste. Marie. After portaging around St. Mary's Falls there, they headed across Lake Superior to Grand Portage or Fort William. On that journey, the cargo and the canoes had to be carried over at least thirty-three portages, and the canoes had to be unloaded each night and repacked every morning.[3]

Alexander Mackenzie noted in his journals the multiple portages and "decharges," which, he explained, were places "where the goods alone are carried" over a rocky path while the empty canoes could be towed by ropes through difficult passages. When both goods *and* canoes had to be carried overland, it was called a "portage."[4] One section of the journey that Mackenzie described, not far from Montreal, gives an idea of the difficulties faced by voyageurs and traders: "Over this portage, which is six hundred and forty-three paces long, the canoe and all the lading is carried. The rock is so steep and difficult of access, that it requires twelve men to take the canoe out of the water: it is then carried by six men, two at each end of the same side, and two under the opposite gunwale in the middle."[5] On one forty-five-mile section of the Mattawa River, Mackenzie described eight portages and two decharges, ranging from 83 paces to 456 paces. Near the last portage, he said, "is Mauvais de Musique [Bad Music], where many men have been crushed to death by the canoes, and others have received irrecoverable injuries."[6]

At Grand Portage, later Fort William, the voyageurs who manned the Montreal canoes turned over the provisions they had brought to the *hiv-*

ernants (or winterers): the voyageurs, wintering partners, and clerks of the North West Company who had brought their furs from their posts in the interior to the great annual rendezvous at the west end of Lake Superior. Because these winterers traveled much smaller rivers and lakes and faced more difficult portages, they didn't employ the Montreal canoes. Instead, they used a smaller version known as the North canoe, or *canot du nord*.

At the peak of its business, the North West Company employed roughly 180 North canoes to ferry supplies and trade goods to the more than eighty wintering posts. These lighter canoes were approximately 24 feet long and could carry 1½ tons of cargo and four to six passengers. The North canoe could be carried over portages by as few as two men.[7] The *hivernants* used the North canoes to haul the furs they obtained during the winter to the company's summer rendezvous, first at Grand Portage and later at Fort William. Once the rendezvous was over, they headed back into the interior in the same canoes, carrying trade goods, basic supplies, and some food provisions that had been brought to the rendezvous by the Montreal canoes.[8]

When out on the large lakes, canoes would sometimes be fitted with sails. Blankets or oil cloths were rigged as sails to catch a light breeze on Lake Superior. Voyageurs relaxed, smoking, singing, or sleeping while their canoes were propelled across the water by a gentle wind. "It was *La Vielle*, or 'the old woman of the wind,' who thus blessed the voyageurs with favoring breezes and lightened their toil," writes historian Grace Lee Nute.[9] Other, more substantial sailing vessels also plied the waters of Lake Superior and the other Great Lakes during the fur-trade era. In the late eighteenth century, the North West Company had "two vessels upon the Lakes Erie and Huron, and one on Lake Superior, of from fifty to seventy tons burthen," Mackenzie reported. The company shipped some of its goods south through Lake Ontario, portaging around Niagara Falls, then across Lake Erie to Detroit, where more food provisions were available. Then the journey went north on Lake Huron and eventually onto Lake Superior, using the larger sailing ships wherever possible. This was less expensive—and no doubt required less manpower—than using canoes exclusively to ferry goods across the large lakes, according to Mackenzie. But it was also riskier and generally took more time, and so it didn't become the primary method of transport.[10]

Alexander Henry and his partners in a copper-mining exploration venture, including Jean-Baptiste Cadot Sr., spent 1770–1771 building a barge and a small sailing ship on Lake Superior.[11] The sloop, launched in 1772, was to carry miners to a vein of copper or on the north side of the lake. But the mining operation proved uneconomical, and by 1774, it was disbanded and the sloop discarded.[12]

The earliest sailing ship on Lake Superior is believed to have been built by Louis Denis, Sieur de la Ronde, perhaps as early as 1734, to undertake copper mining on the south shore of the lake and to carry provisions from the Sault to La Ronde's post on Madeline Island. One report said it was capable of carrying twenty-five tons and had at least two sails, while another said it could haul as much as forty tons. Although constructed from local timber, its iron work and rigging were all ferried by canoe from Montreal. It was actually used very little for the aborted mining venture, but La Ronde used it to carry freight between Sault Ste. Marie and his Madeline Island trading post. It's not clear what became of the ship, but several reports tell of a French vessel sinking on Lake Superior around 1763, just as the British were gaining control of the region.[13]

Two other kinds of craft were also important on Lake Superior and other large lakes in the latter years of the fur trade: the bateau and the Mackinac boat. The first was a boat made of red cedar wood that was pointed at both ends but had a flat bottom. It did not have a keel and was similar to a canoe, but it was built sturdier because it was to be used in deep water and was not meant to be portaged.[14] The Mackinac boat was essentially a barge, usually constructed of red or white oak. It had a flat bottom and blunt ends, as well as a rudder and a removable mast.[15] One voyageur commented on the great speed advantage these vessels had when the wind was right: "With a mild breeze these boats will sail from 60 to 70 miles per day, while they cannot be propelled with oars more than one-half that distance."[16] For most of the fur-trade era, though, on Lake Superior and other large lakes, and on the rivers and lakes of the interior, the canoe was king.

CHAPTER 11

THE NORTH WEST COMPANY

The fur trade of the late eighteenth and early nineteenth centuries was a rough-and-tumble business in which Native people, voyageurs, and traders regularly risked their lives to collect beaver pelts and other hides. They paddled canoes across large lakes and dangerous rivers, made portages over rugged terrain, and spent winters in far-off spots where starvation was a real possibility. Attacks by Native people or opposing traders also occurred.

However, the fur trade wasn't only about adventurous men and women facing risks in the backcountry. It was also a global business, incredible in its complexity and as dangerous financially as it was physically. Consider this report from Alexander Mackenzie, someone who faced more than his share of physical dangers while traveling for the fur trade. In his journal, Mackenzie offered the following example of how the business would work to supply provisions to traders operating in the backcountry in the winter of 1798–1799:

> The orders for the goods are sent [from Canada to England] 25th Oct. 1796.
>
> They are shipped from London March 1797.
>
> They arrive in Montreal June 1797.
>
> They are made [packed for canoe transport] in the course of that summer and winter.
>
> They are sent from Montreal May 1798.

They arrive in Indian country, and are exchanged for furs the following winter 1798–9.

Which furs come to Montreal Sept. 1799.

And are shipped to London, where they are sold in March and
April, and paid for in May or June 1800.[1]

The process Mackenzie described required nearly four years between the
time provisions for the 1798–1799 season were ordered and the furs from
that season were sold in London. During that time, all manner of catastrophes could occur in every part of the supply chain. Little wonder that Mackenzie called the fur trade "a very heavy business."[2] But it was a profitable
business if all went well. For instance, Jean-Baptiste Cadot Sr. noted a profit
of 80 percent in his account book for 1785, which lists goods he purchased
and delivered to his trading post in Michigan's Upper Pennisula.[3]

The fur trade was also critical to the economy of Britain's Canadian
territories, especially when the American Revolutionary War began. In
April of 1780, while the revolution was in full swing, Québec merchant
Charles Grant prepared a report at the behest of General Frederick Haldimand, governor of Québec, regarding the status of the fur trade in Canada.
The trade produced an annual return to Great Britain "in Furrs [sic]" of
approximately 200,000 pounds sterling, Grant wrote, "which is an object
deserving of all the encouragement and protection which Government
can with propriety give to that trade."[4] If, as a result of the war or new
regulations, the fur trade "should be under great restraints, or obstructed
a few years, the consequences would prove ruinous to the commercial part
of this Province and very hurtful to the merchants of London," he added,
"besides the loss of so valuable a branch of trade in Great Britain."[5]

Britain had wrested control of Canada from the French during the
Seven Years' War, known as the French and Indian Wars in the colonies.
At the conclusion of that war, France gave up its claim to Canada with the
Treaty of Paris of 1763. Almost immediately, Alexander Henry and like-
minded adventurers such as Peter Pond, Benjamin and Joseph Frosbisher,
and others began tentative incursions into the old French fur-trading territories. Despite initial antagonism from many of the Native nations—
such as with Pontiac's War—they soon developed trading relationships

with many of the nations, and the British fur trade flourished.

As Grant's report shows, by 1780, the fur trade was already a critical enterprise for Great Britain's northern colonies; in fact, it was the primary revenue producer for Canada. Merchants in Montreal and Québec were buying goods from London and elsewhere and trading their furs to satisfy the fashions of Europe. They relied on ships that brought goods from Europe and the Caribbean and occasionally traded in China. They depended on financiers in England who provided start-up money and multiyear operating loans. But in 1780, English and Scottish merchants were just beginning to define and organize the fur trade as it had never been before.

The North West Company would significantly change the way the fur trade was conducted. Unlike the stodgy Hudson's Bay Company, which initially demanded that Natives bring their furs to its main posts on Hudson Bay, the North West Company followed the old coureurs de bois practice of taking the trade to the Indians, however far from Montreal they might be. But the new company did so in a much more systematic manner than did the early French traders. In the four decades the company existed, the men of the North West Company were said to have "conquered half a continent and they built up a commercial enterprise the like of which North America, at least, has never seen."[6]

"Conquered," though, is not the correct verb in this instance because there was no military or civilian conquest. Instead, the North Westers traveled, traded, and effected alliances, often where no Europeans had previously been, and they did so in a much more organized manner than did earlier traders.

Mackenzie, a partner in the North West Company, traveled overland to the Pacific Ocean a dozen years before Lewis and Clark started their famed journey in 1804. Before that, Mackenzie followed unnamed rivers to the Arctic Ocean. The Mackenzie River in the Northwest Territories of Canada—the second longest river in North America—was named for him. Other partners and agents of the North West Company encountered Native nations that had never before seen Europeans and made the first European visits to the northern Rocky Mountains. They surveyed and produced maps that were extremely accurate for the time, and they recorded detailed geologic and ethnographic descriptions of their surroundings. Many kept journals that provide invaluable insight into this period of the fur trade. But mostly, they maintained a difficult and complicated business enterprise operating through wars, Indian uprisings, political changes, and economic difficulties.

All this, despite the fact that the North West Company was always an ambiguous corporate enterprise. "The North West Company never was a company in the modern sense," according to historian Marjorie Wilkins Campbell. "It had no charter. It was, rather, a series of co-partnerships between small groups of men who were promoters, merchants or fur-trader-explorers, or all three together or in turn."[7] Most of the principals in the company were Scottish immigrants who had left their homes for North America. Others were British colonials who had moved from New England, New York, and other parts of what would become the United States. A few were French Canadians, including members of the Cadotte family, who were involved with the North West Company for much of its existence.

In 1795, Jean-Baptiste Cadotte Jr.—eldest son of Athanasie Cadot and Jean-Baptiste Cadot Sr.—became a clerk with the North West Company in charge of the Fond du Lac division.[8] In that capacity, he oversaw much of the company's business at the southwestern end of Lake Superior, including trading and trapping on the Upper Mississippi River and its drainages. He became a partner at the company's annual Grand Portage meeting in 1801.[9] Only one other French Canadian is listed among the partners at that time: Charles Chaboillez.[10]

While Jean-Baptiste's brother Michel was never a partner in the North West Company, he did work with it, primarily as an independent trader who maintained a post on Madeline Island that traded exclusively with the company. He also oversaw much of the firm's business into the interior of what is now north-central Wisconsin. Minutes of the company annual meeting at Grand Portage in July 1802 include three pages of terms spelling out the agreement between Michel Cadotte and the North West Company. Those terms contracted him for three years to engage in commerce on the company's behalf at "pointe Chaguamigon"—at Chequamegon Bay—as well as the Chippewa River and Lac Courte Oreilles.[11]

But before the brothers Cadotte could tie their fortunes to the North West Company, it had to be created, and that occurred piecemeal. The years immediately after 1763, when Britain gained control of Canada, amounted to a free-for-all in the fur business. The government of the Canadian prov-

inces attempted to regulate traders, for instance, by granting Alexander
Henry and Jean-Baptiste Cadot Sr. the first exclusive license to trade on
Lake Superior. Soon, however, there were many others operating with and
without licenses in that region and territories farther west, elbowing each
other aside to get the first chance at pelts offered by Indians, building trading posts almost on top of one another, poaching Native people en route
to trade with the Hudson's Bay Company, encouraging voyageurs to leave
the employ of other traders to bring their goods and/or Indian relatives to
them. On the Saskatchewan River alone in 1774, four different groups "were
struggling for the trade," Henry wrote. "But fortunately they had this year
agreed to join their stock, and when the season was over, to divide the skins
and meat."[12] That was among the earliest trader confederations that led to
establishment of the North West Company.

It wasn't just competition among the traders that created problems for
the merchants. Government authorities reacted to war with the Americans
in ways that threatened traders' livelihoods. Even so, in May 1778, at the
request of the traders, the government in Québec sent an officer and twelve
men from Michilimackinac to Grand Portage to protect the traders' invest-
ments during the summer rendezvous. The traders also wanted the military
to help them track down voyageurs who had abandoned their responsi-
bilities to the traders. The government, for its part, "was suspicious about
the quantities of guns, ammunition, and blankets being shipped to Grand
Portage, which might easily find their way into the wrong hands," meaning
the hands of the American rebels or those sympathetic to their cause.[13]

In 1778, the government in Québec was late in issuing licenses for fur
traders. The following year "it was rumoured, the governor at Québec
would issue no licenses at all on the ground that only by such restrictions
could he ensure that no goods would reach the rebels."[14] To prevent that
possibility, several Montreal merchants, led by Simon McTavish, prepared
a petition to Governor Haldimand, urging him to allow the trade to continue with the guns and ammunition necessary to barter with Indians and
protect traders. That petition prompted Haldimand to request that Charles
Grant prepare his report on the fur trade that is cited above.

In the meantime, the traders sought a means of working together
rather than ravaging one another's business in competitive endeavors.
Around 1783–1784, according to Mackenzie and a history of the company,

the various fur trade merchants joined together and called themselves the North West Company.[15] It was divided into sixteen shares, but the principals didn't deposit any capital into it, Mackenzie noted. Instead, each party furnished a portion of the goods necessary for the trade.[16]

Mackenzie didn't join the North West Company until July of 1787, after a year of bitter competition with it. Initially, the principals in the company included Simon McTavish and Benjamin and Joseph Frobisher, all experienced traders and merchants.[17] The sixteen shares were divided among nine groups or partnerships: the Frobisher brothers had two shares, as did Todd & McGill; McGill and Paterson; McTavish & Co.; Holmes & Grant; Wadden & Co.; and McBeath & Co. Two other smaller partnerships, Ross & Co. and Oakes & Co., held one share apiece.[18]

The partnerships involved in the North West Company changed frequently over the years, and the number of shares grew. Although Alexander Henry was closely involved with many of the people who formed the company and sometimes bought and sold its furs, he wasn't an original partner of the firm. However, in 1792, when the North West Company expanded its stock to forty-six shares and took in several new partners to eliminate potential competition, Henry and his nephew Alexander Henry the Younger decided to sign up.[19]

The North West Company also sought government protection from competition. As early as 1784, the company was petitioning Governor Haldimand for a ten-year exclusive right to trade in the Northwest region, which included Lake Superior and almost everything west and north of it. In October of that year, Benjamin and Joseph Frobisher wrote a letter to Haldimand, laying out their case. They made it abundantly clear that the fur trade was critical to British interests in the New World, especially because by then the thirteen colonies of the United States had won their independence and removed those territories and their economic resources from the British sphere of influence.[20]

The Frobishers also attempted to show Haldimand how difficult and complicated the fur trade was. For instance, they wrote that travel from Montreal to the company's trading posts beyond Lake Superior "is perhaps the most extensive of any in the known World, but is only practicable for Canoes on account of the great number of Carrying places" or portages.[21] "Two setts [sic] of men are employed in this business, making together upwards of 500" working for the North West Company, the Frobishers explained. Half of that number were employed in transporting goods from Montreal to Grand Portage, at the west end of Lake Superior; "the other half are employed to take such goods forward to every Post in the interior Country to the extent of 1,000 to 2,000 miles and upwards, from Lake Superior."[22]

Voyageurs who handled the Montreal to Grand Portage leg of the trip were known as *mangeurs de lard*, or pork eaters, so called because they usually had lard to add to their dried peas or corn meal and frequently had bacon and other pork meat during their voyages in the great canoes. They were looked down upon by the *hivernants*, or winterers, the more experienced voyageurs who took the goods from Grand Portage to the interior posts and spent the winters there, trapping and trading. Wild game and fish, as well as pemmican made from bison, moose, and other large game, supplied most of the protein in their diets, rather than pork.[23]

But it wasn't just voyageurs who spent winters in the interior. Many partners in the North West Company, such as Jean-Baptiste Cadotte Jr., and clerks who served with them at trading posts were also known as winterers. At the Grand Portage rendezvous in 1794, those wintering partners and clerks complained vociferously about the conditions they had to endure—the poor food and trade goods they often received—along with relatively low pay or minimal shares in the company, while senior partners spent winters in relative luxury in Montreal or even London. A new agreement was hammered out to alleviate those concerns.[24]

Making money off the fur trade was the first order of business for the North West Company, but the principals also recognized how much they depended on the voyageurs to help them become profitable. Thus, in the early years of the nineteenth century, they created a retirement program of sorts for the primarily French Canadian voyageurs. According to the company minutes from an 1810 meeting, "The Agents represented the unfortunate Case of many Old Voyageurs lately discharged from the Companys Service, who have no means of Support—and [are] too Old and Infirm to work in Lower Canada [the region from Montreal eastward]." The partners opted to do something to help "these objects of charity" and agreed to set aside a total of one hundred pounds a year, "to be divided in such manner, as in their Judgment appeared best, but no Individual to receive more than Ten pounds Currency in One Year."[25]

Supplying all those involved in the North West Company trade was difficult, whether they were winterers or the summer crews traveling from Montreal to Grand Portage, as the Frobishers made clear in their letter to Haldimand: "The large Canoes from Montreal always set off early in May . . . [T]he utmost dispatch is required that everything may be ready in point of time to send off their supplies for the Interior Country. . . . Goods, Provisions and everything else required for the Outfits of the year, must be at Grand Portage early in July." It could take up to fifteen days, they noted, for the winterers and their crews to carry all of their provisions for the coming winter across the 8.5 miles of the Grand Portage itself. And those wintering crews sought to leave the western end of the portage, on the Pigeon River, between July 15 and August 1.[26]

If the physical realities of supplying the fur-trade crews were daunting, so were the financial requirements for obtaining provisions from the other end of the supply chain, as Alexander Mackenzie's example demonstrated. When so much time was required between the date provisions were ordered and when furs were sold, a financial middleman was needed to "pay the manufacturers as the goods were delivered and send them on to his customers in America, and who was willing to tie up his own capital until the New World customer had sold the goods and remitted his payments."[27] These middlemen were crucial for businesses throughout colonial America, but they were especially important for the fur trade, not only providing the necessary capital for the trade, but also taking responsibility for marketing the furs in England and the rest of Europe.

Two of the most important merchants, as far as the North West Company was concerned, were John Strettell and John Fraser. These two men were critical to the North West Company's success, even though "Strettell probably never set eyes on Canada, and Fraser was probably never west of Montreal. [T]he influence they had on Canadian business in general, and the fur trade in particular, was great and lasting."[28]

Strettell had business interests and customers from Canada to Bermuda, but he acquired his wealth largely from the fur trade.[29] His connections in Canada included Benjamin and Joseph Frobisher; Québec merchant Charles Grant; and Isaac Todd and James McGill, who formed the business Todd & McGill, which was one of the founding partnerships of the North West Company. Through his customers, Strettell controlled several shares in the North West Company and helped design its organization shortly after its founding. In the early years of the firm, Strettell was "the most important source of capital" for the company.[30] After Strettell died in 1786, John Fraser took on the critical role for the company, even though he had gone bankrupt in 1784. Fraser's financial problems stemmed from the American Revolutionary War and the disruptions it caused in the Canadian fur trade, where Fraser was heavily invested.[31]

A few years after Fraser assumed Strettell's financial role, around 1790, Simon McTavish approached Fraser about becoming a partner "in a new London firm of commission merchants, which would take over the supplying of goods to the North West Company." He agreed, and McTavish, Fraser & Company was born, with Fraser assigned to manage the firm's affairs in London, while McTavish oversaw operations from Montreal.[32] Through this arrangement, McTavish also became the guiding partner of the North West Company, the closest thing to a chief executive officer the firm had. Fraser supervised the preparation of supplies to be sent from London to Montreal each year, leasing or purchasing ships to carry the cargo and hiring captains to sail them. He also marketed the North West Company furs in London, and managed its cash flow. He died in 1825, outliving McTavish and the North West Company itself.[33]

While complex global transactions were critical to the fur trade, agreements with individual traders were also important and far from simple. The 1796 agreement between the North West Company and Jean-Baptiste Cadotte Jr. offers some insight into these arrangements. It was an extension of the 1795 agreement in which Cadotte became a clerk for the company, and it takes up four pages in the record of the company's minutes from its Grand Portage meeting of 1796. As per the agreement, "The said North West Compy [sic] by their said Agents agree to furnish, fit out & Provide at this Place or the Fond du Lac, all such goods as the said Jean-Baptiste Cadotte may require for the said Trade or Adventure." The company agreed to provide "a yearly Assortment of Merchandize not exceeding Six Canoes Load" to Cadotte. It would also hire "Clerks, Interpreters & Men [voyageurs] as may be required for this Concern" and handle the financing.[34]

In return, Cadotte promised to use the goods he received to "Trade, vend, Sell & barter such goods . . . in the best and most advantageous manner" for himself and the company. Further, he agreed to keep accounts of all of his transactions, and he pledged to trade only within the geographical limits set out for him by the company, without infringing on the territory or dealing with Native people who traded with other North West Company posts. Finally, the company agreed to receive Cadotte's furs, "either at this place [Grand Portage] or Fond du Lac . . . at regular, fair & Stated Prices, which prices shall be fixed upon by the Parties themselves Yearly at the time of making the outfit."[35]

A decade after that agreement was signed, a variety of events—geopolitical and financial—conspired to start the North West Company on a downward spiral. In one instance, Alexander Mackenzie decided to go into direct competition with the organization. After his Pacific and Arctic journeys, Mackenzie went to London, where he published his journals. He also became an eighteenth-century celebrity, with his dashing good looks and his tales of Indians, exploration, and adventure. In February 1802, while still in London, he was knighted. When Sir Alexander Mackenzie returned to Montreal, he left the North West Company, joining a partnership and eventually becoming the head of what was known as the XY Company, which competed directly with the North West Company. The new firm was consolidated into the older company in 1804, but the business battle of several years had drained the resources of both firms in the process.[36] The North West Company also survived changes in leadership that included the death of Simon McTavish, who controlled the company through the partnership firm of McTavish, Fraser & Co. He was replaced by his nephew William McGillivray.[37]

Faced with new international boundaries established at the end of the American Revolutionary War and formalized in the Jay Treaty of 1794, the North West Company moved the site of its annual rendezvous and critical meeting place from the Grand Portage—which was part of the United States—to the Kaministiquia River at what is now Thunder Bay, Ontario. Fort Kaministiquia would soon be renamed Fort William, in honor of William McGillivray.[38] Unfortunately for traders, it required a longer, more difficult trip for winterers to reach the backcountry than the Grand Portage site and thus added costs to the company's activities.

The company briefly expanded to the Pacific Ocean, with a fur-exporting site on the Columbia River in what is now Oregon. The British company used the location jointly with John Jacob Astor's American Fur Company, providing an important shipping point to fur markets in Asia. But the conclusion of the War of 1812 made it off limits to the British North Westers.[39]

There were more difficulties, both financial and physical. None was more troublesome than Thomas Douglas, the Earl of Selkirk, and his effort to move settlers onto the Red River, in the middle of some of the North West Company's prime trading territory. That years-long battle was fought economically and legally, and occasionally with violence.[40] One of those involved in the fight with Selkirk, working on behalf of the North West Company, was Joseph Cadotte, believed to be the younger son of Jean-Baptiste Cadot Sr. and a half-brother to Michel Cadotte and Jean-Baptiste Cadotte Jr. He was implicated in the murder of one of Lord Selkirk's men, eventually taken to Montreal to stand trial, indicted, but ultimately never brought to trial.[41]

Simultaneously, there was fierce, sometimes violent, competition with traders associated with the Hudson's Bay Company. At one point, the opponents of the North West Company briefly took control of Fort William and "arrested" North West Company officials there. These lengthy battles drained needed resources from the company as it confronted other problems.[42] Furthermore, the leaders of the North West Company could never convince authorities in England to officially guarantee them a piece of the huge economic and territorial pie that was granted to the Hudson's Bay Company more than a century earlier by King Charles II. Nor could they obtain the protection from competition that they desired. The combined consequences of all these factors were too much for the fragile business arrangements by which the North West Company operated. Its trade—and its business model of taking the trade to Native people in the backcountry—was assumed by the Hudson's Bay Company. The North West Company ceased to exist in 1821.[43]

Those who had been involved with the company were not happy about its demise. In the early 1820s at the Hudson's Bay Company trading post at Rainy Lake, on the border between Canada and Minnesota, many employees were former North West Company men and were "much dissatisfied with the present concern."[44] But that unhappiness could not bring the North West Company back to life.

The North West Company "was no more than an association of commercial men, agreeing among themselves to carry on the fur trade, unconnected with any other business," Mackenzie said.[45] But in its relatively short history, it enabled the exploration and commercialization of the northern third of this continent.

CHAPTER 12

GRAND PORTAGE

Grand Portage is not an easy trek, even in the twenty-first century. The trail as it leaves the site of the old North West Company trading depot and heads west is initially fairly flat but quickly climbs more than six hundred feet to Fort Charlotte eight and a half miles to the west. It takes hikers up and down hills, across streams and through boggy areas. In places, sharp rocks bit at the soles of our shoes. As my wife and I hiked, the irregular surface of the trail made twisting an ankle a real possibility. We survived, however, using hands and hiking sticks to maintain balance. We had planned on only a short trek, not the full seventeen-mile round trip, and it's a good thing. Not only was our gear inadequate, but my physical capability at the time was limited due to a bad knee. Our experience wasn't unique. Other recent travelers on the trail have mentioned how difficult it is.[1]

I can't fathom making that round-trip journey—clad in moccasins, a woolen shirt, and buckskin leggings—day after day for a week or more, carrying ninety-pound packs each way. Particularly hardy voyageurs could carry *two* ninety-pound packs each way. That's what explorer and North West Company partner Alexander Mackenzie described near the end of the eighteenth century. During the course of several days, each voyageur was expected to carry eight packages of ninety pounds apiece over the rugged trail from the North West Company depot at Grand Portage, on the western shore of Lake Superior, to tiny Fort Charlotte on the Pigeon River. At Fort Charlotte, the packages—goods to trade with the Indians and provisions for the long winter in the interior—would be loaded into the midsized North canoes to begin the journey to the northwestern trading territories. On the return trip to Lake Superior, the voyageurs usually carried packs of furs bound into ninety-pound bales to be sent east to Montreal and Europe.[2]

David Thompson, a sometime colleague of Mackenzie, said it required "five days of hard labor" for his team of voyageurs to carry four canoes and all of their gear from Lake Superior to Fort Charlotte in August of 1796. Because Thompson was embarking on a surveying expedition for the North West Company, he and his men also had to transport a large sextant, two telescopes, several thermometers, and drawing instruments.[3] Thompson surveyed Grand Portage again in 1821 as part of an international boundary expedition. Nearly two centuries later, an archaeological group explored Grand Portage and determined that "Thompson's 1821 portage data . . . compared closely with the present portage configuration."[4]

Others who trekked over the Grand Portage during the fur-trade days offered less than glowing descriptions of it. One traveler in 1800 described the portage as being "very bad in some places, knee deep in mud and clay, and so slippery, as to make walking tedious."[5] Another traveler around the same time complained that "where it is not rock, it is mud" and described the mosquitoes as "ferocious." Humans, rather than more conventional beasts of burden, had to haul the goods over Grand Portage because, Mackenzie said, both horses and oxen were tried on the Grand Portage trail, "without success."[6]

Having ridden and packed horses a good deal in the Rocky Mountains and nearby deserts, I can understand that. Although hooves can be protected from sharp rocks with shoes or even special boots, swamps and bogs drain the horse's energy quickly. Animals may even become mud-bound, unable to move.

It's likely that Jean-Baptiste Jr. and Michel Cadotte made the trip over *the* Grand Portage at some point during their careers. We know from their contracts with the North West Company that they traveled to the firm's Grand Portage depot many summers to pick up their trade goods and provisions for the following winters. But the Grand Portage trail itself was primarily a route to northwestern regions such as Saskatchewan and the Lake Athabasca country. It did not lead to the lands now known as northwestern Wisconsin and northern Minnesota, where the Cadotte brothers did most of their trading.

Grand Portage (on Lake Superior) as it might have appeared in 1792, when the North West Company was in full operation. HOWARD SIVERTSON

However, there was *another* Grand Portage, and it's clear the Cadottes traveled there. It was on the St. Louis River, about twenty miles upstream from where the river empties into Lake Superior at what was then called Fond du Lac, now Duluth, Minnesota. The St. Louis River portage was known as one of the most difficult and treacherous in the region, being more than seven miles long and extending over steep hills and through marshes. It could take up to five days for a crew of traders and voyageurs to carry all of their gear and fur bundles around the falls on the river. Climbing the steep, often muddy, clay hills adjacent to the rocky gorge where the falls raged was especially treacherous, frequently requiring those doing the portaging to scramble on hands and feet.[7] Jean-Baptiste Jr. and Michel traversed the St. Louis River Grand Portage in the autumn of 1792, when they were embarking on a lengthy expedition to the headwaters of the Mississippi River and on to the Red River.[8] Four years later, Jean-Baptiste Jr. lost a canoe and three of his ten packs of furs when his voyageurs were attempting to navigate the St. Louis River Grand Portage during the spring. Luckily, several men and one woman in the canoe were able to make it safely to shore before the canoe was lost.[9]

This replica of the old North West Company depot is maintained by the National Park Service as part of Grand Portage National Monument, Grand Portage, Minnesota.
ROBERT SILBERNAGEL

When Michel and Equaysayway were heading toward winter quarters along the Chippewa River, they would likely have taken a different route. Several old trails lead south from Chequamegon Bay to the interior lands of northwestern Wisconsin, including one that follows the Bad River south, then across a portage to the Chippewa River. But even these routes involved lots of hard work and occasional danger. Michel lost two of his voyageurs in a canoe wreck at Chippewa Falls.

I've not been to the Pigeon River end of Grand Portage, where Fort Charlotte once sat, but I have journeyed in the Boundary Waters Canoe Area Wilderness of northern Minnesota, west of the Pigeon River, and in Quetico Provincial Park just across the border in Ontario. And I have experienced the dubious pleasure of making repeated trips over the same portage to carry canoe, clothes, and camp provisions from one lake to another. The longest portage I've made was probably no more than a half mile, but the repeated hikes over the same trails—some steep, many wet and slippery—were by far the most unpleasant parts of the journey.

Portaging was just part of life for early fur traders and their Native allies. Whether traveling from Montreal to Lake Superior, over Grand Portage to the lands of the northwest, or taking a different route into the interior of northern Wisconsin and Minnesota, the traders, voyageurs, and Native people accepted carrying heavy burdens on the trail as part of the journey. Many voyageurs even boasted of their prowess on the portage.[10]

CHAPTER 13

THE ITCH TO TRADE

A certain romanticism accompanies the idea of traipsing on paths where fur traders like Michel and Equaysayway once trod. My wife, Judy, and I have hiked on several such trails, on Madeline Island, at Grand Portage, and on the mainland of Wisconsin, in Minnesota, on Michigan's Upper Peninsula, on Isle Royale, and near Thunder Bay, Ontario. But any romantic notions or historic sentimentality can quickly evaporate when you're being attacked by hordes of hungry mosquitoes.

Those blood-sucking creatures have been annoying people in the fur-trade regions for a long time. Consider the following account from John J. Bigsby, regarding a trip he took to Lake Superior in 1823. The events described occurred on the Pigeon River, at the northwest terminus of the Grand Portage, after travelers had made the 8.5-mile trek from the west end of Lake Superior. It was the typical route of most wintering traders and voyageurs during the height of the North West Company's fur trade: "The mosquitoes were ferocious. . . . Although the heat was very great in these close woods, we wore gloves, veils, and caps over the ears. My pantaloons were tied close down to the boots, or the creatures would have crept up the legs."[1]

After traveling about eighteen miles westward along the Pigeon River, Bigsby's party came upon broad meadows that would have been pleasant, were it not for the mosquitoes. "We slept, or tried to do so, in these meadows. The mosquitoes were in billions," he reported. "As soon as the tread of man gave notice of his approach, I saw them rising to the feast in clouds out of the coarse grass around. We burnt the grass after watering it, and lived in the smoke."[2]

Bigsby's experience was hardly unique. Father René Menard, a French priest who died in 1661 in the woods of what is now northern Wisconsin, was also plagued by mosquitoes. Three French Canadians who accompanied Menard and returned to Québec to tell of their travails reported that the mosquitoes were "so unbearable that . . . there is no other way to ward them off than to run without stopping."[3] Even drinking water was an ordeal. As the French Canadians explained, "[I]t was even necessary for the two others to busy themselves driving away those little creatures whenever any one of them wished to drink, for otherwise he could not have done so."[4]

It wasn't just Lake Superior and nearby lands that harbored mosquitoes, of course. Henry Rowe Schoolcraft offered a heartfelt description of mosquito torment when he wrote of his time near Sandy Lake in what is now Minnesota. According to Schoolcraft, it rained on the evening of July 26, 1820, but when the intermittent showers stopped, "[T]he musquitoes [sic] assailed us in such numbers as to forbid the hope of rest." The insects "unceasingly beset us with their stings, and poured forth their hateful and incessant buzzing upon our ears," he added.[5] It required more than normal human courage and temerity to withstand the attacks, Schoolcraft said.

When he worked at Churchill Factory on Hudson Bay in 1785, fur trader and explorer David Thompson discovered that summer could be more unpleasant than the long, dark Hudson Bay winter: "Summer such as it is, comes at once, and with it myriads of tormenting Musketoes [sic]; the air is thick with them, there is no cessation day nor night of suffering from them."[6] Thompson, though just a teenager at the time, was also a budding scientist and explorer. So, he turned his powers of observation on the mosquito. "The Musketoe Bill [beak or proboscis] when viewed through a good Microscope, is of a curious formation; composed of two distinct pieces;" he wrote. Thompson described both, explaining how the insects sucked blood from their victims, and said humans weren't the only ones tormented. "All Animals suffer from them, almost to madness," he said.[7]

Canadian civil engineer and author Thomas Keefer, speaking in 1854 about the flying attackers on the Ottawa River—the fur-trader highway that ran southwest from Montreal—exaggerated only a little in his description of coping with mosquitoes: "If you would sleep [along the river] on a sweltering night in June, nothing short of chloroform will render a novice insensible to the melody of those swamp serenaders, the mosquitoes, or the tactics of their blood thirsty ally, the black fly, who noiselessly fastens upon your jugular while the mosquito is bragging in your face."[8]

Remedies to ward off mosquitoes existed long before modern chemical insect repellents. Keefer mentioned two methods, neither of which was particularly pleasant: "The first cure is the one applied to hams—smoke yourself until your eyes are like burned holes in a blanket, and until you have creosote enough in your mouth to cure a toothache. The second is to smear all your assailable parts with Canadian balsam [oil and turpentine], until after a night's tossing in your blanket, you have wool enough on your face and hands to make you look as well as feel,—decidedly sheepish."[9]

Native people and French Canadian fur traders utilized still other chemical concoctions to repel mosquitoes and other bugs. One sounds particularly noxious. It was described as "a mix of bear grease and skunk urine."[10] Alexander Henry the Younger said buffalo dung—the only burnable material to be found on the northern plains during part of his journey—proved to be an adequate repellent. "The buffalo dung was tolerably dry, and we made a shift to keep up a smudge to drive off the swarms of mosquitoes."[11]

David Thompson, however, said this technique was useless against the aggressive mosquitoes near Hudson Bay. "Smoke is no relief, they can stand more smoke than we can," he wrote. Later in his narrative he added, "Oil is the only remedy, and that frequently applied; the Natives rub themselves with Sturgeon Oil, which is found to be far more effective than any other oil."[12] Thompson also said smoke was ineffective because "smoke cannot be carried about with us."[13] But, of course, the voyageurs did just that, always keeping their pipes and tobacco handy, ready to smoke when they had a brief respite in their paddling or portaging. In addition to providing a measure of pleasure, the pipes helped keep the bugs away, at least for a brief time.

Smoke, oil, and grease weren't the only weapons in the mosquito wars. Simply being several yards from shore on a big lake like Superior, where a steady breeze is the norm, tends to keep the bugs at bay. Moreover, recent research suggests that the Ojibwe and other Native people of the northern United States and Canada found a natural mosquito repellent that we have only recently rediscovered. Sweet grass, a plant found throughout much of North America, produces a chemical compound called "coumarin," and its odor repels mosquitoes.[14] Plains Indians made braids of sweet grass that they wore and hung in their homes. Indians of the Great Lakes, including the Ojibwe, made baskets, bowls, and mats from sweet grass.[15]

Additionally, some recent evidence suggests that a person's attractiveness to mosquitoes—or lack of appeal to the insects—may be inherited.[16] If that is the case, it is possible that evolution may have helped Native people such as the Ojibwe develop a genetic natural repellent to mosquitoes in their sweat and body odor. Over generations, their mixed-ancestry relatives, like the Cadottes, may have developed a similar genetic barrier.

But for Judy and me and other modern explorers who find they are attractive to mosquitoes, Deet-based repellents or similar products are recommended. Dressing as Bigsby did in 1823—with hats and gloves and the bottoms of pant legs tied—certainly doesn't hurt.

CHAPTER 14

JEAN-BAPTISTE CADOTTE JR.

In the spring of 1798, as he was surveying the Red River region on behalf of the North West Company, David Thompson encountered Jean-Baptiste Cadotte Jr., and he was impressed. The thirty-five-year-old French Canadian-Ojibwe trader had received a good education in Montreal and spoke fluent Ojibwe, Latin, French, and English.[1]

Like Thompson, Jean-Baptiste worked for the North West Company when Thompson visited him at the mouth of the Clearwater River in present-day Minnesota. Thompson consulted Jean-Baptiste about whether he and his party should continue on foot as the snow and ice rapidly melted, or wait until spring had fully arrived and then proceed eastward by canoe. The surveyor ignored Jean-Baptiste's advice to wait, and he soon regretted that decision.

Days after leaving the post, Thompson and his men found that the melting muck was nearly impassable for heavily loaded dogsleds and men on snowshoes. They opted to return to Jean-Baptiste's post, but even that effort became a near disaster as men and dogs were snared in the water and slush. On March 31, Thompson and his party traveled just three miles in three hours as they tried to reach it. They grew so fatigued that they halted the dogs, laid down their packs, and hiked on empty-handed. "At 2 PM, thank good Providence, we arrived at the house of Mr. Cadotte," a weary Thompson reported. Jean-Baptiste immediately sent five men to retrieve all of Thompson's gear and animals.[2]

Given such an amicable beginning to their relationship, it's ironic that five years later, when Jean-Baptiste was dismissed from the North West Company, it would be Thompson who assumed his place as a partner.[3]

Yet it is emblematic of the stormy ride that marked the life of Jean-Baptiste Cadotte Jr.—waves of success and reward followed by dissolution and disgrace. While nearly all sources report that Jean-Baptiste Sr. and his son Michel were steady hands in the fur trade throughout their long careers—adventurous and bold when necessary, but solid and dependable—Jean-Baptiste Jr., in contrast, was the beloved-but-reckless member of the family.

As Thompson noted, Jean-Baptiste was an exceptional linguist, a skill that proved invaluable throughout the latter's life. He also explored important territories for the British fur traders, and he was fearless in dealing with Indians, even when his life was in peril. He won many accolades from people involved in the fur trade near Lake Superior, but sometimes he acted rashly, giving money and goods freely to voyageurs and Indians alike.[4] He also drank excessively on some occasions. Alcohol, it turned out, would be his undoing.

Jean-Baptiste Cadotte Jr. was born on October 25, 1761, at Sault Ste. Marie. He was the third child of Athanasie and Jean-Baptiste Cadot Sr., but their first son.[5] He was baptized by a Jesuit priest on June 29, 1762.[6] The young Jean-Baptiste, along with his brother Michel and an older sister, Marie-Renée, were sent as children to Montreal to be educated, along with another brother, Joseph-Marie, and sister Charlotte, both of whom died young. Their mother accompanied them while their father remained most of the time at Sault Ste. Marie. The family account book shows special care was taken to ensure that mother and children had provisions to live comfortably in Montreal.

A page in the ledger for June and July 1772 discusses items provided to Athanasie and her children by a Montreal merchant.[7] Among the provisions listed on the ledger for mother and children were one pound of "Cotton thread for making Stocks [stockings] for the children" and "1 quire [about 25 sheets] paper for Jean-Baptiste."[8] In February 1773, the account book recorded payments for eight months of boarding school for young Jean-Baptiste. But there was also a note listing several payments to the head of the boarding school "for his trouble" in providing loans to Jean-Baptiste.[9] The spendthrift ways and reliance on credit that would dog Jean-Baptiste later in life were already making an appearance when he was eleven years old.

By the following year, 1774, Jean-Baptiste may have begun helping with his father's fur business. Two pages of the family ledger for 1774 contain an invoice for goods that the senior Cadot sent to an employee at a fur-trade post in Michigan's Upper Peninsula. The handwriting is different from that of earlier entries, and it was penned in a "neat, school-boy hand," according to James F. Edwards, archivist of Notre Dame in the early twentieth century, who provided notes on the account book.[10]

Five years later, it wasn't the fur trade but the priesthood that Jean-Baptiste, now seventeen years old, was preparing to enter. However, he didn't become a priest, for reasons that are unclear. Perhaps British authorities helped dissuade him. In October 1779, Lieutenant Governor Patrick Sinclair, the officer in charge of the British fort at Michilimackinac, took note of the younger Cadotte, who was already displaying his language skills. Writing to the aide-de-camp for Governor Haldimand, Sinclair said Jean-Baptiste was in Montreal preparing to enter the priesthood. He added that the young man had a "very honest father" and suggested it might be wise to send the youngster "to our new Establishment, & in time [he] might answer other good purposes."[11]

In 1778 and 1779, Haldimand was considering the creation of a corps of Native Canadians to help defend Québec and western Canada from a possible American invasion.[12] Jean-Baptiste may have been considered a potential recruit for this endeavor. That's not clear in Sinclair's correspondence, but return letters show that the authorities in Québec liked Sinclair's idea and instructed him to proceed with it. The documentation ends there, however, and it doesn't appear that young Cadotte became part of the British war effort.[13]

Whatever the British leaders or the Catholic Church might have had in mind for Jean-Baptiste, he joined the family fur business instead. Sometime in the early 1780s, he received forty thousand francs from his father to begin work in the fur trade. He wintered at Chequamegon Bay and acquired a substantial amount of beaver and other skins in his first years in the business.[14] The family account book for July 7, 1783, lists more than fifty packs of beaver skins that the senior Cadot's employees secured at winter posts, along with packs of mink furs, raccoon, otter, Canadian lynx, bearskins, and more. However, listed separately from all the other furs were "5 Beaver Robes," "40 Brown Marten," and "5 Bearskins" that were credited to "J Bte Cadot, son."[15] The senior Cadot was apparently proud enough of his twenty-two-year-old heir to have the furs that his son acquired noted separately from all others on the ledger. The next year, he put his son in charge of a new post near the upper St. Croix River in present-day Wisconsin.[16]

The early years of Jean-Baptiste's fur-trade career were much like those of any independent trader. It was a period of shifting partnerships and alliances, of multiple wintering sites, and of long canoe trips on Lake Superior and the rivers of the interior. In spring came voyages back to Sault Ste. Marie, Michilimackinac, and, later, Grand Portage to trade the furs and resupply for the coming winter.

Jean-Baptiste and Michel both worked briefly with their father under the company name of *Mssrs Cadot et compangnie*.[17] Their older sister, Marie-Renée, remained in Montreal but stayed involved in the family business, working with their father's Montreal friend and business associate Maurice-Régis Blondeau.[18] By 1787, Jean-Baptiste Sr. had largely retired from the fur trade. His accounts were turned over to an organization called the *Société générale de Michilimackinac*, and both sons went to work for the new outfit, as shown on invoices from the family ledger.[19] The organization was formed in 1785 by a number of fur traders, including the senior Cadot. It concentrated on the trade south and west of Lake Superior, but it lasted only a couple of years and was dissolved after 1787.[20]

Another young trader, Jean-Baptiste Perrault, who would later become a friend, sometime partner, and colleague of Jean-Baptiste Jr., also worked briefly for the *Société générale* beginning in 1785.[21] It's not clear when Perrault first met Jean-Baptiste, but Perrault undoubtedly knew him by the summer of 1787, when Perrault witnessed a battle reenactment during a ceremony at Michilimackinac to celebrate a treaty signing among the Dakota, the Ojibwe, and other nations. Perrault described the ceremony, saying that "Mr. Cadotte" led a large flotilla of Ojibwe warriors in canoes around the eastern side of the point of Mackinac Island. Meanwhile, another trader paddled around the western side of the point with a convoy of Dakota and other Native people. Wearing war regalia, the opposing fleets attacked each other in mock combat, first firing muskets, then wielding lances and spears. As they completed the battle, the Native people whooped loudly and glided to the shore, while English cannons saluted them.[22]

Two years later, Jean-Baptiste and Perrault were involved in a new trading venture. According to Perrault, six traders—including himself and "cadotte baptiste"—joined forces in July 1789 and agreed to establish a half-dozen winter posts in northeastern Minnesota. Each partner contributed his trade goods, and they agreed to equally divide the proceeds of their fur trading the following spring.[23] The traders drew lots to determine where each should winter. Jean-Baptiste drew Red Lake in Minnesota, where he was to become a familiar trader. In the spring of 1790, the traders headed for Sandy Lake, where they dissolved their partnership.[24] But they re-formed it the following autumn, with Jean-Baptiste this time going to Leech Lake in Minnesota.[25] He was trading at Leech Lake again during the winter of 1791–1792, this time with the backing of Alexander Henry.[26]

Henry's financial support was critical for the young Jean-Baptiste, but it would also become troublesome as the latter dug himself ever deeper in debt. Jean-Baptiste "soon expended in dissipation" the profits he made in the trade, wrote his grand-nephew William Warren. As he became ever more indebted to Henry, the trader eventually halted Jean-Baptiste's credit, and Jean-Baptiste was forced to look elsewhere for funds.[27] Before his relationship with Henry soured, however, Henry bankrolled a large expedition, led by Jean-Baptiste, to the Upper Mississippi and Red River country, probably beginning in the summer of 1792.[28] About sixty men and a few women joined the expedition, including Jean-Baptiste, Michel, and Equaysayway.[29]

At the time, despite the peace ceremony Perrault had witnessed five years earlier, the Dakota were seen as hostile and dangerous, especially in the area of today's northwestern Minnesota. Fear of antagonizing the Dakota prevented most traders from establishing posts in the headwaters of the Mississippi or farther west. But Cadotte, who had a solid reputation for courage and evenhandedness with the Native peoples, recruited traders, trappers, voyageurs, Ojibwe, and others to join his expedition.[30]

The group left Sault Ste. Marie in late summer and traveled uneventfully along the south shore of Lake Superior to Fond du Lac. There the group entered the St. Louis River, made the long, difficult portage around the falls of that river, and continued to Sandy Lake. Led by Jean-Baptiste, the party ascended the headwaters of the Mississippi River, then traversed westward to the Red River, which today forms the border between Minnesota and North Dakota before flowing into Canada. According to Equaysayway, most of the women on the expedition remained at Fond du Lac for the winter because of the anticipated danger from Dakotas.[31]

There was good reason for caution. Not long after the group established winter quarters at Red River—a small fort consisting of log cabins surrounded by a wooden stockade—a large party of Dakota warriors appeared, well-armed and wearing war paint. Jean-Baptiste initially alleviated the potential threat by raising the British flag, then meeting with the Dakota and assuring them the expedition had come only to trade.[32] The Dakota warriors seemingly accepted the traders. They invited Jean-Baptiste and his men to visit the Dakota winter camp, a day's march away. Jean-Baptiste did so, with thirty men. They were greeted warmly by the Dakota, feasted, and carried on a brisk trade, gathering many furs. But the visit nearly ended in disaster, because on the trip back to Cadotte's camp, the Dakota chief concocted a plan to have some of his warriors rush ahead to a densely wooded area along the trail and ambush Jean-Baptiste's party.

Jean-Baptiste suspected nothing until one of his voyageurs warned him of the trap. But once informed of their perilous situation, he acted quickly and forcefully. Jean-Baptiste cocked his musket, pointed it at the Dakota chief, and declared that the chief would be the first to die unless he immediately sent a runner to order his men to retreat. After some hesitation, the chief did so. Jean-Baptiste took the chief back to his own winter post and held him hostage until he could warn all his trappers and Ojibwe colleagues to beware of Dakota treachery. His decisive action deterred farther conflict. He and members of his expedition remained at their post throughout the winter, trading and trapping, with no further threats from the Dakota.[33]

Late in the summer of 1793, the members of Cadotte's expedition made their way to Grand Portage, site of the North West Company's annual rendezvous. During the gathering, Jean-Baptiste and his comrades told of the country they had explored the previous winter. Those discussions, Warren would later write, convinced the North West Company that it could successfully expand its operations into the Upper Mississippi and Red River country.[34]

Warren may have embellished the importance of this expedition and Cadotte's influence, however. The North West Company was already operating farther west than the Red River, dealing with nations west of the Saskatchewan River, as far west as today's Canadian province of Alberta. But the expedition was still important. The company's trade at the time did not include western regions of the United States, and it had little interaction with the Dakota. The Cadotte expedition helped open the territories southwest of Grand Portage, in what is now Minnesota, to the North West Company.

David Thompson, who visited Jean-Baptiste on the Clearwater River in 1798, is credited with opening the Upper Missouri territory and trade with the Mandan for the North West Company. That was one result of his four-thousand-mile surveying trip in 1797–1798. On the same trip, he surveyed the Upper Mississippi and Red River regions.[35] It's conceivable he undertook that work as a direct result of information provided by Jean-Baptiste and his colleagues after the 1792 expedition. Additionally, Cadotte's friend Perrault helped build a permanent North West Company post at Fond du Lac in 1793 and 1794. According to an early history of Minnesota, that post "was established as the result of the information gathered by J.B. Cadotte's expedition of 1792 to the sources of the Mississippi."[36]

With the success of the expedition and his trading experience, Cadotte's reputation flourished, enough so that in August of 1795, he and the North West Company signed an agreement for him to work as an independent trader under contract with the firm.[37] The agreement bound Jean-Baptiste to trade exclusively on behalf of the North West Company for three years, and he spent his first winter working at Red Lake.[38]

It was a good winter for trading, but on the way back to Lake Superior the following spring, Jean-Baptiste lost part of his trade goods in a wreck on the St. Louis River (see chapter 12). Mishaps on the St. Louis River portage were not uncommon, even for experienced backcountry travelers like Jean-Baptiste, because it was one of the most difficult and treacherous portages in the region.[39]

Perrault, who joined Jean-Baptiste at the dangerous portage in the spring of 1796, briefly described the accident, the rescue of the canoe passengers, and the recovery of the furs.[40] Perrault's matter-of-fact recounting of the event doesn't convey the drama that must have ensued as those on shore rushed to save the passengers in the ill-fated canoe, along with its valuable cargo. Nor did Perrault explain how the wreck occurred. Did the canoe capsize in the calmer, but still-swift, waters above the falls? Were the voyageurs attempting to descend to the brink of the falls before hauling the canoe out of the water?

In any event, the accident didn't significantly injure Jean-Baptiste's reputation. He impressed officials of the North West Company enough that they not only renewed his contract in 1796 but extended it for five years and expanded the territory in which he was authorized to trade. The new contract was signed on behalf of the North West Company by two of its leading partners, Alexander Mackenzie and William McGillivray. The contract they signed with him noted "the high opinion entertained of the integrity and ability of the said Jean-Baptiste Cadotte."[41]

Jean-Baptiste's first years trading on behalf of the North West Company were unquestionably successful. He worked vigorously, traded effectively, and won the confidence of the firm's partners.[42] Eventually, though, his penchant for alcohol would wind up disrupting his work. In the fall of 1798, Perrault was given a peculiar assignment by the North West Company. He was told to halt his preparations for his own winter post and proceed to where Jean-Baptiste was supposed to be establishing his winter headquarters, once again near the Clearwater River. Perrault was also given two additional canoes full of supplies and three extra men "to go to the assistance of mr. Cadotte who was subject to allowing himself to be overcome by drink."[43] Exactly how North West Company officials learned that Jean-Baptiste was in trouble that autumn is unknown, but their intelligence proved accurate.

Perrault's report shows his frustration with his friend. When he arrived at the post in late autumn, with winter looming, Jean-Baptiste and his seven men were either drunk or recovering from earlier revelry. They had already consumed a quarter of the rum that was meant to be used as trade material with the Native people throughout the long winter. And the clearing next to the river where they were to build their winter post was a disaster. There were no buildings constructed, just a few partially hewed logs, with scattered supplies and half-empty packs lying around haphazardly.

Perrault presented a letter from the North West Company to Jean-Baptiste, who blanched upon reading it. Then he turned his post over to Perrault, declaring, "'I have nothing to do Henceforth but to drink and to eat All winter.'" Perrault, however, rejected that idea. He urged Jean-Baptiste to work hard through the winter to reestablish his reputation with the company. As part of his effort to drag his friend out of his alcoholic malaise, Perrault told Jean-Baptiste that "I relied more on him than on myself."[44] Aided by Perrault's oversight and encouragement, Jean-Baptiste did not spend the winter just drinking and eating. Together, the two men and their voyageurs completed his post by mid-December. Throughout the winter, they sent men out to shoot bison, and they visited the lodges of nearby Indians to trade.[45] The two men journeyed together to Grand Portage the following spring.[46] With Perrault's assistance, Jean-Baptiste maintained his position and good standing with the company.

Later that same year, Jean-Baptiste earned a reprieve on the excessive debt he had accumulated with Alexander Henry. Early in 1799, Alexander Mackenzie purchased Jean-Baptiste's debt from Henry—at a discounted price—during a Montreal dinner party the two legendary explorers attended. Henry was tired of holding loans for Jean-Baptiste, but Mackenzie was willing to take them on. During his conversation with Henry, Mackenzie praised Jean-Baptiste's courage and spoke of the high esteem in which the Ojibwe held him. Even so, the two men agreed not to tell Jean-Baptiste of their arrangement because they feared his reaction if he discovered his debt had been sold at a discount. The mercurial Jean-Baptiste might take it as a personal insult, they feared, and might then angrily confront Mackenzie or Henry.[47]

Later that year, during the summer rendezvous at Grand Portage, Mackenzie found yet more reason to value Jean-Baptiste's service. He was having difficulty explaining to Ojibwe leaders why the company's summer rendezvous spot at Grand Portage would have to be moved to the Kaministiquia River (today's Thunder Bay, Ontario). The Jay Treaty, signed in 1794 by Great Britain and the United States, had taken effect in 1796. It stipulated new boundaries that placed Grand Portage in the United States and therefore off limits to the British North West Company unless it paid hefty tariffs. This complicated geopolitical arrangement initially didn't make sense to Ojibwe leaders. They knew it was much easier to get to the western lakes and rivers from Grand Portage and the Pigeon River at the west end of that portage than from the Kaministiquia River. Moreover, they viewed the entire region as belonging to them, not to either the United States or Great Britain.

Jean-Baptiste was preparing to leave Grand Portage for his winter post when he learned of Mackenzie's predicament. He returned to the great hall at the North West Company's depot and offered his services as interpreter. His offer was quickly accepted, and in short order he was able to explain the intricacies of international treaties and politics "to the entire satisfaction of all parties."[48]

Jean-Baptiste then returned to his canoe, where Mackenzie handed him a sealed paper, saying it was payment for the services he had just rendered. Jean-Baptiste was some distance out in Lake Superior before he stopped to read the paper Mackenzie had given him. It explained the transfer of his debt from Henry to Mackenzie and then said the debt had been entirely forgiven. Overwhelmed by this generous act, Jean-Baptiste continued to his winter post, eager to repay Mackenzie's kindness by demonstrating his business acumen and showing that he was a dependable trader for the firm. He vowed to return the following spring with a greater-than-normal accumulation of furs.[49]

According to William Warren, Jean-Baptiste proved his leadership with the Indians in another fashion when he had to deal with a murder committed around 1798. A Canadian voyageur working at Lac Courte Oreilles in north-central Wisconsin was killed by an Ojibwe. Jean-Baptiste, then heading the North West Company trading post at Fond du Lac, sent word to Ojibwe leaders, telling them the suspect must be turned over to him or traders would stop visiting them, and they would lose access to critical trade items such as guns, tobacco, and cotton fabric.[50] The following spring, the man in question was delivered by an Ojibwe chief. The accused was tried by a jury consisting of North West Company clerks, traders, and voyageurs, was found guilty, and was sentenced to die by stabbing, just as his victim had died.

The execution took place the next morning. But despite being stabbed several times, the man leapt to his feet and ran to the shore of Lake Superior, where he expired in the arms of Equaysayway and Saugemauqua, Jean-Baptiste's mixed-ancestry wife, who also went by the French name Jeanette Piquette. The two women had rushed out to comfort the dying man. The clerks and voyageurs at Fond du Lac hunkered inside their post, fearing the Ojibwe would retaliate for the man's death, but there was no attempt at revenge. When Jean-Baptiste Cadotte explained the reasoning behind the execution to them, the Ojibwe leaders accepted his form of justice.[51]

Perhaps because of such events as well as his success as a trader, the North West Company continued to reward Jean-Baptiste. In June of 1801 he was made a partner in the company, along with five other men. Each of the five received a 1/46th share of company stock. Jean-Baptiste was only the second French Canadian to become a partner in the company, which was dominated by Scottish, English, and Irish traders. It was a great day for the proud eldest son of Jean-Baptiste Cadot Sr.[52]

However, on the same day that Jean-Baptiste became a partner, the North West Company adopted a resolution that must have been aimed in part at him—as a warning about his excesses. The resolution noted that many North West Company employees were frequently drunk and therefore unable to adequately perform their duties: "to prevent therefore this (*greatest of Evils*) from gaining Ground and, if possible, *to root it out altogether*," the resolution decreed that any partner who was too drunk to fully perform his duties would be expelled from the company. Any clerk or interpreter found guilty of the same would forfeit his wages for the year.[53]

It was an emphatic statement at a time when alcohol, especially rum and brandy, were part and parcel of the fur business. Jean-Baptiste was not the only trader who got drunk regularly and sometimes neglected his duties. Several fur-trade journals describe either the drinking habits of traders or the manner in which alcohol was used to trade with, and sometimes cheat, Indians.[54] One Hudson's Bay Company trader, working at a post in the interior, complained that even though he had plenty of ammunition and other desirable trade items, and despite the fact that he offered better prices than nearby competitors, "[t]he Indians would not trade their furs because I had no brandy."[55] A decade later, the North West Company passed a resolution emphasizing the need for the continued use of alcohol in the trade, just as Parliament was contemplating a law to forbid alcohol throughout the industry.[56] Alcohol was viewed as a necessity for trading with Indians, but the company didn't want its own employees and partners abusing it—hence the 1801 resolution.

More than likely, Jean-Baptiste left the 1801 rendezvous fired with the same enthusiasm he had experienced after Alexander Mackenzie forgave all his debts: he planned to do the best job possible to prove to the North West partners that their confidence was not misplaced. Yet, as for so many people plagued by alcoholism, his good intentions were overwhelmed by his addiction. So it was that two years later, the North West Company elected to enforce the expulsion rule against Jean-Baptiste. He was the first partner expelled for alcoholism.

No records exist detailing any specific event that tipped the scales against Jean-Baptiste. His friend Perrault reported only that Jean-Baptiste was working northwest of Lake Superior "when, having misbehaved through drink, he lost his place" with the company.[57] The lengthy expulsion resolution passed by the North West Company in 1803 provided few particulars about Jean-Baptiste's offense. It said only that the previous winter he had "indulged himself in drunkenness and Riot," which had resulted in a significant loss to the company.[58]

Whether a formal hearing was held and whether Jean-Baptiste was given a chance to testify on his own behalf were not reflected in the resolution. Rather, the document demonstrated the finality of the decision. It asserted that the company expelled Jean-Baptiste from the firm and deprived him "of every Share, Right and Interest and expectation" with the company as effectively as if Cadotte had never been a partner.[59] Also in July of 1803, the North West Company accepted David Thompson as a partner, giving him the same number of shares that Jean-Baptiste was forced to relinquish.[60]

The North West Company's action regarding Jean-Baptiste meant that, after at least twenty years in the fur trade, at the age of forty-one, one of the boldest, most well-connected and successful French Canadian traders of the time was effectively booted out of the business. The promise of his younger years evaporated with the alcohol. Fortunately for Jean-Baptiste and his family, however, his linguistic skills were still valuable and would later land him a job as an interpreter for the Indian Department of the British government. But until that position materialized, the North West Company demonstrated it was *not* run by heartless merchants worried only about their bottom line. For ten years, from 1803 through 1813, the company paid Jean-Baptiste a pension of one hundred pounds per year, purely at the firm's discretion. It discontinued the pension when the company learned he had obtained the job of Indian interpreter for the British government and was able to support himself without the company's help.[61]

But this new opportunity didn't mean that his problems with alcohol were over. Jean-Baptiste continued to drink heavily. He abandoned his wife, Jeanette Piquette, and their five children in about 1810.[62] He was briefly appointed storekeeper of Fort St. Joseph, on Lake Huron southeast of Sault Ste. Marie, in February of that year. But once again, his drinking cost him his job. Lieutenant Governor Francis Gore sent a letter to the governor general of Canada, objecting to Jean-Baptiste's appointment, noting that "the dissipated habits and extreme intemperance of the Interpreter Cadotte render him unfit for any trust."[63]

Jean-Baptiste Cadotte Jr. died in Canada in 1818, near Fort George in Ontario.[64] Both his career and his family had suffered greatly from his alcoholism. Even so, he made important contributions to the fur trade, to the North West Company, and to the legacy of the Cadotte family as a trader, explorer, interpreter, and friend of the Ojibwe.

CHAPTER 15

THE SUGAR BUSH

Eliza Morrison enjoyed the seasonal changes in activity around Madeline Island, where she grew up in the first half of the nineteenth century. But few things evoked happy memories of her childhood like maple sugar: "And then I use[d] to be happy," she wrote. "We all live[d] quite well in going to the place where we make sugar."[1]

Spring marked the start of the new year for Ojibwe in the Lake Superior region, and with it came the making of maple sugar. As Frances Densmore explains in her study of Minnesota's Ojibwe people: "The first and one of the most enjoyable events of the [Ojibwe] industrial year was the making of maple sugar."[2] Eliza Morrison was very much attuned to these sorts of events at the west end of Lake Superior. She spent much of her life with her Ojibwe relatives or those of her husband. She was born Eliza Morrin in November 1837, just a few months after Michel Cadotte died on Madeline Island. Her father was Scottish, and her mother had Ojibwe ancestry. Eliza married a man named John Morrison, who was the great-grandson of Jean-Baptiste Cadotte Jr.[3]

The sugar ritual continued for Morrison and her young family when she was a busy mother. She described traveling with her husband, sisters, and small children in March 1877 to make sugar. Using dogs and foot power, they hauled sleds a distance of twelve miles, working quickly to get to the sugar bush before the ice and snow began to melt in earnest. But it was all worth it, she said, because of the wonderful scenery, the family collegiality, and the sugar produced. As Morrison wrote to a friend, "I think there is a quite peculiar charm in this business."[4]

The charm hasn't evaporated in the twenty-first century. Roger Cadotte, seven generations descended from Michel and Equaysayway, lives near Bay-field, Wisconsin, and is an enrolled member of the Red Cliff Ojibwe tribe. Each spring, he and his sons tap maple trees on their property and bring in syrup with other family members. As he explains, "When February rolls around, the topic of conversation between my brothers and three of my sons is usually speculation about the upcoming syrup season. On average, tapping usually begins about mid-March here. When the taps are out, there are usually evening phone conversations around the question: How much sap did you get? We all look forward to the first boil of the season."[5]

During the fur-trade era, making sugar was more than a pleasant activity. It was a means of ensuring survival at a time when there was often little other food available. Major Arent DePeyster, commander of British forces at Michilimackinac in early 1779, wrote to the governor of Québec in June of that year regarding the lack of food for the Europeans and Indians in the region. "Were it not for the sugar in the spring many would starve," he said.[6] Alexander Henry told of making sugar in 1768 on Michipicoten Island, on the northeast side of Lake Superior. The effort began in early April, he noted, and "[s]ugar-making continued till the twelfth of May. On the mountain, we eat nothing but our sugar, during the whole period. Each man consumed a pound a day, desired no other food, and was visibly nourished by it."[7]

It's difficult to imagine living on nothing but maple sugar for more than a month and being "visibly nourished by it." However, nutritional information about maple syrup, the main product made today from maple sap, shows that it is high in carbohydrates but also high in minerals such as manganese, potassium, and calcium. Furthermore, it's a natural source of certain beneficial antioxidants, providing more per serving than raw tomatoes or cantaloupe. According to one industry report, it "delivers more nutrition than all other common sweeteners and has one of the lowest calorie levels."[8] Even so, not all the early traders shared Henry's enthusiasm for maple sugar. George Nelson, an early-nineteenth-century trader in northern Wisconsin, complained "When Sugar time came, we lived near a month upon that deleterious article alone . . . deleterious I say, because it affects so much the stomach."[9]

Whether or not one was partial to maple sugar, however, it was an important trading commodity for both Native people and fur traders. Alexander Mackenzie emphasized the importance of Ojibwe sugar-making, explaining that sugar was not only life-sustaining, but also an important economic item, something "they exchange with traders for necessary articles."[10]

In addition, sugar-making provided a critical cultural connection for the Ojibwe living near Lake Superior. Following a long winter spent hunting and trapping in small bands or isolated family groups, the sugar bush provided an opportunity for communal activity. It also allowed for courtship and the arranging of marriages. After a month or more making sugar, the Ojibwe would migrate to even larger gatherings, often along the shores of Lake Superior, to fish and later in the year, gather wild rice.[11]

Making the sugar required tapping the trees with hand-carved wooden taps in the spring, when the sap was beginning to run.[12] It was collected in birch-bark containers made specifically for that purpose, then poured into large copper or iron kettles. According to Densmore, "The sap was boiled to a thick syrup, strained, replaced in the kettles, and heated slowly. When it had thickened to the proper consistency it was transferred to a 'granulating trough,' where it was 'worked' with a paddle and with the hands until it was in the form of granulated sugar." One confectionary treat involved allowing the syrup to thicken and harden in small birch-bark cones or even in a portion of a duck's bill. It could then be sucked on or eaten in small pieces, much like hard candy today.

Roger Cadotte recalled his father's method of collecting sap and making syrup when Roger was a young boy. His description of that process is very similar to what Densmore and earlier authors have described. "In the early years he would whittle the taps for the trees and drill a small hole through them for the sap," Cadotte said. "The spouts were quite large compared to the modern day metal versions. They were probably close to an inch in diameter. He would use any type of metal pail such as a coffee can for a sap bucket. A nail was driven into the tree below the wooden spout and the bucket hung there. Each day we would gather the sap into larger buckets to bring home."[13]

Roger's father, he recounts, used a variety of stove systems for boiling sap, but the most common one involved constructing a stove from an old metal barrel. A hinged door was cut into the bottom so that wood could be shoved in to the burner area. Another opening was cut near the top to allow placement of a large pot that contained sap to be boiled: "Dad would keep track of the amount of sap being added to the pot so he knew approximately how much syrup would be the finished product, based on a 40-to-1 ratio. . . . When enough sap had been added to produce at least a gallon he would remove it before it was completely done and finish it indoors on the stove."[14]

Although commercial syrup producers nowadays utilize more complex and mechanized systems, things haven't changed tremendously for small-scale syrup makers in the modern era. As Roger explains, "Today, we are using 7/16-inch metal spouts and a hanger that holds a plastic bag to catch the sap. The bag also keeps the sap pure if it rains or snows. . . . As in the early days, I still gather on snowshoes, at least in the early part of the season. . . . This year I had 20 taps and will probably net about 3½ gallons of syrup."[15]

From Alexander Henry's time to the present, those who lived on Madeline Island or the surrounding shores of Lake Superior have spent a good deal of time each spring making syrup or sugar from the sugar maples of the region. In the late nineteenth century, Indian schools in the region often closed during the sugar season because so many students had gone with their parents to the sugar bush.[16]

It was hard work, as Eliza Morrison made clear when she described an 1882 trek to a friend's sugar bush. The trip involved a hike of several miles through trees, brush, and snow. Eliza carried her three-year-old daughter in a pack on her back along with other supplies. Her fourteen-year-old son accompanied her and carried blankets. "I know some people would think this was [a] hard life," she wrote years later. "We do not think it is hard at all. We think it is just charming."[17]

CHAPTER 16

MICHEL AND EQUAYSAYWAY: THE EARLY YEARS

A utumn in the forests of northwestern Wisconsin can be stunningly beautiful—burnt-orange maple leaves, bright yellow birches, and crimson sumac bushes mixed with the deep green of evergreen trees. But in 1788 the forest also held threats for Michel Cadotte and his Ojibwe partners, not just from the natural world but from the Dakota, whose enmity with the Ojibwe had smoldered for more than a century. Furthermore, it wasn't the beauty of the forest that attracted twenty-four-year-old Michel to this country, but the bounty of its fur-bearing creatures, especially beaver but also white-tailed deer, moose, bear, fox, ermine, and more. Autumn was the critical time for venturing into the backcountry and establishing winter headquarters. From there, daily excursions could be made to trap the animals whose pelts would bring money and trade goods when they were hauled back to Lake Superior in the spring.

Michel was more than four hundred miles from his home base, which in 1788 was his father's trading headquarters at Sault Ste. Marie, the eastern entrance to Lake Superior. He was roughly eighty miles upstream from where the Chippewa River empties into the Mississippi River in northwestern Wisconsin. The only way back home was by canoe and grueling portages, as long as the rivers and lakes remained open, or by the drudgery of trekking on snowshoes, perhaps accompanied by dog sleds, once the frigid winter set in.

Michel did not travel alone, however. More than one hundred Ojibwe were with him in 1788, as well as a number of French Canadian voyageurs.

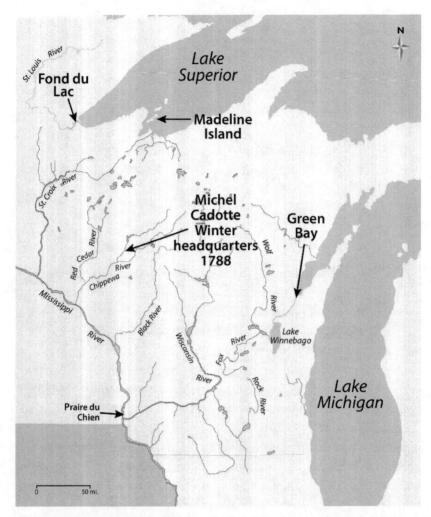

The Wisconsin region in the fur trade era. The Cadottes' winter headquarters in 1788 was not far from the present-day town of Chippewa Falls, Wisconsin. ROBERT GARCIA

The French Canadians, along with Ojibwe men, women, and children, would trap, hunt, and gather food, as well as prepare the furs for the return trip to Lake Superior in the spring. The Ojibwe were Michel's friends and partners. Many were also his family—blood relatives or relations through marriage. Equaysayway likely accompanied him on this particular winter-long expedition as she had on other trips.

The fur-trade career of Michel's brother Jean-Baptiste Jr. was like a rough ride down a whitewater river. It was swift and dangerous, marked by quick decisions and hasty actions that sometimes created problems but also frequently produced jubilation and success. It ended when his alcoholism drove him to disaster. Michel's career followed a much different trajectory. It was more like a long, upstream paddle characterized by some rough water and occasional disturbances but few self-created catastrophes.

With Equaysayway beside him, Michel's career survived international changes that forced him to alter his political allegiance and his business methods. The couple managed to navigate massive cultural changes that could easily have divided their family over religion or other issues. They accomplished all this without being prone to flamboyant actions or hasty decisions. Michel was shrewd and diplomatic. He was thoughtful when making key decisions, and he nearly always sought conversation over conflict.

Consequently, he was trusted enough that French Canadian voyageurs who had been severely mistreated by a rival trader fled to Michel for relief, and he had sufficient influence with the Ojibwe to calm serious tensions between nations on several occasions. Yet, despite his solid reputation, Michel was not above using subterfuge to take advantage of another trader. And, while he was respected by most people in the region, he angered some competitors, one of whom fired guns at Michel and his men while they were traveling on Lake Superior.

All of that would occur later. In 1788, although Michel and Equaysayway were a relatively young trading couple, they weren't newcomers to the Chippewa River basin. The previous autumn their first child, Michel Jr., had been born near Chippewa Falls, where they established their trapping and trading headquarters that winter. Their winter trading post in 1788, downstream from the 1787 camp, was not in unknown country, but it *was* in disputed territory. For several years, the Cadottes and their Ojibwe colleagues had pushed deeper into the rich fur-bearing lands along the Chippewa River and closer to the amorphous border of territory to the west claimed by the Dakota. In 1788, the Cadottes were closer than ever to that border, and caution was required.

Over the decades, the Ojibwe and Dakota had fought multiple skirmishes in this disputed territory along the upper reaches of the Mississippi River and its tributaries. Thus, in that autumn of 1788, the Cadottes built a cabin protected by a log stockade, as did their French Canadian and Ojibwe companions.[1] It proved to be a reasonable precaution because during the winter a band of Dakota warriors approached the camp, outfitted as if ready for combat. But they apparently intended only to threaten and never actually attacked. Even so, Michel, fearing his Ojibwe and French Canadian workers might abandon the camp due to the Dakota threat, decided to seek a truce between the trading groups. He assembled one hundred well-armed men to accompany him and embarked on a half-day hike down the snow-covered river valley to the Dakota camp.[2] Michel and his men approached cautiously, displaying peace pipes and a white flag. It was one of many times in his career that the stolid and pragmatic Michel showed his penchant for diplomacy over conflict.

The peace mission was a success. No fight ensued because Michel and an older French trader named La Roque, who partnered with the Dakota, brokered a winter-long truce between the two enemies so that each side could benefit from the fur-gathering season. The peace lasted only until summer, when tribal members on both sides looked for opportunities to settle old scores. But it was reinstated the following winter and for many winters after that.[3] In establishing a temporary truce, Michel and La Roque were following a century-old French pattern of attempting to maintain peace among Native nations in order to ensure a productive trade.[4]

Michel didn't deal with these situations alone. Equaysayway was with him through most of these events, although there is little documentation of her activities. She joined Michel on his expeditions to the Chippewa River in the late 1780s, and she and other women joined Michel and his brother Jean-Baptiste on the first part of their journey to the headwaters of the Mississippi River in 1792–1793.[5]

Once Michel and Equaysayway established a permanent trading post on Madeline Island, around the turn of the nineteenth century, it's probable that she spent most of her time at the family compound there. With six children under fourteen years of age by 1800, Equaysayway no doubt found it increasingly difficult to travel into the backcountry. Even at the family home, however, Equaysayway impressed people. Thomas McKenney, the US Superintendent of Indian Affairs who visited Madeline Island in 1826, described her as "a worthy, well-disposed woman."[6]

Equaysayway was born around 1760, four years before her husband and three years before the French ceded most of what is now Canada to

An illustration of the Chippewa River as it flows into the Mississippi. HENRY LEWIS, "INDIAN TRIBES OF WISCONSIN," LOT 2575 (G) LIBRARY OF CONGRESS

the British. Her Ojibwe lineage, as well as Michel's, helped the couple develop critical partnerships with the Indians. Additionally, as the son of Jean-Baptiste Cadot Sr., Michel was a member of one of the most respected French Canadian fur-trading families around Lake Superior. With all of their family connections, Michel and Equaysayway were a powerful couple near southwestern Lake Superior, even if Michel initially operated in the shadow of his more flamboyant brother.

Michel was neither the precocious youngster nor, apparently, the apple of his father's eye that his older brother was. There are no entries in the existing family account book indicating that school materials were purchased specifically for Michel, and there is no separate ledger item detailing how many pelts Michel acquired on his first fur-trading expedition. Nothing indicates that British authorities took a special interest in Michel at a young age, as they did his older brother. And it doesn't appear he was ever hired to serve as a government interpreter.

But Michel's name actually appears more frequently in the family ledger than does his brother's, beginning with an entry listing a number of bills "[s]ent to Mr. Maurice Blondeau, Merchant at Montreal." Seven of the listed bills are under the category "1781 by Michel Cadot son," and they include payments made to some of the most important fur traders of the time: "Mr. Alex Henry," "Messrs. frobisher and Co.," "Mr. McTavish."[7] Michel turned seventeen in July of 1781, and like his brother and older sister, he had been sent to Montreal as a youngster to be educated. Evidently, his father trusted him enough as a teenager to allow him to take on some important administrative duties for the family business. Many of the family-ledger entries with Michel's name attached were made after Jean-Baptiste Cadot Sr. began to turn over his fur business to his two eldest sons. No entries exist for this time with the name of Jean-Baptiste Jr. attached, so it may be that the younger Michel assumed bookkeeping duties for "Messrs. Cadots and Company" and the trading entities the Cadottes were involved in during subsequent years. If so, he performed these duties with little concern about consistent spelling, grammar, or legibility.[8]

The family account books also offer clues about when the family name "Cadot" morphed into "Cadotte," although the ultimate reason isn't clear. Michel's father, Jean-Baptiste Cadot Sr., didn't adopt the anglicized spelling, as is demonstrated throughout the account books. Neither did Michel initially. All of the early references to him in the family ledger spell his surname as "Cadot." It was not until 1798 that the account books used the spelling "Cadotte," although even then it reverted to "Cadot" in at least one entry.[9] Michel's 1803 contract with the North West Company, written in French, spells his name "Cadotte." His brother's 1795 contract with the company— both the original French and an English translation—also uses the surname "Cadotte."[10] Whatever the reason, both brothers had largely jettisoned the name Cadot and had become Cadottes before the eighteenth century ended.

Michel probably met Equaysayway in the early 1780s, after he left his father's Sault Ste. Marie home and ventured into the north woods of Wisconsin. Their meeting may have occurred at Michel's first post, on the Namekagon River southwest of Madeline Island near present-day Hayward, Wisconsin, where Michel began trading in 1784, not far from the St. Croix River area where Equaysayway was born.[11] By 1787, Michel and Equasayway were living as husband and wife—based on Ojibwe tradition—on the Chippewa River. It was there Michel Jr. was born on September 6, 1787.[12] A few years later, as the Cadottes continued to trade in the Chippewa River region, warriors from the Sauk and Fox nations trekked from southern Wisconsin to the Chippewa basin to challenge the Ojibwe and their Cadotte trading partners and to try to take control of the fur-rich area. After a desperate fight and significant casualties on both sides, the Ojibwe repulsed the intruders. Fox and Sauk Indians never returned to that part of northern Wisconsin to challenge the Ojibwe for their lands.[13]

Meanwhile, for Michel and his family, danger didn't come just from enemy Indian nations. According to William Warren, in 1787, Michel and Equaysayway survived a life-threatening incident caused by a leader of one of the Ojibwe bands who were their allies. As was customary at the beginning of the fur-trapping season, Michel had brought with him fruit brandy to share with the Indians and French Canadians for one great celebration before the long, difficult winter's work began. There would be much revelry and drunkenness, but it would be controlled. A few warriors would be appointed to serve as tribal security guards to ensure that weapons were stored away and that violence was kept to a minimum. Only one of the two bands of Ojibwe who were to join the Cadottes that winter had arrived when the civil chief of that band approached Michel and suggested he hand out the liquor immediately. Michel refused, saying they must wait for the second band. After two more days of waiting, the tribal leader again approached Michel, and this time he was more demanding. When Michel again refused, the chief stormed angrily away. He paddled swiftly to his camp across the river, tossing threats and curses in Michel's direction.

When he reached his camp, the chief ran into his lodge and grabbed his musket, then fired at Michel's camp across the river, nearly hitting Equaysayway. The band's war chief (a different leader from the civil chief) rushed up and wrestled the musket from the disgruntled man's hands, preventing bloodshed. The war chief and other members of the band were so angered by the actions of their civil chief that they threatened to kill him. But Michel, displaying a generosity of spirit that was also part of his character, interceded on the chief's behalf and his life was spared.[14]

Sometime later, the second band arrived with a chief who happened to be Equaysayway's uncle. Incensed by news of the reckless shooting, the second band refused to camp close to the first group and instead elected to locate some distance downstream. They invited Michel, his family, and the French voyageurs to join them, which they did.[15]

The following year, during the winter of 1788–1789, Michel helped save the life of fellow fur trader and sometime rival Jean-Baptiste Perrault, the man who later came to the aid of his alcoholic brother (see chapter 13).

Perrault's problems began when two Lac Courte Oreilles Ojibwe were killed by Dakota after they and other members of their band visited Perrault's trading post on the Red Cedar River that autumn. Friends of the men who were killed blamed Perrault and his traders for allowing Dakota into their post at the same time as the Ojibwe were present. They said members of their band would seek revenge on Perrault and his traders, and they showed up at Perrault's small trading post just after Christmas, apparently intent on settling the score.[16]

When the Ojibwe warriors appeared, Perrault and his men expected to be attacked and barricaded themselves behind the wooden walls of their trading post. Suddenly, Perrault saw a letter "fly through the air" and land just outside the door: "I seized it instantly, and opened it. I found it signed by mr. michel Cadot." Michel's letter said he'd recently learned from a friend among the Ojibwe that the Lac Courte Oreilles band intended to kill Perrault and his crew. He warned Perrault that the Ojibwe warriors would destroy the small group of traders unless Perrault treated the Ojibwe with the utmost courtesy and caution.[17] Perrault followed Michel's instructions, allowing Michel's Ojibwe friend to enter the post alone. He explained to the Ojibwe man that Michel was "my great friend." Perrault showered the man with compliments and obtained his promise that the other Ojibwe warriors would not harm Perrault or his men.[18] With the threat of violence gone, Perrault paid the family of the two deceased Indians with cloth, woolen coats, rum, ammunition, tobacco, and other goods. By following Michel's sensible advice, Perrault and his men had survived the potentially deadly encounter and lost nothing but some trade goods.[19]

Despite receiving such valuable counsel from Michel, Perrault described another occasion in which the young fur trader used trickery to put a competitor at a disadvantage. Perrault said he visited trader John Johnston in the spring of 1792, after Johnston had spent the winter trading from a post on the mainland along Chequamegon Bay. This was before Michel and Equaysayway established their permanent trading post on Madeline Island. Johnston had run out of rum to trade with the Indians that winter. He told Perrault he'd sold all his rum at very discounted prices, following advice he received from Michel as they both headed to their winter posts. Michel had told Johnston he could do well if he exchanged one keg of rum for every six beaver pelts the Indians offered, but that equation of rum for pelts was less than a third of what Perrault was willing to accept.[20] Michel, it appears, had hoodwinked a competitor into selling his goods for far below market value.

Additionally, Perrault and Michel sometimes found themselves at odds in the highly competitive fur-trade world. In 1795, Perrault was an employee of the North West Company, while Michel was still an independent trader not yet affiliated with the firm. Perrault set up winter quarters at Lake Pokegama near present-day Grand Rapids, Minnesota. In late October, he discovered another party of independent traders had arrived and planned to set up a trading post to compete with Perrault's North West Company operation. The party included Alexander Henry the Younger, nephew of Jean-Baptiste Cadot Sr.'s friend and partner Alexander Henry; Pierre-Antoine, Comte Dupont de l'Étang; "le grand michel Cadotte" (the Michel of this book); and "le petit michel Cadotte" (Michel's first cousin and employee).[21]

The new arrivals were ill prepared that winter, Perrault claimed, not having brought sufficient provisions. It's hard to believe that the four experienced traders just listed, including "le grande" Michel, were not adequately prepared for a winter's worth of trading at a backcountry post. Perhaps they lost some of their goods on the voyage in, or maybe, as evidently occurred earlier, Michel was not entirely honest about his situation when dealing with a competing trader. In any case, the newcomers asked to buy some additional supplies from Perrault. He agreed, with the stipulation that Michel's group would not attempt to travel into the backcountry to trade with the surrounding Ojibwe but would trade only with those who came to their post.

Both outfits remained through the winter and traded at their respective posts with some success, working peacefully in the same neighborhood, but each striving to get the better of the opposing traders. At one point, Perrault heard that an Ojibwe chief from the Rainy Lake area was approaching the traders' posts. He quickly sent out five men to intercept the Ojibwe leader and his party "before mr. Cadotte heard of It." The chief and his men received a lavish reception at Perrault's post, and Perrault thus acquired the chief's large accumulation of furs and moose meat while Michel got nothing.[22]

Perrault wasn't the only man who went head to head with Michel in fur-trade competition. In 1804, Simon Chorette (also spelled Chaurette),

a former North West Company trader who had joined the offshoot XY
Company, sent men to the Chippewa River to trade in direct competition
with Michel's operation. By then, Michel was trading exclusively on behalf
of the North West Company and maintained his headquarters on Madeline
Island. Chorette even took literal aim at Michel on one occasion, according to François Victor Malhiot, one of the young trader's colleagues with
the North West Company. Chorette and his men "fired small shot at Mr
Cadotte when he passed near them on Lake Superior," though the shots
were not very accurate, and Malhiot added, "I presume they [the shooters]
were intoxicated at the time."[23]

When Malhiot realized that Chorette's men were headed to the
Chippewa River to challenge Michel's traders there, he dispatched one
of his most trusted employees to Madeline Island to warn Michel. Malhiot urged him to send more men to the Chippewa River to compete with
Chorette and to "have him followed, step by step," until spring.[24] It's not
clear whether Michel followed Malhiot's advice, but he continued to trade
successfully on the Chippewa River for many years.

In another instance of competitive backbiting, trader George Nelson
reported that he and others working for the XY Company in July of 1804
camped on Madeline Island "near Grand Michel Cadotte's fort." While
there, one of Michel's men deserted because, he claimed, he had been ill-
treated. He joined Nelson's group and left the island. It should be noted,
however, that Nelson was then working as a clerk for Simon Chorette,
and though he had conflicting feelings about his boss, he had reason to
denigrate an important competitor.[25]

For the most part, though, Michel won the respect and trust of those
he encountered. Malhiot recalled one event that indicated the high regard voyageurs and other fur-trade workers had for Michel. Malhiot was
sent by the North West Company to take temporary control of the Lac
du Flambeau post in 1804. The clerk who had been in charge of that post,
Charles Gauthier, was a drunkard who reportedly abused his men and
the Indians around him. He forced the men to live on starvation rations
while he feasted. Malhiot said he met the fleeing employees of the Lac
du Flambeau post when they reached Lake Superior about twenty miles
southeast of Madeline Island. The men were "thin and emaciated like real
skeletons," and they told Malhiot they were on their way to Michel's post

to seek his assistance.[26] They believed they would be well treated by him.

Michel overcame obstacles he encountered in the fur business, even though he was not a great soldier or warrior, nor was he a powerful politician or a business leader with a major fur-trade company. He also didn't have any direct connections to the governments in charge. Still, Michel's calm and diplomatic nature allowed him to defuse tense situations. Consequently, he was personally respected by the Ojibwe, French Canadian voyageurs, and most people involved in the fur trade. Later on, he would be consulted by fellow traders and others on matters relating to the Lake Superior region. He and Equaysayway won praise from government officials and private citizens who visited their home at Madeline Island. And well after his death, Michel remained "dear to the hearts" of Ojibwe hunters and leaders who knew him.[27]

Michel and Equaysayway's business continued to grow in the final years of the eighteenth century, and so did the number of inland trading posts operated by his employees and relatives. William Warren listed more than a dozen trading-post locations in Minnesota and Wisconsin where "the marks of this old pioneer" were "still visible" when Warren wrote in the late 1840s.[28] A half-dozen more of Michel's trading locations in both present-day Minnesota and Wisconsin have been listed by other sources.[29]

In 1798, Michel aligned his fur-trade business with the North West Company and began to trade in the Fond du Lac district. He later traded for the North West Company at Turtle Lake and Rainy Lake in present-day Minnesota. In 1802, he signed a formal contract with the company that limited his trading area to the regions around Chequamegon Bay, the St. Croix River, and Lac Court Oreilles.[30] He was neither an employee of the company nor one of its partners; rather, he was a contract trader who agreed to buy all his goods from the North West Company, sell all of his furs to the company, and work exclusively within the territory the firm prescribed for him.

Sometime during this period, Michel and Equaysayway established their trading post and their family home on Madeline Island. The exact date is not known, although different sources have put it as early as 1792 and as late as 1803. The Cadottes may have begun trading on the island at an early date, without initially making it their full-time home. Independent traders rarely had fixed abodes in those days, since it was necessary for them to winter at various locations along with their Indian allies to trap and trade for furs. However, once Michel was trading under a contract with the North West Company, he was probably able to maintain a more permanent trading headquarters and home for his family, while sending his employees to trade in the backcountry.[31]

Despite a few detractors, Michel was clearly well respected as a trader and citizen of the Great Lakes region. Grandson William Warren provided glowing accounts of his reputation, calling him "full of courage and untiring enterprise" and reporting that he was a man of "unbounded charitable disposition."[32] Former Wisconsin senator William Vilas declared in a court case in Ashland, Wisconsin, in 1908 that Michel was "[a] great historic character of the Lake Superior region. Cadotte was not a warrior, nor a statesman . . . but he was a big man, trusted alike by the Indians and the white men, and a man of integrity."[33]

Intrepid North West Company explorer and surveyor David Thompson consulted with Michel in 1798, while attempting to determine the number of Indians who lived along the entire southern shore of Lake Superior.[34] Even after Michel retired and turned most of his trading business over to his sons-in-law, he was considered an elder statesman and was consulted on many matters related to Indian policy.[35] But this trust and respect didn't insulate the trader from trouble. In the first decade of the nineteenth century, international events provoked one such incident, which nearly led to his undoing.

CHAPTER 17

THE AMERICANS ARRIVE

As the eighteenth century drew to a close and the nineteenth century began, Michel and Equaysayway Cadotte's fur business looked solid. In 1798, Michel had joined forces with the North West Company as an independent trader. Four years later, he signed a contract that gave him the exclusive right to trade with the firm for the next three years in the regions around the Chippewa River, at Lac Courte Oreilles, and at La Pointe on Madeline Island. It was a substantial trading territory that involved multiple villages and bands of Ojibwe.[1] But changes were coming. International and regional upheavals would begin to alter the way the Cadottes did business, and fallout from the international turmoil would lead to a significant financial loss for the traders.

Michel did face some competition, even during those pre-upheaval halcyon days. People like Simon Chorette and George Nelson, working for Alexander Mackenzie's XY Company, tried to poach some of his trade. There were probably a few unaffiliated traders as well. But the North West Company was unquestionably the dominant firm in the region, and with its backing, Michel's business did well.[2] Plus, there must have been some familial anguish when his brother Jean-Baptiste Jr. was dismissed as a partner from the North West Company in 1803, though that unfortunate event apparently didn't have any impact on Michel's association with it. In fact, there are indications that his allowed territory with the firm expanded in the following year.[3]

In any event, by 1806, Michel and Equaysayway's business was steady. The North West Company records for July of that year show the firm had twenty-two "departments," from the Athabasca Region in today's Alberta,

Canada, to Sault Ste. Marie at the east end of Lake Superior. The La Pointe
Department, operated by Michel, was midsized among those twenty-two
departments. The La Pointe Department listed five clerks, three of whom
were named "Michel Cadotte": they were *Le Grand Michel*, the man married to Equaysayway; (presumably) *Le Petit Michel*, cousin of *Le Grand
Michel*; and Michel Cadotte Jr., son of *Le Grand Michel* and Equaysayway.
Also listed as a clerk for the La Pointe Department was Leon St. Germain,
a son-in-law of Michel and Equaysayway, who had married their daughter
Margarete. Finally, there was J. B. (Jean-Baptiste) Corbin, who would play
a key role in later developments that affected the Cadottes' business.[4]

In 1806, the La Pointe Department received four large Montreal canoes'
worth of goods for the upcoming trading season. Several other departments received only two, while some large departments, such as the one
serving Lake Winnipeg in today's Manitoba, received ten or more canoes'
worth of goods. All of the goods were delivered to the company's annual
rendezvous point at the Kaministiquia River at what is today Thunder Bay,
Ontario.[5] Michel or his agents traveled there to pick up the trade goods.
The rendezvous point had been moved north from the previous site at
Grand Portage due to treaty requirements between Great Britain and the
United States. Consequently, Michel had to travel farther north than he
had a few years earlier to receive his trade goods from Montreal. But a
more significant change was coming for Michel and other traders on the
south shore of Lake Superior.

A new fur-trading entity called the Michilimackinac Company was
formed sometime in 1805 or 1806. It included many partners of the North
West Company, as well as other Montreal merchants, and it was created
specifically "as a means of protection against American interference following the Louisiana Purchase of 1803." The Michilimackinac Company
did its trading and obtained its furs in the United States, but its headquarters were in Montreal.[6]

On December 31, 1806, the new company executed an agreement with
the North West Company delineating boundaries where each could conduct its trade. The agreement said that the North West Company could not
"carry on any Trade at any of the Posts on the south side of Lake Superior"
from Sault Ste. Marie to Madeline Island. The North West Company also
agreed to relinquish trade along the Chippewa River. Much of the terri-

tory relinquished was Michel's designated trading area.[7] But he and his employees weren't abandoned. The same agreement included a clause that required the Michilimackinac Company to "assume the Contract entered into by the said North West Company and Michel Cadotte," as well as the contracts of several other traders who worked on behalf of the North West Company south of Lake Superior.[8]

Michel still had a fur-trading business, and he still had a contract with a Montreal-based company made up primarily of British Canadians, but his family's long association with the British fur traders, which had begun more than forty years earlier when his father partnered with Alexander Henry, was drawing to a close. At the same time, other regional conflicts were developing that would soon jeopardize Michel's relationship with his Ojibwe colleagues.

It wasn't long after Europeans arrived in North America that they started to fear a general Indian uprising in which multiple Native nations would unite to slaughter as many Europeans as possible and drive the remainder back across the Atlantic. This fear was formed out of Europeans' misunderstanding regarding the difference among Native cultures, but it was also fed by the expressed desires of a few Native leaders to accomplish just what the Europeans feared. Those desires occasionally manifested themselves in military engagements in which the Indians were led by charismatic and adept leaders such as Pontiac, Black Hawk, or Crazy Horse.

One of the most successful attempts to unify Native people against the European interlopers occurred in the first decade of the nineteenth century. It began in the Ohio River Valley but spread as far as the Mississippi River Valley and much of the Great Lakes region, led by a Shawnee man who called himself Tenskwatawa ("The Open Door"), though he was known to most Europeans as "the Shawnee Prophet." He was assisted by his warrior brother, Tecumseh.[9]

Tecumseh, according to Canadian historian Robert S. Allen, "was both frank and honest" and "was impressive. Where the Prophet was charismatic, Tecumseh was dedicated and disciplined. His absolute priority was to preserve and defend the lands and cultural values of his people."[10] The Prophet preached a message of purification that included Indians eliminating white influences from their world: metal implements, flints for fires, alcohol, and European-style clothes. He even urged Native people such as the Ojibwe to put aside their sacred Midewiwin practices, arguing that the entire system had been corrupted by Europeans. Ultimately, the Prophet directed most of his animosity toward the Americans. One of his followers explained the reasons for this after supposedly receiving a revelation. The Great Spirit, he said, was "the Father of the English, of the French, of the Spaniards and of the Indians." However, the Great Spirit reportedly told this man, "the Americans I did not make. They are not my children but the children of the Evil Spirit . . . they have taken away your lands which were not made for them."[11]

The Shawnee Prophet's message spread rapidly among many Indian nations, including the Ojibwe of Lake Superior's southern shoreline and much farther west. John Tanner, who was captured by Shawnee Indians as a young boy and spent thirty years living among the Ojibwe after he was traded to them, recalled learning of the Prophet while he and his Ojibwe wife were staying with a band near the Assiniboine River in present-day Saskatchewan. Tanner learned "of a great man among the [Shawnee], who had been favoured by a revelation of the mind and will of the Great Spirit."[12]

After some time, most of the Ojibwe of Tanner's group had adopted the Prophet's teachings and had abandoned most European goods. The Prophet's influence was not without benefit, Tanner noted: "For two or three years, drunkenness was much less frequent than formerly; war was less thought of, and the entire aspect of affairs among them, was somewhat changed by the influence of one man." However, he said, the Prophet's doctrines had little tendency "to unite them in the accomplishment of any human purpose."[13] The Prophet's influence also affected the Ojibwe along the south shore of Lake Superior and the interior of northern Wisconsin—those to whom Michel Cadotte and his employees were related, and with whom they worked and traded.

The Prophet's doctrine "spread like wild fire" throughout Ojibwe country, including around Chequamegon Bay, wrote Michel and Equaysayway's grandson William Warren.[14] Proof of his power was the fact that he persuaded so many Ojibwe to throw away their medicine bags, "which the Indian holds most sacred and inviolate." Near Chequamegon, "the Ojibways collected in great numbers" to engage in the practices espoused by the Prophet. According to Warren, "[n]ight and day, the ceremonies of the new religion were performed, till it was at last determined to go in a body to Detroit, to visit the prophet." They were actually heading toward an Indian community that became known as Prophet's Town, north of the present-day city of Lafayette, Indiana, and southwest of Detroit. Tenskwatawa and Tecumseh founded the village in 1808, and they encouraged members of all tribes to join them there.[15]

Some 150 canoes of Ojibwe warriors left Chequamegon Bay that summer to answer the Prophet's call. The flotilla made it as far as Pictured Rocks on Lake Superior's southern shore, approximately 195 miles east of Madeline Island, when they encountered Michel Cadotte. He was returning from Sault Ste. Marie, and he persuaded the Ojibwe to return to their homes and forsake the Prophet. Michel also instructed these Ojibwe about Tenskwatawa's "real motives," Warren reported.[16] Exactly what those real motives were, Warren didn't say, but he described how disillusioned other bands of Ojibwe later were after they visited the Prophet. Those Ojibwe told of hunger, illness, and other suffering at Prophet's Town.[17]

They weren't exaggerating. The winter of 1808–1809 was a difficult one for the Indians from the northwest, especially the Ojibwe and Odawa, who had joined Tenskwatawa at Prophet's Town. Harsh conditions and near-starvation food rations left many people weakened. An influenza epidemic swept through the community that winter, killing many Odawa and Ojibwe and leaving the survivors of those two nations convinced that the Prophet was a fraud.[18]

Support for the Prophet and his mission gradually disappeared among the Ojibwe, including those with whom Tanner lived. As he wrote in 1830, "[M]edicine bags, flints, and steels, were resumed; dogs were raised, women and children were beaten as before, and the Shawnee prophet was despised. At this day he is looked upon by the Indians as an impostor and a bad man."[19]

However, before the Ojibwe near Lake Superior abandoned the Prophet's ways, a group of them used his teachings as an excuse to pillage Michel's trading post at Lac Courte Oreilles. The exact timing of this attack is unclear. Warren said it occurred in 1808, but whether that was before or after Michel met and halted the flotilla of warriors headed to join the Prophet is uncertain. Another source says the attack at Lac Courte Oreilles took place in 1807.[20] According to Warren, the attackers were young men from the Lac Courte Oreilles village who were captivated by the Shawnee Prophet and the excitement he created.[21] But Warren also blamed Jean-Baptiste Corbin, Cadotte's clerk and the man then in charge of the Lac Courte Oreilles post, for enraging the Indians by severely beating his Ojibwe wife.

Corbin's actions so angered the Ojibwe that "the young men leaped into their canoes" and paddled across the lake to Cadotte's trading post, where "they broke open the doors and helped themselves to all which the store-houses contained." Corbin then fled for his life, aided by an elderly Ojibwe woman, who gave him a blanket, moccasins, and ammunition. He made his way to safety at Cadotte's headquarters at La Pointe, roughly one hundred miles to the north. Later, Corbin returned to Lac Courte Oreilles and lived there for decades with his Ojibwe wife (her name is now unknown).[22]

The attack on Cadotte's trading post infuriated the chief of the Lac du Flambeau Ojibwe village about ninety-five miles east of Lac Courte Or-eilles. According to Warren, "in open council, he addressed the ringleaders with the most bitter and cutting epithets. . . . It came near being the cause of a bloody family feud." However, goodwill between the two Ojibwe bands was restored "through the exertions of the kind-hearted Michel Cadotte." Once again, Michel demonstrated his ability as a peacemaker and his ca-pacity to soothe enraged tempers, even when he was the victim of hasty action.[23] He lost an estimated five thousand dollars' worth of goods in the attack, and his business suffered "irreparable damage." Even so, he continued to trade with the Indians under the auspices of the Michilimack-inac Company, although the number of trading posts he operated and the number of men he employed decreased significantly.[24]

In 1811, more changes arrived from another quarter. John Jacob Astor, who would become America's first multimillionaire, negotiated with the Michilimackinac Company to create still another company, the South West Fur Company, which would operate only in the United States. Michel was still trading through the Michilimackinac Company, even as Astor began a concerted effort to purchase that firm from the Montreal mer-chants who controlled it. Simultaneously, Astor lobbied to get Congress to enact a law that would make it illegal for noncitizens of the United States to engage in the fur trade within US boundaries.[25]

Meanwhile, relations between the English and the United States were deteriorating. With the Napoleonic Wars raging across the Atlantic, block-ades started affecting the ability of the British to sell their goods in France and elsewhere. The British retaliated by stopping merchant ships from reaching neutral nations such as the United States, confiscating cargo and impressing sailors into the Royal Navy. A contingent of "War Hawks" emerged in the US Congress, arguing that the only way the United States could protect itself was to drive the British entirely from North America and assume control of Canada.

The Americans also accused the British of fomenting Indian unrest and encouraging them to attack American settlers in places such as the Ohio Valley. British authorities denied that charge, but they remained in close contact with leaders of various Indian nations, recruiting them for the British side in the event war broke out.[26] That occurred on June 18, 1812, when President James Madison formally declared war on Great Britain and approved the US invasion of Canada. The War of 1812 was underway, and the British depended heavily on their Indian allies for assistance against the Americans. Tecumseh was one such ally, offering his allegiance and all the Native warriors he could muster to the British cause, once his own brother had fled Prophet's Town in late 1811 and the dream of a powerful Indian confederacy was dead. When war ultimately broke out, Tecumseh and his men played an important role in the fall of Detroit in August of 1812. He was killed at the Battle of the Thames, across the border from Detroit in Ontario, in October 1813.[27]

Thousands of warriors from a variety of nations joined in the war, mostly on the British side. By one estimate, more than three thousand Odawa, Potawatomi, and Ojibwe from the Great Lakes region made a military contribution to the British war effort. In fact, according to Allen, "The employment of Indian allies by the British crown during the War of 1812 was the single most important factor in the successful defence of Upper Canada."[28]

William Warren, writing in the mid-nineteenth century when important treaties between the Ojibwe and the US government were being negotiated, tried to put a positive spin on Ojibwe loyalty to the Americans during the war. He disputed the notion that large numbers of Ojibwe fought for the British during the War of 1812: "not more than one or two warriors" from Lake Superior and the Upper Mississippi regions "are mentioned as having joined the British."[29]

But other evidence, some of which involves the Cadottes, contradicts his claim. When the Americans surrendered at the first Battle of Michilimackinac in July of 1812, there were fears on both sides that the Indians who had joined the British forces in the battle would attack the American soldiers and their families as they departed the fort. That didn't occur, however, and one person who helped prevent the violence was Michel Cadotte Jr. In an August 1812 letter to British military leaders, John Askew Jr., a storekeeper who assisted the British military at Michilimackinac, said three men, including "M. Cadotte Jun. have rendered me a great service in keeping the Indians in order."[30] As a result, Askew noted, the Indians didn't drink excessively, and they refrained from stealing livestock or other property from the Americans, much less harming them.[31]

Warren maintained that Michel Cadotte Jr. and his brother Jean-Baptiste—both sons of Michel and Equaysayway—were captured by the British at Drummond Island on Lake Huron and were given the option to be imprisoned or act as interpreters and recruit Ojibwe for the British cause. According to Warren, "They accepted the latter alternative, and were actors in all the principal Canadian battles, and were present on the occasion of Tecumseh's death."[32] It wasn't only Michel Jr. and Jean-Baptiste who joined the British effort, however. Their brother Augustin also joined, and aside from Warren's account, there is no indication that their service was involuntary. Michel Jr. may have even led a contingent of Ojibwe warriors to fight with the British at Michilimackinac.[33]

Further evidence that suggests significant involvement by the Ojibwe on the British side includes the fact that the Indian force at Michilimackinac was led by John Johnston, the man who had traded at Chequamegon Bay before Michel established his trading post on Madeline Island. Johnston's wife was an Ojibwe and daughter of an important war leader from the Chequamegon area. It is likely that he, along with the Cadottes, recruited Ojibwe from that region.[34] Additionally, one of Michel's cousins, Chief Buffalo of La Pointe, fought with the British at the Battle of the Thames when Tecumseh was killed. He was an influential leader who would have brought Ojibwe warriors with him.[35]

A number of people with ties to the Chequamegon region—including several Cadottes—joined the British effort during the War of 1812. And, despite Warren's protestations, it's also likely that substantial numbers of Ojibwe from the area followed them. After all, the Ojibwe had been trading partners and allies of the British for half a century when the war broke out.

It would have been unusual for them to abandon their allies in the face of American aggression.

After two and a half years, the war ended, with more of a whimper than a bang. Both sides could claim a measure of victory when the Treaty of Ghent was signed in December of 1814, even though the boundaries between the two countries had not changed from those established in 1794.[36] British Canada had held off the American invasion and had become more unified, while the United States had solidified its independence from Great Britain. The greatest losers in the war were probably the Indians on the United States side of the international boundary. Their alliance with the British left them suspect in the eyes of the Americans who now controlled the region. More importantly, US settlement on what were previously Indian lands in the Upper Midwest and Great Lakes region began to explode soon after the war ended.

One person who certainly benefited from the war was John Jacob Astor. In the wake of the conflict, with anti-British sentiment still smoldering, he finally won approval for legislation making it illegal for noncitizens to engage in the fur trade in the United States. That gave him a near-monopoly over the fur trade in the United States from 1816 until 1834.[37] Astor's efforts to purchase the Michilimackinac Company were no longer necessary. His American Fur Company, created in 1808, simply assumed the trade that had once belonged to the Montreal interests.[38] Michel and his fur-trade business thus again faced major changes. He would either have to capitulate to the Americans or move to Canada. He eventually chose the former alternative, and in 1820 he began trading directly with the American Fur Company. That summer, he purchased his US citizenship for five dollars.[39]

By 1821, sons Michel Jr. and Augustin were working as interpreters for the American Fur Company, beginning at the Lac du Flambeau outfit.[40] That same year, New England brothers Lyman and Truman Warren each married one of Michel and Equaysayway's daughters.[41] The brothers entered the region as traders in 1819, and in 1823, after having sold their independent trading operation at Lac du Flambeau to Astor's American Fur Company, they were able to purchase their father-in-law's operation at La Pointe on Madeline Island. In time, the trading post on the island became a part of the American Fur Company network, with Lyman Warren as its agent.[42]

The American Fur Company Warehouse, 1922. PHOTOGRAPHER UNKNOWN. WHI IMAGE ID
36808

   Michel didn't abandon the trade altogether, however. A federal record
of licenses granted to fur traders shows that in 1831, Michel, listed as "Michael Cadotte, sen.," still had a license to trade at La Pointe on Madeline
Island. In the same document, Lyman Warren also received a license to
trade at La Pointe, while one of Michel's sons, listed as "Michael Cadotte jr.,"
received a license to trade at the Montreal River in northern Wisconsin.[43]

CHAPTER 18

RELIGIONS COLLIDE

Early Europeans and Americans who encountered Ojibwe people conducting Midewiwin ceremonies, also called Grand Medicine ceremonies, were often startled by what seemed so foreign to the Christian rituals that they understood. In the Midewiwin, drums were pounded, rattles were shaken, and participants chanted repeatedly. Death and resurrection were frequently portrayed. But the newcomers usually misunderstood the significance of the ceremonies. As Canadian scholar and Anishinaabwe author Basil Johnston, one of the few Anishinaabe scholars who have written about the Midewiwin ceremony and rituals in detail, explains, Ojibwe cultural taboos and European antagonism toward Native health practices have made discussing such issues problematic for Anishinaabeg authors.[1] Thomas Peacock, introducing a chapter on traditional Ojibwe health practices in his 2002 book, *Ojibwe Waasa Inaabidaa: We Look in All Directions*, put it this way: "This chapter was difficult for me to write for several reasons. Traditional Ojibwe health practices, particularly those combined with prayer and ceremony, have been closeted in mystery for generations because they were banned for many years by the colonizers. Both governmental officials and agents of the church considered the ancient combination of herbal and spiritual care to be sorcery, so this subject is not one Ojibwe people openly discuss. Furthermore, some of us believe that to bring up unpleasant topics (or unpleasant spirits for that matter) is to will them."[2]

Anishinaabe scholar Benjamin V. Burgess said he first learned of the Midewiwin while he was in college, attending a camp in Wisconsin for Ojibwe students who might become teachers: "After camp ended I returned home and asked my mother about the Midewiwin [and] she replied, 'They are medicine people.' She added, 'Your aunt was Mide; she was taken aside at a very young age. They kept her out of school. They hid her from social workers that would have taken her away for sure.'"[3]

Equaysayway and Michal Cadotte and their family had to negotiate similar cultural conundrums as they stepped between their Ojibwe world, their French Canadian Catholic heritage, and later, the introduction of Protestant theology by their son-in-law Lyman Warren and the religious leaders he enticed to Madeline Island.

These sorts of conflicts may have even helped precipitate the 1868 killing of a noted Minnesota Ojibwe leader by fellow Ojibwe. When Bag-one-giizhig the Younger, or Hole in the Day, was killed, "He was in the middle of a tense feud between Catholic missionaries . . . and Protestant missionaries . . . over missions and political ambitions," explains Anish-inaabe author Anton Treuer. "Bagone-giizhig flirted with conversion to Catholicism but always maintained his traditional Ojibwe beliefs, to the chagrin and frustration of the missionaries."[4]

Despite non-Native frustrations with traditional beliefs, a few Europeans began to write about those beliefs soon after first contact. French explorer Nicholas Perrot, who first visited Lake Superior about 1665, talked of Native people in the region revering animal-like deities, especially the Great Hare, whom he said they viewed as the creator of the world. In the twenty-first century, Anishinaabeg author Michael Witgen lends credence to Perrot's observations when he writes that Nanabozho, a shape-shifting hare and trickster, was "the true culture hero of the Ojibwe peoples." Nan-abozho is also linked to the Ojibwe creation story for Chequamegon Bay. He is said to have created the peninsula that forms the bay in order to trap beaver.[5] In addition to the Great Hare, Perrot said the Native peoples he encountered near Lake Superior worshipped serpents, panthers, bears, and certain birds, and they honored the sun as "the author of light."[6]

The Ojibwe had their own group of spirits, which they called *manidog* (singular: *manido*). In this system, they consulted and offered sacrifices to these spirits, seeking success in hunting, calm waters while canoeing, and relief from illness and more. Sacrifices also were made to appease evil spirits believed to have caused misfortune. Dreams played an important role in determining what action should be taken.[7]

Johnston detailed a similar, though more detailed pantheon, in which there were four orders to creation: the physical world; the plant world; the animal world; and lastly, the human world. In the physical world, Father Sun and Mother Earth were most revered, followed by Grandmother Moon and Grandfather Thunder. The Northern Lights also occupied a special place to illuminate soul-spirits headed to the Land of Peace.

Plants were revered for their ability to sustain life, to heal and for use in ceremonies. But it was animal spirits, such as the bear, eagle, crane, loon, and snake, that the Ojibwe communed with most frequently, even though they could be confounding. Animal spirits could shift to represent good or evil, birth and death, young and old, day and night and more. Animal beings were part of the Midewiwin ceremonies, Johnston writes: "Often animal beings were represented as contraries or contradictions."[8]

The Midewiwin and its ceremonies were employed in a number of forms by various Native nations of North America, especially around the Great Lakes. But the Midewiwin is most closely associated with the Ojibwe.[9] In the early twentieth century, Frances Densmore spent fourteen years visiting five different Ojibwe reservations, in part learning about the Midewiwin Society. Most of her information on the society came from three Ojibwe men, "all of whom were members of the Midewiwin, and were in good standing at the time of giving their information."[10] In the mid-nineteenth century, however, it was important to some people that Ojibwe religious practices not sound too foreign to American Protestants. William Warren wrote his *History of the Ojibway People* in the 1840s and early 1850s as the Ojibwe were negotiating major treaties with the United States government. At the time, assimilating Native people into white culture and turning them into what whites viewed as "civilized people" was at the heart of US Indian policy. Perhaps because of this consideration, Warren sought to demonstrate that Ojibwe beliefs were similar to Old Testament biblical stories. "The writer has learned enough of the religion of Ojibways to strengthen his belief of the analogy with the Hebrews," Warren wrote.[11] Densmore learned of similar edicts when she interviewed Midewiwin elders sixty to seventy years after Warren conducted his research. Midewiwin members were to always respect the Midewiwin Society and its ceremonies and were required to show respect to women. As Densmore noted, "Lying, stealing, and the use of liquor are strictly forbidden." Male members of the society were taught to be quiet and unassuming, to refrain from acting hastily, and to avoid speaking recklessly.[12]

Similarly, in his look at the Midewiwin Society and ceremonies, Johnston lists nine provisions in the Midewiwin "Code for Long Life and Wisdom." They include honoring the elderly, honoring women, honoring life in all its forms, honoring one's promises and kindness, being peaceful, courageous and moderate in all things.[13] The inner workings of the Midewiwin are revealed only to members. Even William Warren, who learned of the society and some of its rituals from tribal elders and his own relatives, admitted that much about the society remained a mystery to him: "Amongst the Ojibways, the secrets of this grand rite are as sacredly kept as the secrets of the Masonic Lodge among the whites."[14] Still, Warren took issue with "[m]issionaries, travellers, and transient sojourners amongst the Ojibways" who had witnessed parts of the Midewiwin rites and reported that they were "composed of foolish and unmeaning ceremonies." Ojibwe could just as easily view Christian rituals and conclude "that they consist of unmeaning and nonsensical ceremonies," he declared.[15]

Some twentieth-century students of Ojibwe culture such as Christopher Vescey and Harold Hickerson, have concluded that the Midewiwin Society and its ceremonies were a postcontact response to European intrusions into their territory and the challenges these intrusions posed to traditional beliefs. These historians maintain that the Ojibwe created a new religious system that incorporated many ideas of Christianity brought by the Jesuits, along with traditional spiritual beliefs.[16] Warren believed otherwise, maintaining that Midewiwin rites were based on ancient traditions that had been used for "a long line of generations."[17]

Recent archaeological information suggests that the Midewiwin Society and its ceremonies were functioning before the first Europeans arrived.[18] Additionally, Hickerson may have had reasons to dismiss the historical importance of the Midewiwin, according to Treuer. The research Hickerson used in his book was developed while he was working for the Indian Claims Commission, "established by Congress in 1946 to hear tribal cases against the federal government concerning ceded lands and monetary reparations. Historical briefs were used to support the government's contention that various Native people had only recent and therefore limited use of the lands they claimed, and thus deserved only minimal compensation."[19]

Furthermore, Treuer notes, there is no evidence that early European leaders were alarmed by a new spiritual ceremony that might have drawn potential converts away from Christianity or challenged European authority. While "the advent of other religious societies after European contact, such as the Ghost Dance, received much attention . . . ," he explains, "there are no references to the creation of midewiwin in European missionary or explorer texts." Finally, Treuer agrees with Warren that Native peoples' oral histories say the Midewiwin existed long before the first contact with Europeans.[20]

If Native ceremonies and beliefs were disturbing to some of the first American missionaries to arrive in Ojibwe country during the early decades of the nineteenth century, so was the Catholic faith practiced by most French Canadians and many of their mixed-ancestry relatives. In the 1830s, Presbyterian missionary Edmund Ely fought a two-pronged personal religious war in northwestern Wisconsin and northeastern Minnesota against Catholics on the one hand and the Ojibwe on the other. Ely believed that Catholics were leading Native and mixed-ancestry people straight to hell, and he hoped to convert the Native people to his own version of the one true faith.[21] He was particularly alarmed by one Catholic French Canadian interpreter named Pierre Cotté, who, he believed, was working with Satan to convince the Ojibwe to join the Catholic Church. In his journal for February 5, 1836, Ely wrote, "O, let not the ungodly [Catholics] pervert thy truth to the ruin of the blind heathen [Indians]."[22] Yet, those he referred to as "blind heathens" had their own long-held spiritual beliefs, which they were not eager to abandon for Christianity, especially not the tight-fisted, fire-and-brimstone version that Ely preached.

When cholera struck the region in 1835, Ely worried about the souls of the Ojibwe near Fond du Lac; as he wrote on June 8, "The poor Indians are sick and do indeed suffer." If only they would accept his brand of Christianity, there would be hope for them, he argued, "but they are bound in chains of superstition."[23] Ely was just one of the numerous Protestant missionaries and religious leaders who arrived at Lake Superior in the middle decades of the nineteenth century. He left a detailed journal that shows he was exceedingly intolerant of any religious beliefs but his own. His ongoing conflict with both Catholic and Native beliefs is emblematic of the clash of religions that occurred on a much larger scale in this region.

Members of the Cadotte family, with their Native traditions and French Canadian Catholic backgrounds, and their later exposure to Protestant beliefs, were sometimes caught in a theological crossfire. For instance, Presbyterian minister–teacher Jedediah D. Stevens visited Madeline Island in early 1830 at the behest of Lyman Warren, son-in-law of Michel and Equaysayway Cadotte. Warren was undergoing a spiritual awakening and would eventually join the Presbyterian Church. Stevens found reason to hope for Warren's salvation; however, he despaired for Warren's wife, Mary, and her sister Charlotte—two of Michel and Equaysayway's daughters—"led as they were by their Catholic faith to 'the very threshold of destruction.'" During his visit, Stevens held conversations with the women and with sixty-five-year-old Michel about their religious beliefs but reported that he was "unable to remove the veil from their hearts and the scales from their eyes."[24]

Like his brother Jean-Baptiste Jr., Michel was sent to Montreal as a youngster to attend school. He joined his brother at Montreal's College of Saint Raphael, a Catholic high school that prepared young men for the seminary, although it's not clear how long he continued his studies.[25] Later, he and Equasayway had their children baptized as Catholics, and years after that, the couple were married in the Catholic Church. It's not known how they viewed traditional Ojibwe religious ceremonies or whether they participated in them, but Michel had connections to Ojibwe traditions through his mother, Athanasie, although she was also a practicing Catholic. Equaysayway was equally connected to Ojibwe culture through her prominent family and its ties to Madeline Island at the western end of Lake Superior, which was once the center of Ojibwe spiritualism. They were both familiar with Ojibwe beliefs, even if they weren't active adherents to those beliefs or participants in their rites. They knew that the Ojibwe around Lake Superior, like other Native groups in the region, focused their beliefs on a variety of spirits rooted in the natural world.

The Jesuits who arrived in the western Great Lakes region in the mid-1600s initially claimed some success in converting Native people to Catholicism. In 1679, Father Claude Dablon, superior of the Jesuit missions in New France, wrote of a priest at Green Bay, Father Louis André, who had baptized thirty-four people in 1673. In 1674, he added 100 people to the list of converts, and the following year, another 140. According to Dablon,

St. Joseph's Catholic Church. PHOTOGRAPHER UNKNOWN. WHS IMAGE ID 36883

"At the present time, he Counts more than 500 christians on the whole bay."[26] But Dablon's report also pointed to one of the problems the Jesuits faced: large numbers of their converts were children or old people on their deathbeds. Dablon said André was "peopling paradise with many children, who died after baptism."[27]

The Jesuits also briefly maintained a mission at Chequamegon Bay in the late 1660s. It was abandoned in 1671 amid threats of potential attacks from the Dakota. There would not be another permanent Catholic clergy presence in the Chequamegon region until more than 150 years later. Soon after the first Protestant missionaries arrived, Father Frederick Baraga established a Catholic mission on Madeline Island in 1835, and a small log church was built that same year.[28] A larger building, known as St. Joseph's Catholic Church, was built nearby in 1841.

Despite the absence of missions or priests, Catholicism continued to be practiced around the western end of Lake Superior during that century and a half when there was no Catholic church or mission. Many of the French Canadian traders and voyageurs in the area, as well as their mixed-ancestry families, remained loyal to the Catholic Church. Many, including Michel and Equaysayway, traveled east to Sault Ste. Marie, Michilimackinac, or even Montreal to have their children baptized by Catholic priests or have their backcountry marriages recognized by the Church. The records of the Catholic mission at Michilimackinac show many baptisms of French Canadian and mixed-ancestry children during these years. For instance, Jean-Baptiste Marcot Jr., baptized on June 13, 1762, was "born in the winter quarters at la pointe de Chagouamigoun on the twelfth of January last."[29]

When the first Protestant missionaries arrived at Madeline Island, other transformations were also occurring in the Ojibwe world. The Protestants' arrival coincided with the push for treaties between Native nations around Lake Superior and the US government. Beginning in 1818 and continuing for more than thirty years, these efforts sought to establish hard geographic boundaries and ever-decreasing territory for each nation.[30]

Edmund Ely wasn't the first or the most important Protestant missionary in the region. One of the first was Frederick Ayer, who arrived at Madeline Island in 1830 to teach at the school Lyman Warren created. He later moved on to northern Minnesota. Sherman Hall came to Madeline Island a year later and remained until 1853. William Boutwell initially joined Hall on Madeline Island before proceeding westward into Minnesota. But the task of gaining converts wasn't easy for any of them.

A report by one missionary discussed the efforts and results at Yellow Lake, Minnesota, and La Pointe, Wisconsin: "During the winter of 1835-6, both at La Pointe and Yellow Lake there was much religious interest. Several conversions are mentioned at each place," wrote Reverend Stephen R. Riggs. But those "several conversions" didn't come easily. The Indians converted "are of course persecuted and opposed by their heathen relations, and they are branded with the name of 'Praying Indians.'"[31]

By 1838, a spiritual awakening reportedly had been experienced in the small community of Pokeguma, in what is now Minnesota. There, first Ayer and later Boutwell attended the Native people, but this awakening and the increasing number of Christian converts, Riggs wrote, "aroused the opposition of the heathen party, who proceeded greatly to annoy the missionaries, by killing their cattle, and threatening to drive them from the country."[32] One reason for the Indians' hostility toward the missionaries, he added, was the fact that they had ceded land to the United States through a treaty negotiated in the summer of 1837. It was not ratified by Congress until the following year, but that didn't stop non-Indian settlers; therefore, "[I]mmediately, before the Treaty was ratified, white people began to take possession" of lands still technically owned by the Ojibwe.[33]

Conversions on and around Madeline Island were equally hard to come by for the Protestants. During the first thirty-four years of the Protestant church on Madeline Island, fewer than ten Ojibwe or mixed-ancestry individuals became members of the Presbyterian Church.[34] The Protestants labored under a number of burdens as they sought converts. For one thing, large numbers of the French Canadians and their mixed-ancestry families had long-standing ties to the Catholic Church. Also, the Protestants required a lengthy period of study before accepting a new member. Equally important was the style of worship.

The Protestants' "rather bleak faith," as represented by missionaries, such as the austere Reverend Sherman Hall, didn't appeal to the Ojibwe or those of mixed ancestry as much "as the ritual and pageantry of Catholicism," said Hamilton Nelson Ross, who began visiting Madeline Island in 1894.[35] Additionally, the Indians were perplexed by the fact "the white man had so many different sects in the worship of a common Diety," and it angered them that leaders of each sect claimed theirs was "the only true course to salvation."[36]

Sherman Hall, like Edmund Ely, worried about the Catholics' influence. Even before he arrived at Madeline Island, he wrote to his father, saying that "I have more fears that the Catholics will cause us difficulties, than the Indians will."[37] Hall's fears may have been realized when Father Baraga arrived at Madeline Island in July of 1835. Unlike the Protestants, Baraga found the region fertile for Catholics. With enthusiastic local help, he had a church built in twelve days, and by October 1 of that year, he had baptized 148 new Catholics. The first child he baptized was nine-month-old Elizabeth Cadotte, a relative of Michel and Equaysayway through Michel's distant cousin, Benjamin Cadotte. Baraga may have thought it prudent to start with a relative of Madeline Island's still-important leading couple.[38]

The priest's success was worrisome for the Protestants, who were so concerned that they sought to remove constitutional protections for Catholics in their neighborhood. Hall, Ayer, Ely, and Boutwell sent a letter to

Henry Rowe Schoolcraft, the US Indian agent at Mackinac Island who had authority over the Indian nations of southern Lake Superior, asking him to refuse Baraga a license of residence to continue his Madeline Island church and mission. They wanted Schoolcraft to advise the priest to relocate and "confine his labors to some of the fields not pre-occupied."[39]

Baraga remained on Madeline Island, however, apparently without interference from Schoolcraft or other US government officials. He remained the priest at La Pointe until 1843 and later became a bishop serving Michigan's Upper Peninsula. Other priests followed him and kept the small congregation active. Despite the theological conflict between the Protestants and Catholics, cooperation also occurred in the small community on Madeline Island. For example, in 1838, when the wife of the Presbyterian school teacher on the island suffered the loss of a stillborn baby, Baraga joined the funeral procession with Protestant mourners.[40]

Additionally, according to Hall, Baraga encouraged Catholic, Ojibwe, and mixed-ancestry parents on the island to send their children to the Protestants' mission school, where they could learn to read and write in both English and their Native language. But he did so with caution, warning the Protestants not to meddle with the religious beliefs of the Catholic students or he would remove all of them from their schools.[41]

Both Protestant and Catholic churches remained on and around Madeline Island throughout the turbulent years of the nineteenth century and into the twentieth century—and they continue in the twenty-first. Still, the traditional ways haven't disappeared. "Several midewiwin lodges, including those still active today at Bad River, Wisconsin, and Lake Lena, Minnesota, revitalized their societies and resumed their ceremonies. The number of participants there and in other communities with active lodges has increased," Treuer wrote.[42]

CHAPTER 19

A METHOD TO THEIR MARRIAGE

Nothing in the record of Michel Cadotte's life suggests that he was impetuous or that he and his partner Equaysayway were prone to making spur-of-the-moment decisions. So when they decided to get married in a Catholic church in 1830—more than forty years after they first became husband and wife under Ojibwe custom—they must have had a good reason.

In fact, they had multiple reasons to have their marriage recognized under European American rules, notably: important court cases were changing how marriages between European men and Native women were viewed by authorities; treaties had been forged that made marriage issues more significant for mixed-ancestry couples like the Cadottes; and substantial cultural changes were on the horizon as the first of the Protestant missionaries began to arrive at Lake Superior.

When I initially learned that Equaysayway and Michel had been married in the European tradition late in life, I found it curious, but I didn't give it a lot of thought. Soon, however, the oddity of that late-in-life marriage, also known in the trade as "marriage rehabilitation," began to trouble me. Although many other traders and their Native wives had their "marriages in the custom of the country" formalized in the European sense sometime later, I wondered what made the Cadottes do so more than forty years after they were joined by Ojibwe tradition.

To try to understand the Cadottes' choice, I visited St. Anne's Catholic Church to view the official record of the wedding.[1] I also wondered what else was happening about the same time that might have made a marriage recognized by European and American authorities more urgent. It became apparent that Michel and Equaysayway were responding to the changing circumstances of their world. They were demonstrating the same adaptability and resiliency they had shown at different periods in their lives when situations demanded change.

Little is known about how and when Equaysayway and Michel were wed under Ojibwe tradition. That had occurred before the autumn of 1787, when Michel Jr. was born near Chippewa Falls. But there is no documentation of when that union was recognized by their Ojibwe family. That's hardly surprising, given the Ojibwe tradition of recording important events orally, rather than with written documents.

Although Ojibwe tradition did not require a formal wedding ceremony, a number of authors have recorded rituals that often preceded an Ojibwe marriage. Frances Densmore outlined some of those rituals in her 1927 ethnographic study, *Chippewa Customs*: "If a young man's intentions were serious, he killed a deer or some other animal and brought it to the girl's parents. This was to indicate his ability and intention to provide well for his family. If the parents approved of the young man, they asked him to stay and share the feast. This was understood as an acceptance of his wish to marry their daughter, and he was allowed to come and go with more freedom than formerly."[2]

It seems likely that Michel offered such a gift to Equaysayway's father, La Grue, to win his approval for the marriage. However, many decades later when Equaysayway related stories about her early life with Michel to their grandson William Warren, his account includes no information about their Ojibwe marriage.

Densmore relied on Warren's sister, Julia Warren Spears, to describe how one newlywed couple obtained their own lodge in the 1840s on the Bad River Chippewa Indian Reservation at the south end of Chequamegon Bay: "The Chief had a daughter, of whom he was very fond. . . . His wife built a wigwam for the young couple near their own, making it as pretty as possible and furnishing it with new floor mats and other articles. When the young couple were ready to begin life together, they quietly took up their abode in the wigwam which had been provided for them."[3]

Michel's nominal home in those early years was still at his father's trading headquarters at Sault Ste. Marie. But he understood the importance of traditions and rituals to the Ojibwe. Therefore, it's not hard to imagine that he and Equaysayway maintained a bark-covered lodge near Equaysayway's parents or other family members prior to establishing their permanent home and trading post on Madeline Island.

None of this suggests that Michel Cadotte abandoned the Catholic faith in which he was raised. He didn't, and that's demonstrated by the fact that he took his young children to Mackinac Island to be baptized in the Roman Catholic faith. But if he and Equaysayway ever contemplated having their marriage consecrated by the Catholic Church on one of these occasions, they apparently didn't take action. Or if they did, the documentation has been lost. So, the couple found it prudent to be married by a Catholic priest in 1830, when they were both in their late sixties. Around the same time, they obtained a marriage license from the county clerk's office on Mackinac Island, thus ensuring that their marriage would also be recognized by US civil officials.[4]

Perhaps the most important reason for that decision was judicial. In 1824, a Michigan territorial judge named James Doty, presiding at what would become Green Bay, Wisconsin, had determined that marriages between people of European descent and Natives were not valid if they were consecrated only by Indian custom. Doty convened the first grand jury ever held in Green Bay, according to historian Jacqueline Peterson: "At Doty's instigation, the muddled jurors indicted thirty-six of the town's principal male inhabitants for fornication and two for adultery. The majority pleaded guilty to escape the fine [and] stood before a justice of the peace to legitimize their sexual unions."[5] The judge rejected the defendants' claims that they were legally married because they had lived many years with their wives and had large families and that their marriages had been legitimized "according to the customs of the Indians."[6]

There were no newspapers on Madeline Island to bring reports of Judge Doty's decision, but communications among the many fur traders likely carried the news. Whether the court case initially caused Michel and Equaysayway anxiety is not known. But it was worrisome in retrospect. Although the French had long honored such marriages, and the British did for the most part, Doty's ruling was among the first of several court cases in the United States over the next few decades that would cast doubt on the legitimacy of marriages created under Native customs.[7]

In addition to the court case in Green Bay, substantial political and cultural upheaval arose near Lake Superior in the first decades of the 1800s that raised questions about Native marriages. Treaties with the US government created considerable turmoil, and the 1826 Treaty of Fond du Lac may have added urgency to questions regarding the Cadottes' marriage.

The Treaty of Fond du Lac was the first of the agreements between the United States and the Lake Superior Ojibwe to include provisions for people of mixed Ojibwe and European descent, or "half-breeds," as the treaty called them. Article IV of the treaty began by saying: "It being deemed important that the half-breeds, scattered through this extensive country, should be stimulated to exertion and improvement by the possession of permanent property," sections of land would be set aside at Sault Ste. Marie for some of them.[8]

It's more than a little condescending to argue that Michel and Equaysayway—as well as many other people of mixed ancestry—needed to be "stimulated to exertion and improvement" by the US government. The Cadottes had already experienced long lives marked by hard work and danger. They had achieved financial success and setbacks, and they had developed solid reputations based on their own endeavors. Nevertheless, of the forty-six mixed-ancestry individuals or families named in the treaty as "half-breeds" who were due to receive a section of land at Sault Ste. Marie, five of the listings were for Michel and Equaysayway and their heirs.[9]

Under the treaty terms, Equaysayway and Michel were each due one section of land, as were each of their children living in the United States. Ossinahjeeunoqua, the wife of Michel Cadotte Jr., was assigned a section, and so was grandson William Warren. None of the granddaughters was named in the list.[10]

Congress failed to approve that provision of the treaty, however, and the land grants at Sault Ste. Marie for people of mixed heritage never materialized. But it is worth noting that both Equaysayway and Ossinahjeeunoqua were listed in the treaty as the *wives* of their respective husbands, rather than individuals due a section of ground in their own right. Perhaps the realization that future treaties might have similar provisions—and might require proof of marriage—was an added incentive for both couples to have their marriages recognized by the Catholic Church and civil authorities, especially in the wake of the Green Bay court ruling and the imminent arrival of Protestant proselytizers.

The first recorded instance of a Protestant missionary arriving at Madeline Island was in early 1830, when Presbyterian minister Jedediah Stevens visited the Cadotte compound. It was after talking with Michel Cadotte and his daughters that Stevens declared he was "unable to remove the veil [of Catholicism] from their hearts and the scales from their eyes."[11]

Michel and Equaysayway were married according to Catholic doctrine a little more than six months later. It's understandable that they weren't willing to abandon Catholicism for the new version of Christianity that Protestants such as Smith were promoting. But realizing that this sort of evangelizing was on its way to the western end of Lake Superior may have been another reason for the couple to have their union recognized under European rules.

The first Protestant preachers had arrived near the *east* end of Lake Superior, at Mackinac Island, earlier in the nineteenth century, and a permanent mission was established there in 1823. Both Michel Sr. and Michel Jr. would have known of that development from their frequent trips to Mackinac Island and to Sault Ste. Marie. They probably also had some understanding of the brewing conflict between Protestants and Catholics in the region. It was one more reason to ensure their marriages were recognized under the Catholic religion they had followed their entire lives.

Additionally, Michel and Equaysayway were protecting their own assets and those of their descendants by having their marriage officially sanctioned. In 1824, they had bequeathed land on Madeline Island and nearby to each of their four sons then living in the United States, and in 1827, they had provided more land for their daughters and their grandchildren from those daughters. The land on Madeline Island, roughly the southern third of the island, came to them through Equaysayway's family and other Ojibwe leaders. It was formalized in a deed registered on Mackinac Island in 1827, through which Michel and Equaysayway agreed to give a portion of the land—roughly two thousand acres—on the island to their son-in-law Lyman Warren, who, in turn, gave a parcel to the new Protestant mission on the island.[12] Ensuring that their marriage was recognized by the proper authorities—so that the land given to Equaysayway was clearly considered Michel's also—may well have been another factor in their decision to be married in 1830. The fact that they chose to do so after their eldest son formalized *his* marriage makes the timing of their marriage all the more intriguing.

Before Michel and Equaysayway were married at St. Anne's Catholic Church on Mackinac Island in July of 1830, their son Michel Jr. married Ossinahjeeunoqua—who went by the Anglo name Esther—in the same church. At least one witness was present at both ceremonies. Perhaps it was the younger Michel who convinced his parents that they needed a formal Catholic wedding.[13]

In 1826, son-in-law Lyman Warren had begun efforts to recruit a Protestant mission and school for Madeline Island. Although he wasn't successful in that effort until 1830, he no doubt spoke with his in-laws about what he hoped to do. It's possible that Lyman Warren, realizing the changes that would arrive with the Protestants and understanding his in-laws' devotion to their Catholic faith, acted in concert with his brother-in-law Michel Jr. to push for the wedding.

How much celebration attended the Cadottes' wedding on Mackinac Island is impossible to determine. There were no newspapers on the island then and few on the nearby mainland. The registry at St. Anne's Church that records the marriage is fairly straightforward. The contracting parties for the marriage that occurred on July 26, 1830, on Mackinac Island were listed as Michael Cadotte and Marie Magdelaine, daughter of La Grue. Michel's parents were recorded as Jean-Baptiste Cadotte and "une sauvagesse."[14] The witnesses were William McGulpin, Alexis Corbin *père*, and Alexis Corbin *fils*. The latter two were fellow fur traders, while McGulpin was a well-known resident of Mackinac Island and a baker for the American Fur Company. The presiding official was a priest named Jean Dejean.[15]

Although they had been married for decades under Ojibwe custom, Michel and Equaysayway Cadotte were now officially husband and wife in the eyes of the Catholic Church, and perhaps more importantly, under the auspices of the US government, which would affect their lives in a multitude of ways.

Michel and Equaysayway continued to live at their family compound on Madeline Island. The last of their eleven children, Joseph, was born there in 1807. All but one of their children survived to adulthood, and the couple had multiple grandchildren, many of whom lived near them on Madeline Island.[16] Michel Cadotte died there in 1837 and was buried in the cemetery beside Father Frederick Baraga's new Catholic Church.[17] Equaysayway lived more than a decade longer and was alive when William Warren was interviewing Ojibwe elders about their tribal history.[18] Census records show her living at La Pointe in 1850, with her age listed as ninety. But Equaysayway is not buried beside Michel, her husband of more than fifty years. It is believed she is buried elsewhere on the island that was named for her.[19]

CHAPTER 20

LYMAN WARREN'S PREDICAMENT

I n September of 1838, Lyman Warren wrote a letter to his friend and fellow trader, William Aiken, concerning the trouble they faced from their former employer, the American Fur Company. Warren put his return address on the envelope—La Pointe, Wisconsin. Underneath, in a clear script, he added this plaintive declaration: "'We have no friends' &c."[1]

The late 1830s were a difficult time for fur traders in general and for the American Fur Company, which employed Warren on Madeline Island and Aiken in northwestern Minnesota in particular. They were particularly troublesome years for Lyman Warren, Michel and Equaysayway's son-in-law.

Warren claimed a proud heritage, tracing his ancestors back to the Pilgrims at Plymouth Rock. He had successfully engaged in the fur trade for two decades, and he had married into the important Cadotte family. He worked hard to bring religious instruction, a church, and the vestiges of civilization—at least as he understood them—to his isolated community and fur-trading outpost. Warren also sought to ensure that his children and others he was responsible for had solid educations. Despite being respected by his fellow traders, as well as religious and civilian leaders, everything came crashing down on him in 1837–1838, leaving both his reputation and his finances in tatters. His problems coincided almost exactly with the end of the fur trade as the major industry defining Lake Superior and Madeline Island.

Lyman Marcus Warren was born on August 9, 1794, in Massachusetts.[2] His family moved several times before settling in East Clarkson, New York, where his father, Lyman Warren Sr., operated a successful business as a tanner and shoemaker.[3]

In 1818, Lyman Warren and his younger brother, Truman, headed west to engage in the fur trade. They worked first for Charles Oakes Ermatinger, an independent Canadian trader operating out of Sault Ste. Marie. Thanks to the law passed by Congress in 1816, only US citizens could legally trade with Indians within the boundaries of the United States. Ermatinger needed US citizens to represent him in the trade south of the Canadian border, and the Warren brothers arrived at an opportune time.[4]

In 1819, the brothers purchased Ermatinger's trading post at Lac du Flambeau, Wisconsin. But by 1821, tired of competing with John Jacob Astor's American Fur Company and the near monopoly it held on the fur trade around the southern shore of Lake Superior, they arranged to sell their business to Astor's company. A year later, they went to work for that same company. Truman stayed at Lac du Flambeau while Lyman was employed at Fond du Lac.[5]

Anyone involved in the fur trade around Lake Superior in those years became acquainted with Michel and Equaysayway Cadotte and their substantial trading operation headquartered on Madeline Island. By the 1820s, the size of that business was considerably reduced from what it had once been, but the Cadottes were still a force to be reckoned with in the business. Furthermore, several of the Cadottes' sons worked for the American Fur Company at posts such as Lac du Flambeau, so it was inevitable that the Warren brothers would meet the family.

In 1821, the same year they decided to sell their business to the American Fur Company, both of the Warren brothers married daughters of Michel and Equaysayway Cadotte. Lyman joined with twenty-one-year-old Marie, who became known as Mary, while Truman married sixteen-year-old Charlotte.[6] Lyman Warren didn't formally tie the knot with Marie, at least according to European ritual, until 1827, when they were married on Mackinac Island.[7] Truman had already been married to Margaret Bazinet, the daughter of a French Canadian trader who also worked for the American Fur Company, with whom he had two children.[8]

By 1823, the two brothers were able to purchase their in-laws' La Pointe trading post on Madeline Island. The American Fur Company, which had long carried on trade with the Cadottes, soon appointed the Warren brothers as its agents on the island.[9] The post became the company's headquarters for most trade around southern Lake Superior, while the Fond du Lac post served the western end of the lake. American Fur Company traders from posts in the interior brought their furs to Madeline Island and received supplies there.

The Warren brothers also began raising families with the Cadotte sisters. Truman and Charlotte Warren had twin boys named Edwin and George and a daughter named Nancy. Lyman and Mary Warren had six children who survived to adulthood: four daughters (Charlotte, Julia, Mary, and Sophia) and two sons (William and Truman).[10]

Lyman's son Truman Warren was born after tragedy struck the family in 1825. That year, Lyman's brother Truman died from what William Warren described as "a severe cold caused by the extreme exposure incident to an Indian trader's life." He expired while on board a vessel bound for Detroit, where he hoped to obtain medical treatment.[11] With his brother's death, Lyman Warren assumed responsibility for all of Truman's children, as well as his widow, Charlotte. This additional burden was lifted when Charlotte remarried, this time to James Ermatinger, the nephew of trader Charles Oakes Ermatinger.[12]

All of the Warren children received a good education for youngsters living at an isolated outpost. First, they attended schools at Sault Ste. Marie and then on Madeline Island after Lyman persuaded a Protestant organization to open a school there. Eventually, with the aid of Lyman Warren's father, most of the Warren children studied in New York.[13]

The Warren children and their cousins grew up primarily at the Cadotte–Warren compound on Madeline Island. In 1832, US Army Lieutenant James Allen, on a survey expedition to the Upper Mississippi River region, was impressed when he stopped at the island, where Lyman Warren then operated the trading post. Allen wrote that Warren "has given to the spot an appearance of civilization. He has built a large and comfortable dwelling, a store house and eight or ten other buildings, which with the houses of Cadotte and family . . . make almost a village."[14]

Allen also noted that, as the primary trader for the American Fur Company in the region, Warren oversaw a large trading realm south and west of Madeline Island, including the St. Croix and Chippewa rivers and the area from Lac Court de Oreilles to Lac du Flambeau.[15] It was much the same territory where Michel Cadotte once traded when he worked under contract with the North West Company.

Edmund F. Ely, the missionary and teacher, stopped at Madeline Island in August 1833 on his way to his first posting at Sandy Lake, Minnesota. He complained frequently about the people and landscape he encountered during his sixteen years in the Lake Superior region, but he had no complaints about La Pointe and the Cadotte-Warren compound. Noting that Warren was "one of the most extensive traders" in the Lake Superior region, Ely wrote with underlined astonishment that this important person allowed the missionary, Reverend Sherman Hall, to live "in the best half of Mr. Warren's house *rent free*." Ely also described a small community with "10 or 12 houses & stores, built in the Canadian manner—covered sides & roof with bark (cedar is the common kind)." He also said Warren had a good farm near the buildings, where he raised wheat and berries. And, although he saw livestock, Ely observed, "Grass is poor for cows."[16] In the same portion of his journal, Ely wrote that "Mr. W. has been the most essential help to the mission."[17] He was referring to Sherman Hall's mission on Madeline Island. Indeed, Lyman Warren was instrumental in its founding.

Before Lyman's brother Truman died, the two of them had become interested in religion and what they deemed a proper education for their children. Writing letters regularly to the American Board of Commissioners for Foreign Missions in Boston, Lyman eventually persuaded the group to send both teachers and missionaries to the small community on Madeline Island.[18]

The first to arrive and stay, in 1830, was Frederick Ayer, a lay teacher whom Warren had met at the mission school on Mackinac Island. Ayer began teaching a small group of students in a building Warren provided to house the school. The following year, the Foreign Missions board approved a permanent mission at the school. Presbyterian minister Sherman Hall and his wife arrived at Madeline Island in August of 1831.[19]

Like most who visited, Hall was favorably impressed by what he saw on the island. "We were agreeably disappointed on finding the place so much more pleasant than we had anticipated," he wrote.[20] A few months later, in a letter to a family member, Hall extolled Warren's virtues: "He charges no rent for the house or furniture. We are almost daily receiving some new measure of kindness from him, though he has given $100 to the mission for this year, besides many things of which he has made no account. We ought to be peculiarly grateful that God has given us such a friend in him."[21]

Warren eagerly joined the new congregation led by Hall when it was first created, even though his wife, Mary, remained a Catholic. The family apparently worked around any theological differences, and Lyman Warren was elected clerk of the new Protestant church at La Pointe. The following year, he was appointed deacon.[22]

Life on Madeline Island proceeded with the steady seasonal rhythms of the fur trade. Winters were relatively quiet, as traders and trappers spent the cold months in the backcountry. Spring brought trips to the maple sugar groves, and when the ice broke up, the trappers began arriving to deliver their furs and resupply for the next year. Although it didn't match the revelry of the old North West Company rendezvous at Grand Portage, a boisterous commerce continued at La Pointe through summer and early autumn.

During these years, Warren performed important functions beyond trading. He reported trouble between the Dakota and Ojibwe to the appropriate Indian agents and worked with Ojibwe Chief Great Buffalo of La Pointe to help prevent farther confrontations.[23] He personally refused to employ liquor in his fur trade with the Indians, even though other independent traders did so.[24] In 1833, when John Jacob Astor sold the American Fur Company to Ramsay Crooks and several of Crooks's associates. Warren was made a partner, with ten of the company's one thousand shares.[25]

Warren wasn't universally esteemed, however. Lawrence Taliaferro, Indian agent for the Dakotas at Fort Snelling (present-day Minneapolis), described Warren as a "dastard." During negotiations for the Treaty of 1837, when Warren showed up with a group of Ojibwe to demand money he claimed was due to him from trading with Indians, Taliaferro pulled his revolver and threatened to shoot Warren, accusing him of attempting "to intimidate this Commission." He didn't shoot only because Henry Dodge, by now territorial governor of Wisconsin and the head of the treaty commission, ordered him to hold his fire. Taliaferro was chagrined that twenty thousand dollars was set aside in the treaty for Warren.[26]

Twenty-first-century Ojibwe author Anton Treuer described Warren as unscrupulous for the manner in which he sought money for himself in the 1837 treaty negotiations: "Warren was following an established European trader practice of inflating Indian debts, creating false claims, and using them to gouge money from the Indians' government annuities."[27] However, Treuer also noted that Warren was among those who believed that the Ojibwe received a poor deal in the 1837 treaty, in part because of the antics of Taliaferro and the rhetoric of an Ojibwe man called Hole in the Day the Elder, which cowed many Ojibwe leaders into keeping silent about the problems they saw with the treaty.[28]

A little more than a year after he became a partner in the American Fur Company, Warren moved the location of the company's headquarters on Madeline Island from the Cadotte family compound near the southeastern point of the island to a spot several miles away, on the western shoreline. The new site was about two and a half miles across Lake Superior from the mainland, where the town of Bayfield would eventually be built. This location offered a better harbor for fishing vessels as the company planned diversification into the commercial fishing business.[29]

Warren oversaw the construction of a dock at the new company site on the island but miscalculated its length and thereby cost the firm money. He acknowledged his own mistake in a letter to Ramsay Crooks early in 1835, saying "I almost feel ashamed to confess that I did not last fall examine the location of our Wharf with sufficient care."[30] Aware that the fur trade was starting to decline, Warren personally became involved in the timber business. He invested in a sawmill near Chippewa Falls with Henry Sibley, a friend and fellow trader who later became territorial governor of Minnesota.[31]

Lyman Warren was a successful trader and an important leader in religious and educational matters and, following in the footsteps of his father-in-law, he was arguably one of the most important men at the western end of Lake Superior during the early decades of the nineteenth century. He had no idea, however, that his career, his reputation, and his finances would all come crumbling down within a few years.

Changing fashions in Europe and the eastern United States were already reshaping the fur trade, as men's beaver felt hats lost their appeal. By 1838, the industry was beginning to retreat across the continent. The last great Rocky Mountain Rendezvous for fur traders in the western United States was held in 1840, and fur-trading posts closed throughout the next decade.[32]

The American Fur Company didn't shutter its trading post on Madeline Island until 1849.[33] By 1835, however, company executives could see that the future for the fur trade looked bleak. In the mid-1830s, company president Ramsay Crooks ordered Warren to begin converting the firm's

Madeline Island post into a commercial fishing and processing center, with fur trading as a secondary endeavor. However, the fishing venture also proved less profitable than the company had hoped, for a variety of reasons, including Warren's purported mismanagement. Thus, when Crooks and others began looking for someone to blame, Lyman Warren found himself in the crosshairs.

In addition to Warren's mistakes in constructing the new dock for the fishing venture, Ramsay Crooks viewed his involvement in the Sibley saw-mill as an act of disloyalty to the American Fur Company. Crooks wrote to a colleague that "our ablest agents have criminally preferred their individual interest to those of the Company." Making clear just who he was talking about, he decreed that Warren be expelled from the American Fur Company. Notices of Warren's dismissal—and the fact that the company would no longer honor any documents with his signature—were ordered to be placed in key newspapers of the region.[34]

It wasn't only Crooks who believed Warren's actions were criminal. Federal charges were even levied against him. Daniel Bushnell, who was the government's Indian subagent serving the Ojibwe in the western Lake Superior region, had been at Madeline Island since 1836, and he was no fan of Warren. He claimed that Warren had illegally engaged in private business with Indians while he was employed by the American Fur Company, in violation of an 1834 congressional act.[35] Such activities were not uncommon among traders, but Warren's precarious position with the American Fur Company and Bushnell's personal animosity toward him made him an easy target.

Gabriel Franchère, an agent of the American Fur Company sent by Crooks to investigate problems at La Pointe, was surprised at the turn of events he encountered when he appeared on Madeline Island in the late summer of 1838. "On my arrival here I found Mr. Warren under a military guard, with orders for his immediate removal from the country, focused on some complaints made by Indians to the sub-agent Mr. Bushnell," Franchère wrote to William Aiken in August.[36]

In April 1839, Warren and Michel Cadotte Jr. went to court in Mineral Point, Wisconsin, on charges stemming from Bushnell's accusations. After several months, the charges were dismissed for insufficient evidence of criminal intent.[37] However, before that case went to court, Warren offered a very different explanation for his legal troubles than what Bushnell alleged. As he wrote to Henry Sibley, "I shall soon leave for Green Bay under the escort of a military guard to answer a charge of breaking the laws of the land." Warren suggested bitterly that the law, as interpreted in his case, prevented him from even communicating with his in-laws Michel and Equaysayway Cadotte to obtain a parcel of land on Madeline Island for Warren's children. Because Michel was part Ojibwe and Equaysayway was a full Ojibwe, Warren hinted that his dealings with them violated the federal law Bushnell had cited.[38]

Whether Warren's discussions with his in-laws were the source of Bushnell's accusation that he illegally engaged in business with the Indians is unclear. Perhaps, like Lawrence Taliaferro, Bushnell believed Warren had criminally conspired with the Ojibwe to get money for himself through the 1837 treaty. In any event, it is known that Warren had long sought a portion of Madeline Island for his family and for a religious mission and school, and he eventually achieved that goal. The deed for that land was the first official document to use the name "Magdalen Island" (later Madeline) to refer to the island.[39]

A decade later, Warren became involved during negotiations for the 1837 treaty, the one in which Taliaferro took issue with Warren's actions. In addition to seeking money for himself, Warren and other traders who had married Ojibwe women successfully lobbied for a treaty provision that required that some of the proceeds from the sale of Ojibwe land go to the mixed-ancestry children of the traders' marriages. A little over twenty-five hundred dollars would eventually be awarded to Warren for his children and those of his deceased brother.[40]

The Treaty of 1837, also known as the Treaty of St. Peters or the Pine Tree Treaty, awarded a total of fifty-three thousand dollars to Warren and William Aiken, both acting as agents of the American Fur Company, for debts that the Ojibwe allegedly owed to the traders. This was the money that enraged Taliaferro. But that money ended up going directly to the American Fur Company, not to the individual traders. Warren later sued in an unsuccessful effort to recover a share of it. He clearly believed that Ramsay Crooks's company had treated him shabbily.[41]

Warren's concerns about Crooks and the American Fur Company are revealed in his letter to Aiken in September of 1838, in which Warren advised caution. He talked of Crooks's arrival at Madeline Island the previous month, but said he didn't know what the outcome would be for either him or Aiken. He also mentioned "a small claim of $8,000." He urged Aiken against "giving the company one Dollar" and added, "You will do me a great favor to keep secret all my communications to you on the subject of yours and my money. It's best to keep our own business to ourselves, for we have no friends in this business."[42]

In addition to Warren's financial and legal troubles, the small Protestant congregation that he helped found on Madeline Island dismissed him from its fold in 1837 on charges of lewdness. The charges apparently involved a woman of the congregation who was also excommunicated at the same time.[43] Reverend Hall, the same man who had extolled Warren's virtues just a few years earlier, now expressed his frustration with Warren, the congregation's one-time benefactor. "One of the individuals [who was excommunicated] occupied a place of high standing here which rendered the case much more aggravating," he wrote. "[T]his individual had enjoyed our perfect confidence, and had been made our intimate and confidential councellor [sic] from the first establishment of our mission."[44]

Six years later, these transgressions were apparently forgiven after Warren publicly acknowledged his error and after "having satisfied the members of the Church, that he felt sincerely penitent for his past conduct." Warren was reinstated with the church in 1843, but not with the same leadership role he had once held in the congregation.[45]

The difficult times created understandable stress for Warren and apparently strained even some of his closest relationships. In an April 1838 letter to William Aiken, he pleaded with his friend not to end their relationship over some unflattering remarks Warren had made regarding Aiken. In the letter, Warren declared he had never spoken disparagingly about Aiken in public: "When I have spoken unfavorably of you it was here at home amongst ourselves." Warren also said he was ashamed of the way their friendship had deteriorated, and he hoped Aiken would "sincerely reflect" on the situation and agree that it was time to put such behavior behind them.[46]

They apparently did just that, because in letters later that year, Warren spoke of Aiken as a friend and a trusted confidant. In another September 1838 letter to Aiken, Warren told his friend that "if Mr. Crooks consents," Warren planned to travel to upstate New York to see his wife and children, who were temporarily living near his father while the children attended school there. Warren invited Aiken to send his daughters to the same school.[47] One of Aiken's daughters, Matilda, later married Warren's son William.

Meanwhile, Warren's venture into the timber business was proving less successful than he had hoped. In 1841, he asked Henry Sibley to reduce his half share in the Chippewa River sawmill because he could not afford the annual payment of three thousand dollars, and he was not making enough profit under the original arrangement, especially when he was also paying for his children's schooling.[48] His financial difficulties were eased a bit that same year when he was hired as a government farmer for the Ojibwe at Chippewa Falls, but that job lasted only two years.[49]

In July of 1843, Warren's wife, Mary, died at Chippewa Falls, less than a year after the birth and death of their last child, Harriet. Warren took Mary's remains to be buried at Madeline Island the following winter.[50] Soon, his health began to suffer while his financial and legal problems continued. Even so, he attempted to patch up his differences with Ramsay Crooks. In a January 1845 letter to Crooks, he expressed regret for filing a lawsuit against the company. He also told Crooks he and his partners had sold the Chippewa Falls sawmill, and he planned to move to Dubuque, Iowa. But that didn't occur.[51]

Instead, Warren fell ill in 1846. He planned to visit a hospital in Detroit, according to his daughter, Julia Warren Spears. He took two trunks with him that carried all of his important papers and valuable personal items, but the trunks disappeared while Warren was at Sault Ste. Marie, awaiting transportation to Detroit. "Losing all his business papers made father worse," Spears wrote.[52] Warren didn't make it to Detroit. Instead, Lyman Marcus Warren returned to Madeline Island and died at La Pointe on October 10, 1847. He was buried on the island alongside his wife, Mary.[53]

Two years later, the American Fur Company closed its post at Madeline Island. Company employees left La Pointe and moved to St. Paul, Minnesota. As Julia Warren Spears recalled: "The buildings [at La Pointe] were then sold and torn down. As they were tearing down one of the large stores they found my father's trunk in one of the vaults." But the trunk had been broken into, and all of Lyman Warren's valuable papers were gone.[54]

After Warren's death, some members of the extended Cadotte family remained on Madeline Island. A few of them continued trapping ani-

Julia Warren Spears, ca. 1924. PHOTOGRAPHER UNKNOWN. WHI IMAGE ID 115687

mals for their fur but largely as a sidelight to other endeavors. By the time Lyman Warren died, the heyday of the fur trade—and the Cadotte family's extensive involvement in the industry—had ended.

CHAPTER 21

WILD RICE

Paintings and photographs have long captured the idyllic nature of harvesting wild rice—or *manoomin*, as the Ojibwe call it. One person is at the rear of the canoe, usually standing, poling placidly through a rice bed at the edge of a lake or slow-moving river. Another sits near the front of the canoe, bending the rice stalks over the gunwales and slapping them with a special cedar paddle so the rice kernels drop into the canoe.

For biologist Peter David, rice beds on a pleasant autumn day "are beautiful places to be."[1] David works for the Great Lakes Indian Fish and Wildlife Commission (GLIFWC), which represents eleven Ojibwe tribes in Wisconsin, Minnesota, and Michigan in stewarding natural resources on lands ceded by the tribes to the United States through nineteenth-century treaties. Often, the only sounds are bird calls, the slapping of the paddles, and the swish of the canoe as it brushes against tall rice stalks. Through his work and personal experience, David has come to understand the importance of such rice beds to the region's ecosystem, to outdoors enthusiasts, and especially to the Ojibwe of the area. Rice beds are certainly more than just beautiful places for Ojibwe like Marvin Defoe, who works on historic preservation for the Red Cliff Band of Lake Superior Chippewa. "For the Anishinaabeg, those are our gardens," Defoe said. "That's where we go to get our food source."[2]

Furthermore, although it may appear idyllic, ricing is also hard work. After a day of poling a canoe through a rice field with a friend, David reported, "I was bushed. I really enjoyed it, but I was tired."[3] And harvesting the rice is just the beginning. After it is gathered, the rice has to be processed. To do it the traditional way, rather than paying a professional processor, requires a substantial amount of work, as both Defoe and David explained.[4]

Harvesting wild rice. WHI IMAGE ID 133699, STABLER W. REESE

After the rice is gathered into canoes, processing consists of four critical procedures: drying, parching, hulling, and winnowing. Originally,
the drying was done by placing the collected rice on hides, blankets, grass
mats, or birch bark. The rice was exposed to sunlight and air and was then
raked or turned while pieces of stalk, sticks, or other materials inadver-
tently collected with the rice were removed. The drying process could take
from four to twenty-four hours.[5]

Next, the rice had to be parched so that the hulls would loosen in order
to prevent germination and to reduce the moisture content so the kernel
didn't spoil. Then the rice kernels could be kept indefinitely. Once the
Ojibwe began trading with Europeans, parching was usually done in iron
or copper kettles. Prior to European contact, they had used wooden racks
over fires, and many Ojibwe were still using them into the late-nineteenth
and early-twentieth centuries. Either way, the rice was continuously
stirred to prevent grains from popping or becoming scorched. Parching
time could run from fifteen minutes to an hour, depending on the size of

the batch being processed, the size and source of the seed, and how well it had been air dried.[6]

Then the rice had to be hulled—an exhausting physical activity that was often the responsibility of men and boys. The rice was spread in a small pit about eighteen inches deep and two or three feet in diameter. Traditionally, the pit was lined with animal hides, but in later years, blankets, canvas, wooden staves, and other materials were used. Wearing clean moccasins and stepping carefully into the rice pit, the huller started to tread lightly upon the rice. Usually, tree branches were placed on either side of the pit like handrails, so the huller could regulate the amount of weight he placed on the rice as he rhythmically tramped it. The process was called "jigging" or "dancing the rice." The person doing the dancing worked about fifteen minutes continuously on each batch.[7]

Finally, the rice had to be winnowed. The hulls or chaff separated from kernels during the rice dance were isolated and discarded in this procedure, and the rice kernels stored for later use. Often the Ojibwe accomplished this by stirring the rice on a shallow tray of birch bark in a light breeze. Most of the chaff was blown away and the rice kernels remained. Any stubborn hulls that remained were picked out by hand.[8] All this work—this "ricing"—for a grain that is not actually rice at all.

The term "wild rice" is commonly applied to two closely related plants, both of which are part of the Gramineae family of wild grasses. Neither is closely related to the white rice long grown in rice paddies in Asia. Today, scientists designate one plant *Zizania palustris*, sometimes called "northern wild rice"; the other is *Zizania acquatica*, or "southern wild rice." However, the nomenclature has changed over time, and some previous accounts use the two terms interchangeably. While both species are important to wildlife, human harvest is focused almost entirely on *Zizania palustris* due to its larger seed, even though it has a much more limited range.[9]

Manoomin, the Ojibwe name for wild rice, is generally translated as "good berry" or "good seed." However, author Thomas Vennum Jr. questioned that translation in his 1988 book, *Wild Rice and the Ojibway People*, suggesting that, based on a number of linguistic studies, the word is a variation on ancient Algonquin words meaning roughly "any stiff grass bearing edible grain."[10] The early French called the grain *folle avoine*, meaning "fool's oats" or "wild oats," because it reminded them of a weed that frequently invaded wheat fields in their homeland and resembled oats. The Menominee of Wisconsin were sometimes called the *Folle Avoine* because of their proficiency with wild rice. Because it grows naturally in marshy areas, early English-speaking visitors to the Great Lakes likened the grain to the white rice grown in Asia. Hence the name "wild rice" that is still used today.[11]

Although misnamed, wild rice has long been recognized as a highly nutritious food. In a 1901 government study on the grain, ethnologist Albert Ernest Jenks declared, "[wild] rice is more nutritious than the other native foods to which the wild rice producing Indians had access. . . . [I]t is more nutritious than any of our common cereals, [such] as oats, barley, wheat, rye, rice, and maize."[12] Vennum also found rice nutritious, noting that "[i]n the traditional Indian diet, wild rice was more nutritious on the whole than any other naturally available vegetable, grain, animal or fruit source."[13]

A more recent examination of wild rice was somewhat less exuberant in touting the nutritional value of *Zizania palustris* but still gave it high marks. According to a 1997 report by the Universities of Minnesota and Wisconsin, "This grain has a high protein and carbohydrate content, and is very low in fat. . . . The nutritional quality of wild rice appears to equal or surpass that of other cereals. . . . Mineral content of wild rice, which is high in potassium and phosphorus, compares favorably with wheat, oats, and corn."[14]

For Ojibwe living in the Upper Midwest, *manoomin* isn't treasured just for its nutritional value. According to Vennum, "Stories and legends, reinforced by the ceremonial use of *manoomin* and taboos and proscriptions against eating it at certain times, show the centrality of wild rice to the Ojibway culture. . . . These factors suggest that wild rice, at least in the past, approached the status of a sacred food."[15] Even today, when Ojibwe set out to harvest wild rice, "We always do it with reverence," Defoe said. "We always say some prayers. We're always careful about the water. And we usually have a little feast" associated with gathering the *manoomin*.[16]

Whatever its nutritional benefits or sacred status, North West Company explorer and surveyor David Thompson was not overly impressed when he was fed wild rice while visiting trader John Sayer at Cass Lake in present-day Minnesota in the spring of 1798. For two days, Thompson reported, he ate nothing but "a mess of wild rice and [maple] sugar," adding, "I tried to live upon it, but the third day was attacked with heart burn and weakness of the stomach, which two meals of meat cured."[17] Still, Thompson acknowledged that Sayer and his men had survived the entire winter on little but wild rice and maple sugar. Such a diet, he said, "keeps them alive, but poor in flesh."[18]

In his 1901 study, Jenks said wild rice once grew in more than half of the forty-eight states in the continental United States, including the Upper Midwest. He described it growing along the Eastern Seaboard and as far south as Florida. Jenks referred to this grain as *Zizania acquatica*, but he apparently combined the two species when he described the large, historic range of wild rice. The range of *Zizania palustris* was, and is still today, largely limited to northern portions of Minnesota, Wisconsin, Michigan, and areas in Canada.[19]

Early European visitors to the region were awed by the large rice beds and sometimes expressed frustration because the fields were so immense and thick that they made travel difficult. Father Jacques Marquette, while traversing the Fox River from Green Bay, en route to the Wisconsin River, then to the Mississippi River in 1673, complained: "[T]he road is broken by so many swamps and small lakes that it is easy to lose one's way, especially as the River leading thither is so full of wild oats [rice] that it is difficult to find the Channel.[20] North West Company partner and explorer Alexander MacKenzie reported in the late eighteenth century that "[v]ast quantities of wild rice are seen throughout the country [from Lake Superior to Lake Winnipeg], which the natives collect in the month of August for their winter stores."[21] William Warren said that at Prairie Rice Lake (now Rice Lake) in northwestern Wisconsin around 1850, the wild rice was "so thick and luxuriant . . . that the Indians are often obliged to cut passage ways through it for their bark canoes."[22]

There is little question that the areas of prime rice production have diminished considerably since the days when the Europeans first witnessed Native peoples gathering wild rice. Marshes drained for croplands, dams that flooded other rice areas, and, more recently, climate change have all contributed to shrinking the rice areas. "We've lost a lot of the rice resource," Peter David laments. Minnesota lost many of its rice beds but managed to retain some of its most important ones. Wisconsin lost even more, but that has changed in recent years, through reseeding and conservation. As David explains, "I think we've increased the rice fields in Wisconsin 25 percent in the last few decades, but it's getting harder to continue this success, and now *manoomin* is facing new threats from climate change. In Michigan, the bulk of the rice fields have disappeared, although there are efforts now to re-establish them."[23] As Defoe explains, the act of harvesting rice the traditional way is also a means of ensuring its continuation: "You're harvesting, but you're also planting." As paddles knock rice kernels into the canoe, inevitably some kernels fall back into the water, where they may lay dormant for years before sprouting.[24]

Throughout the fur-trade era, ricing was primarily practiced by Native peoples. While many accounts exist of European traders purchasing or trading for wild rice, few of them harvested or processed the grain themselves. As Thompson wrote, "The Natives collect not only enough for themselves: but also as much as the furr [sic] traders will buy from them. . . . Two or three Ponds of water can furnish enough for all that is collected."[25] Jean-Baptiste Perrault, Michel and Jean-Baptiste Jr.'s contemporary, recorded several places in his autobiography about obtaining wild rice during his fur-trade endeavors. In 1786, while traveling southwest from Green Bay, he and a small group headed toward a lake "to get wild rice; we remained there two days; and on the third we took our way to prairie du chien [sic]." He was traveling with a group of Menominee Indians, so it's likely they did the harvesting and processing. They may have done so earlier and had the rice cached so that it could be easily obtained when Perrault and his comrades arrived.[26]

Like David Thompson, Perrault also noted how important wild rice could be in the fur trader's diet. In 1791, while wintering near the headwaters of the Mississippi River, he wrote, "I was obliged to lend three fawnskins of wild rice to my neighbors [fellow traders]; For they would have starved without it. They were reduced to eating moss from pines."[27] A few years later, Perrault reported that he gave twenty-five fawnskins of rice to Jean-Baptiste Cadotte Jr. as the latter was traveling to his winter headquarters near Red Lake in Minnesota.[28]

Whether or not Equaysayway and Michel Cadotte engaged in ricing is unknown. They certainly were familiar with *manoomin*, and no doubt ate it, both for sustenance and as part of the many tribal ceremonies in which rice was involved. However, there were no rice fields on Madeline Island. If the Cadottes gathered wild rice, it's likely they traveled to the rice beds in the Kakagon Sloughs or Bad River Sloughs on the mainland to the south of Madeline Island.

These rice beds were important historically, being used by the Ojibwe and others over the centuries. Eliza Morrison, who spent much of her life with her Ojibwe relatives on the western end of Lake Superior, took note of their value during the latter half of the nineteenth century; Marvin Defoe did some of his first ricing there in the second half of the twentieth.[29] New efforts are underway to protect them in the twenty-first century. The Kakagon and Bad River Sloughs, sometimes referred to as the "Everglades of the North," were recognized as a Wetland of International Importance in 2012, the first such site to be owned by an Indian nation.[30] Moreover, as Michel and Equaysayway and their Ojibwe relatives pushed south and west toward Dakota Territory during the 1780s, they not only gained access to important fur-bearing lands, but also important ricing areas such as Prairie Rice Lake.[31] These days, a bag of store-purchased wild rice was probably grown in Minnesota or California, the two leading producers of wild rice in the country.[32] But this is cultivated wild rice. Because it is grown differently and mechanically harvested and processed, it bears little resemblance to the traditional wild rice of the Lake Superior region.

Throughout the first half of the twentieth century, however, when individuals or even large commercial organizations wanted to obtain wild rice, they usually visited Native peoples and purchased the rice directly from them.[33] For a long time, though, many non-Natives had sought ways to cultivate wild rice on a larger scale and in more controlled environments than in lakes and rivers of the Upper Midwest. In the mid-1960s, researchers at the University of Minnesota began experimenting with seed production and breeding plants that could be commercially grown and harvested by mechanized means. "The results from such research were astonishing," Thomas Vennum wrote. "[I]n 1968 the 900 acres of paddies produced 90,000 pounds of green rice; by 1973 the acreage had not quite doubled to 17,000 acres and the yield increased to 4 million pounds."[34] But those changes didn't benefit Native groups such as the Ojibwe: "[T]he advent of paddy rice production completely distanced them from the lion's share of the profits. . . . Once the wild rice plant was successfully moved inland for farming on paddies, mechanical combines replaced Indian people as harvesters, and the wild rice industry fell almost totally into white hands."[35]

Now if you are looking in food stores or online, you have to do some searching to find wild *manoomin* for sale that wasn't grown commercially in paddies, but it is available. For instance, a five-pound package of "Native American Hand Harvested Wild Rice" from the White Earth Nation of Ojibwe in Minnesota can be purchased directly from the Ojibwe.[36] Alternately, non-Native people may experience the satisfaction of harvesting wild rice by obtaining permits from state agencies such as the Wisconsin Department of Natural Resources to harvest rice on lakes and rivers that are not on Ojibwe reservations. The state agencies in Wisconsin, Michigan, and Minnesota work closely with the Great Lakes Indian Fish and Wildlife Commission to conserve and improve the rice beds.

Each year, thousands of non-Natives take to the rice beds of Wisconsin and harvest wild rice for their own use, but few of them go a step further and process the rice themselves. Instead, most take the rice they have gathered to one of the many professionals who offer custom processing to rice harvesters.[37] Other than Native traditionalists, few are now willing to engage in the hard work of processing the wild rice by hand or have the knowledge to do it well. Still, for many Ojibwe even in the twenty-first century, the physical and spiritual activities associated with harvesting and processing *manoomin* remain an important emotional connection to their ancestors.

Passing those activities on to younger generations is equally important. "It's up to the elders to teach these things to the younger people," said Defoe. "That's how I learned. I went to the older people who knew what to do and learned from them." Defoe and other elders instruct young Ojibwe in ricing techniques and tradition, showing them how to harvest properly, to "dance the rice" to hull it, even how to listen to the many birds that are often present, and to understand that the birds help reduce the bug population that would otherwise prey upon the ricers. They also teach traditional hunting and fishing techniques. Defoe also makes his own traditional birch bark canoes. He believes that "as you get older, you almost have an obligation to pass on this knowledge to others."[38]

CHAPTER 22

TREATY TRIALS

In June of 1850, *The Lake Superior News and Mining Journal* of Sault Ste. Marie responded to President Zachary Taylor's order for the removal of all Wisconsin and Michigan Ojibwe to northern Minnesota. The newspaper predicted the order would result in "the most disastrous consequences."[1]

That prediction was, unfortunately, quite accurate. By the following winter, the 150-mile trail from Sandy Lake, Minnesota, to Madeline Island and beyond had witnessed the deaths of 230 Ojibwe—men, women, and children. The dead were among the thousands of Ojibwe who had trekked eastward from Sandy Lake in the middle of the winter, with few provisions and ravaged by disease, to return to their homes in Wisconsin and Michigan. Another 170 Ojibwe had died at Sandy Lake in the autumn and early winter of 1850.

Because the location of annuity payments had been switched, tribal members from Wisconsin and Michigan's Upper Peninsula were lured to Sandy Lake by territorial agents intent on having the Indians relocate to Minnesota Territory. But provisions at Sandy Lake that winter were woefully inadequate, disease ran rampant, and death was ever present.[2] The events of the winter of 1850–1851 became known as the "Sandy Lake Tragedy" or the "Wisconsin Death March" and caused the deaths of more Native people than either the Sand Creek Massacre in Colorado in 1864 or the Wounded Knee killings in South Dakota a quarter century later.[3]

And yet, despite what many people in Minnesota and Washington, DC, desired, the 1850 gathering of Ojibwe at Sandy Lake did not result in the wholesale removal of Wisconsin and Michigan Ojibwe to Minnesota.

They were not forcibly relocated from their home territories, as were so many other Indians in the United States. Some of the credit for that fact goes to La Pointe Ojibwe leader Great Buffalo, a cousin of Michel Cadotte. Great Buffalo made a remarkable journey to Washington, DC, with Oshogay, another Ojibwe leader, when he was about ninety-three years old to successfully lobby against Ojibwe removal.

By the middle of the nineteenth century, after decades of treaty negotiations, the Lake Superior Ojibwe were convinced they had preserved their homeland. However, a few politicians, traders, and others were eager to relocate the Ojibwe of northern Wisconsin and western parts of Michigan's Upper Peninsula to the headwaters of the Mississippi River in Minnesota Territory, there to join other Ojibwe bands already in Minnesota. A combination of partisan politics and economic interests fueled the push for removal. Additionally, news accounts of traders at La Pointe charging exorbitant fees to Indians who gathered there for annuity payments in 1848 helped make the case that it was time to move the annuity payments and the Ojibwe to a new location in Minnesota.

In 1849, the Whig-dominated legislature of the new Minnesota Territory adopted a resolution supporting the removal. However, in Wisconsin, which had become a state in 1848, many whites wanted the Ojibwe to remain. But voters there didn't support the Whigs as strongly as those in Minnesota did. Consequently, Whig President Zachary Taylor sided with the Minnesota contingent and signed the removal order in February 1850.[4]

Minnesota's first territorial governor, Alexander Ramsey, and others in the territory supported the move because they coveted the economic boost that would come with *all* of the Ojibwe receiving their annual treaty payments in north-central Minnesota.[5] The Minnesota proponents and their colleagues in Washington didn't couch their support for the removal in such avaricious terms, however. Rather, they argued that it was in the Ojibwe's best interests to move in order to protect them from "injurious contact" with the advancing white population of Wisconsin; to remove them from the temptation of alcohol that traders in Wisconsin liberally provided; to protect whites from the "evils" and "annoyances" of having Indian neighbors; and to better promote Anishinaabe civilization by congregating all of the different bands in one location.[6]

Annuity payment at La Pointe, 1870. The man seated second from right is William S. Warren, a nephew of William W. Warren. CHARLES A. ZIMMERMAN. WHI IMAGE ID 48581

Even some Minnesota Ojibwe supported the move. Bagone-giizhig the Younger, also known as Hole in the Day the Younger, was an Ojibwe leader from the area around Gull Lake, Minnesota. According to Anishinaabe historian Anton Treuer, "He pressured and threatened at just the right times . . . to move the annuity station [for the Wisconsin and Michigan Ojibwe] to Sandy Lake."[7] However, after the Sandy Lake disaster, Bagone-giizhig became highly critical of the attempted removal and the government officials he believed were responsible for the disaster, especially Governor Ramsey.[8]

The Michigan and Wisconsin Ojibwe were certain that treaty terms agreed upon thirteen years earlier allowed them to remain on their lands as long as none of their members engaged in violence against the whites.[9] Large segments of the small white population of northern Wisconsin and Michigan—from newspaper editors to local business owners and religious leaders—believed the Ojibwe should remain. They didn't fear the "evils" of the Indians. Instead, they valued them as workers and customers and, like people in Minnesota, wanted the Indians to receive their annuity payments nearby so the latter could spend money in their vicinity.[10]

Hole-in-the-Day the Younger, undated. COURTESY CROW WING COUNTY HISTORICAL SOCIETY

In the fall of 1850, Ramsey and John Watrous, a trader who had been appointed subagent for the La Pointe Indian Agency, concocted a plan to lure the Wisconsin Ojibwe and those from the western portion of Michigan's Upper Peninsula to Sandy Lake, apparently with the support of the Secretary of Interior and the Commissioner of Indian Affairs. Instead of disbursing the annual treaty payments and goods for most of the Wisconsin Ojibwe at Madeline Island, as had been the case for more than a decade, all of the Ojibwe annuities would be dispersed at Sandy Lake that year.

The Sault Ste. Marie newspaper, which opposed the plan, called the idea "a new and ingeniously contrived plan of effecting the removal of the natives." The *New York Times* called the Ramsey–Watrous plan "an iniquitous scheme."[11] In spite of such objections, however, several thousand Ojibwe reluctantly gathered at Sandy Lake in late autumn of 1850, depending on government officials to provide food and other necessities while they awaited the annuity disbursements.

The result was catastrophic. Requested supplies to feed the Indians were delayed, leaving them to subsist on meager provisions of moldy flour and rancid meat. The annuity money from the federal government that was supposed to arrive in October didn't show up until late December.[12] By then, measles and other illnesses had spread through the Ojibwe camps, killing adults and children alike. In the middle of the winter, the Wisconsin Ojibwe and a small number from Michigan decided they would be better off at home, even though the rivers were frozen and they had to hike, carrying their children and sick tribal members with them.

In a petition signed in 1851 by twenty-eight Lake Superior Ojibwe leaders, including Great Buffalo, the Indian leaders described the terrible events of the previous winter. "When we left for home, we saw the ground covered with the graves of our children and relatives," the petition said.[13]

In the aftermath of the Sandy Lake Tragedy, Ramsey and Watrous blamed disease as well as delays from the federal government for the problems. They also targerted the Natives themselves. In one letter, Ramsey suggested the Ojibwe who traveled to Sandy Lake were better off because they had traded their annuity payments for food. If they had remained at home, as a consequence of their "thriftless habits" and their tendency to spend all they had with traders, most of their money would have simply disappeared.[14] Meanwhile, support for the Ojibwe remaining in the Lake

Superior region grew stronger in subsequent years among the white traders, loggers, miners, and others in Wisconsin and Michigan.[15]

The attempted removal of the Ojibwe from Wisconsin and Michigan,
the resulting Sandy Lake Tragedy, and the Treaty of 1854, marked the cul-
mination of a thirty-year period of intense treaty activity. During those
decades, the United States government, fresh from securing control of the
region after the War of 1812, began to assert its authority through a series
of agreements with the Ojibwe and other Native nations. Even though he
was in his sixties when the treaty efforts began, Great Buffalo was a key
player throughout the period.

The treaty years also proved challenging for people of mixed descent—
those like the Cadottes, who were part Ojibwe, part French Canadian, and,
in some cases, part American. Regarded as near equals during the French
and British fur-trade years, they now found themselves defined as something less. Were they Indian or white? Did they have the same rights as
whites? In at least one instance, there was an attempt to limit their ability
to vote (Indians were not made citizens of the United States and therefore
not allowed to vote nationwide until 1924). On the other hand, were those
of mixed heritage due to receive any of the money or other goods that went
to their Indian relatives through the treaties?[16]

Efforts were made in several of the treaties to identify people of mixed
ancestry and determine what they should receive. Throughout these discussions, Ojibwe leaders such as Great Buffalo routinely argued on behalf
of the people of mixed descent, seeking to ensure they received a fair ac-
counting in the treaty arithmetic.

Buffalo was known as "Bizhiki"—or Bison—in Anishinaabe, but he
also went by the Indian name "Kechewashkeen," as well as other names.[17]
French Canadians called him "Le Beouf" (the Beef).[18] He was referred to
as Great Buffalo to differentiate him from several other Ojibwe leaders
also called Buffalo by the whites. He was born sometime around 1759 near
Madeline Island. An obituary printed in a La Pointe newspaper when he
died in 1855 listed him as "aged about 100 years."[19]

According to trader Benjamin Armstrong (Great Buffalo's adopted son
and friend for the last fifteen years of his life), when Buffalo was a youngster, he was a skilled hunter "and the best bow and arrow shot of his time."
He also displayed more wisdom and was less warlike than other famous

Ojibwe leaders of the time, such as Hole in the Day.[20] Great Buffalo was related to the Cadotte family, perhaps on both Michel's *and* Equaysayway's sides, although there are questions about the latter connection.[21] They were also neighbors on Madeline Island.

Although Great Buffalo was once loyal to the British, by 1825, when one of the earliest American-Ojibwe treaties was hammered out at Prairie du Chien in what is now southwestern Wisconsin, he had apparently resigned himself to the American presence. He was the third Ojibwe leader to sign the treaty.[22] (There were three earlier treaties involving the Ojibwe and the US government, in 1817, 1819, and 1820, but they involved lands in lower Michigan and the Ohio River Valley and at Sault Ste. Marie, not the regions around western Lake Superior.)

The 1825 treaty was negotiated not just with the Ojibwe, but with representatives of the Dakota, the Sauk and Fox, Menominee, Iowa, Ho-Chunk, Odawa, and Potawatomi. All of the nations agreed to abide by the Americans' request for peace among them, while the Dakota and Ojibwe agreed to accept boundary lines between their territories. No Ojibwe lands were ceded to the United States in the 1825 Treaty of Prairie du Chien, but the tribal representatives present agreed to recognize the US government as the controlling entity of their region.[23]

Not all of the Ojibwe bands from around Lake Superior were represented at the treaty negotiations, however. So the Ojibwe leaders present asked government officials to hold another meeting with tribal leaders the following year. They agreed, and the government expedition to negotiate the 1826 Treaty of Fond du Lac drew Thomas McKenney, then the US Commissioner of Indian Affairs, to Lake Superior. He visited Madeline Island on the same journey.

In his book about his journey to Fond du Lac, McKenney wrote little about Buffalo or Bizhiki, whose name he spelled "Pe-chee-kee." However, McKenney told one story of seeing Buffalo's son wearing a British medal around his neck, which could have been construed as an expression of hostility to the Americans. McKenney confronted the young man, but said later, "Pe-chee-kee, his father, was near, and spoke, saying, 'It is my medal, he only wears it for ornament.'"[24]

Even though McKenney was spare in his comments about Great Buffalo, the Madeline Island Ojibwe leader spoke eloquently and at length during the negotiations, according to the journal of the treaty proceedings. By then in his late sixties, he emphasized that he was an orator, not a war chief; "I am no chief. I am put here as a speaker," he said at one point. Earlier, he had stated, "The name of speaker has come down to me from my fathers."[25]

Great Buffalo also spoke of the needs of his people—"Our women and children are very poor."—and told the Americans, "Our ears are open to your words. We remember them."[26] At one point he spread a map before the participants, which he said "was given to us by our forefathers." But the journal does not indicate what the map revealed, and no known copy of the map exists.[27]

The Treaty of Fond du Lac included a provision for an annual payment of two thousand dollars "in money or goods, as the President may direct," to be paid to the Ojibwe living in the United States in consideration of their poverty "and of the sterile nature of country they inhabit, unfit for cultivation and almost destitute of game."[28] The last section apparently reflected the beliefs of McKenney, Governor Lewis Cass of Michigan Territory, and other members of the treaty commission. But it would have surprised the Ojibwe and fur traders who had found game to trap and eat, had gathered wild rice and fish, and had cultivated small gardens and farms in the region for centuries. The Ojibwe wanted annuities from the US government in exchange for making certain concessions and forming reciprocal alliances. But they were not as destitute as the treaty suggested.[29]

Having spent centuries dealing with the French and British, they understood the negotiating process with whites as one in which they were expected to speak as children seeking assistance from their "father." In describing seventeenth-century French relationships with the Ojibwe, historian Michael Witgen has written that "[T]he allies needed to recognize one another as family, as inawemaagen. The French placed themselves at the head of this family by assuming the persona of Onontio, the French Father. Their Native allies, in similar fashion, became the children of Onontio." This created "a social and political relationship based on the obligations that members of an extended family owed to one another."[30]

Another Anishinaabe historian and scholar, Cary Miller, explains that "Anishinaabeg approached Europeans in much the same manner as they approached their tribal neighbors with requests for food, clothing, or other items that emphasized continued mutual reliance." But that social understanding was often lost on American treaty negotiators. "The Americans did not understand that as gift givers, the Anishinaabeg expected them to stand by the promises made when the gifts were presented, not just the agreements that ended up in the text of American treaties," Miller wrote. "Gifts had been tangible evidence of the agreements made between the Anishinaabeg, foreign governments, and other tribes at Prairie du Chien and Fond du Lac."[31]

The 1826 Treaty of Fond du Lac contained a measure under which the Ojibwe agreed to "grant to the government of the United States the right to search for, and carry away, any metals or minerals from any part of their country." But it expressly stated that the Ojibwe weren't giving any land to the government.[32] Additionally, the treaty became the first agreement to make arrangements for "the half-breeds, scattered through this extensive country." It proposed to set aside a section of land—640 acres—at or near Sault Ste. Marie for each of the people of mixed ancestry named in the treaty. Included in this list of people who were to receive property were Michel and Equaysayway Cadotte and their children. Saugemauqua, the widow of Michel's brother Jean-Baptiste Jr. was to receive a section, as were each of her five children.[33] But none of them received the land. That provision was rejected by Congress.[34]

A year later, McKenney, Cass, and others were back in the region, this time near present-day Green Bay, Wisconsin, on the Fox River, to complete still another treaty. This one established a southern boundary line for Ojibwe territory, making clear where their lands ended and those of the Menominee and Ho-Chunk began.[35] That was apparently sufficient for the government's needs at the time. A decade later, though, new government officials were back with even greater demands.

In July of 1837, approximately a thousand Ojibwe, primarily from bands of the Upper Mississippi region but also the Lake Superior area, convened at Fort Snelling, near present-day Minneapolis. Negotiations were led by Henry Dodge, governor of what was then Wisconsin Territory. Dodge and many others were convinced that the region that now includes northwestern Wisconsin and northeastern Minnesota *was* rich in minerals and timber and *was* suitable for agriculture, despite what the 1826 Treaty of Fond du Lac had said. So, for the first time, the representatives of the United States came demanding that Ojibwe give up large tracts of land.[36]

The Ojibwe, however, believed they were only leasing land to the Americans, specifically for the removal of white pine. According to historian Eric M. Redix, "From the Ojibwe perspective, it was only natural to assume that the treaty was a lease of resources. There were practically no settlers moving onto the land. Also, the treaty made no mention of Ojibwe people moving onto reservations or removing outside the ceded territory. After all, why would the Ojibwe be allowed to stay on land that did not belong to them anymore?" Additionally, the Ojibwe of the Chippewa Falls area had made similar lease agreements with an individual timber operator only the year before. They had every reason to believe the American government was seeking the same thing.[37]

Poor interpreting, whether intentional or a result of incompetence, added to the Ojibwe's misunderstanding of what Dodge and the other treaty commissioners were demanding.[38] Furthermore, Dodge required that the Ojibwe give up the land in perpetuity, while in return they would receive annuity payments for *only* twenty years. However, they would retain the right to hunt, fish, make sugar, and gather wild rice on the lands they ceded to the government, subject to their removal at the pleasure of the president. This clause, and the verbal discussions that accompanied it, were what the Ojibwe referred to thirteen years later when they vehemently objected to attempts to remove them to Minnesota from their homelands near Lake Superior.

As Benjamin Armstrong wrote of the 1837 treaty: "the Indians were told and distinctly understood that they were not to be disturbed in the possession of their lands so long as their men behaved themselves. . . . [W]ith these promises fairly and distinctly understood they signed the treaty that ceded to the government all their territory lying east of the Mississippi, embracing the St. Croix district and east to the Chippewa River."[39] This did not include Madeline Island, the areas immediately around Chequamegon Bay or the southern shore of Lake Superior.

The money the Ojibwe received for giving up the land—a total of thirty-five thousand dollars each year for twenty years—was viewed as a pittance by many observers at the time. The settlement was barely enough to provide "a breechcloth and a pair of leggings apiece," complained Lyman Warren, who conferred with the Ojibwe during the negotiations, even as he sought money in the treaty for himself and his family. Henry Rowe

Schoolcraft said the Ojibwe had been persuaded "to fritter away their large domain for temporary and local ends, without making any general and permanent provision for their prosperity."[40]

Great Buffalo was present during the 1837 treaty negotiations but spoke little because the lands to be ceded to the government weren't in his home neighborhood. Nonetheless, he was critical of the terms. "The Indians acted as children; they tried to cheat each other and got cheated themselves," he said. "When it comes my turn to sell my land, I don't think I shall give it up as they did."[41]

Great Buffalo's comments reflect the fact that the 1837 treaty also helped fuel a rift between Wisconsin Ojibwe leaders and those living along the Mississippi River in present-day Minnesota, in part because much of the negotiation on behalf of the Ojibwe was conducted by a Mississippi Valley Ojibwe man who was not a recognized leader, while the land ceded (or leased, as the Ojibwe believed) was in Wisconsin. Consequently, several prominent Wisconsin Ojibwe leaders refused to sign the treaty, including Nena'aangabi, the Rice Lake headman who was second only to Great Buffalo in status among Wisconsin Ojibwe at the time.

Much of the problem stemmed from the fact that Dodge insisted on dealing with the Ojibwe as a single nation, with all of those present having equal authority to sell or lease land, no matter where it was. But such a political body was not something the Ojibwe understood or accepted for themselves, and it "contradicted the autonomy maintained by each individual Ojibwe band."[42]

The 1837 treaty also allotted seventy thousand dollars to settle the claims of various traders who maintained they were owed money by the Ojibwe and one hundred thousand dollars in cash for mixed-ancestry children of the region. Lyman Warren had his hands in both of those accounts, seeking money for himself and the American Fur Company from the seventy-thousand-dollar pot and money for his children, nieces, and nephews from the funds set aside for those of mixed ancestry. He was partially successful in both respects but didn't obtain as much money as he believed he was due.[43]

The funds for the mixed-ancestry children were important for the fur-trader families around Lake Superior, and the Cadottes were prominent among them. Of the 880 claims that were submitted for money on behalf of people of mixed descent, approximately 5 percent involved descendants of Jean-Baptiste Cadot Sr.[44] Only 380 of those 880 claims were accepted in hearings held over the next few years, but many of them involved the children and grandchildren of Michel and Equaysayway Cadotte.[45]

The agreements reached by the Ojibwe in the 1837 treaty proved short-lived, however. Demand for timber and farmland drove the push for ever more Ojibwe land. A report by a Michigan state geologist told of vast copper wealth to be found along Lake Superior's south shore. So, in 1842, another representative of the US government, Robert Stuart of Detroit, gathered Ojibwe leaders on Madeline Island and demanded more concessions.[46]

This time the Ojibwe agreed to give up the lands around the south shore of Lake Superior, including lands surrounding Chequamegon Bay, as well as on Michigan's Upper Peninsula. Again the Ojibwe accepted payments that were minimal in exchange for the right to remain on the ceded lands, at least temporarily. And again money was set aside for payments to traders and to people of mixed descent.[47]

As with the 1837 treaty, there was again a misunderstanding about whether land was being sold to the US government or only being leased, in this case for mineral rights for copper. One Lac du Flambeau leader made the Ojibwe position clear when he declared during the negotiations, "I do not give you the land, it is the Mineral only that I sell if there is any to be found on my land. I do not cede the Land."[48] And, as Dodge had done five years earlier, Stuart viewed all of the various Ojibwe bands as a single entity. Although he did agree to distinguish between Ojibwe living in the Mississippi Valley and those in Wisconsin, Stuart told those gathered, "Your Great Father will not treat you as Bands but as a nation."[49]

Great Buffalo was present, and he tried unsuccessfully to protect the interests of the Ojibwe on Madeline Island and nearby areas. A few months later, in a letter sent through Lyman Warren to the Reverend Alfred Brunson, then the Indian subagent at La Pointe, he complained that Stuart had refused to listen to the Ojibwe who opposed the terms of the treaty. Buffalo said he was "ashamed" of the treaty, and he requested that Brunson ask US President John Tyler why he sought to "oppress his children in this remote country."[50]

Buffalo and other Ojibwe leaders from around Lake Superior apparently had good reason for concern. As historian Ronald Satz notes, "The evidence from American eyewitnesses . . . indicates the commissioner [Stuart] used heavy-handed tactics to secure the treaty."[51] According to Brunson, Stuart told the Ojibwe leaders at one point that it made little difference if they signed the treaty because the government could simply take the land if they refused. At the same time, Stuart assured the Ojibwe that they would not be required to leave their lands for a long time. In any event, the treaty was signed. Then it was another five years before government officials came seeking still more concessions from the Ojibwe.

An 1847 treaty between the United States and the Ojibwe, primarily in Minnesota Territory, ceded tribal lands in central Minnesota to the federal government. Although it was negotiated at La Pointe and Fond du Lac, and Lake Superior Ojibwe leaders signed it, the treaty did not greatly impact the Ojibwe living in northern Wisconsin and Michigan. However, one important provision allowed people of mixed ancestry to be eligible for annuities that were due to the Ojibwe if they lived among the Ojibwe. Michel and Equaysayway Cadotte's grandson William Warren was one of those who signed up immediately under the new provision.[52] But that provision diminished the amount of annuities available to other Ojibwe and created friction among Ojibwe leaders.[53]

By 1849, when Alexander Ramsey was appointed territorial governor of Minnesota, officials were already discussing how to arrange for the removal of the Wisconsin and Michigan Ojibwe to Minnesota.[54] A contingent of Lake Superior Ojibwe leaders traveled to Washington that year to present a petition to Congress, seeking to block any removal effort. But no official action was taken.[55] Soon, however, pressure on President Zachary Taylor led to the 1850 removal order and the Sandy Lake Tragedy.

In spite of the failure and tragic consequences of the 1850 attempt to move all the Ojibwe to Minnesota, officials made another attempt to move the Wisconsin and Michigan Ojibwe to Minnesota in 1851. The renewed effort also occurred despite an August 1851 announcement by Commissioner of Indian Affairs Luke Lea that the 1850 removal order was suspended while new President Millard Fillmore (Zachary Taylor had died in office in July) sought to determine whether removal was the best option. However, the 1851 removal effort was far less consequential than that of the previous year. This time, most of the Wisconsin and Michigan Ojibwe knew enough of their opponents' tactics to refuse to budge from their homes.

Most ignored entreaties and threats from John Watrous, who once again argued that the Ojibwe had to move to Minnesota Territory if they wanted to receive their treaty goods and annuities.[56]

By 1852, the Lake Superior Ojibwe, especially Great Buffalo and his allies, had had enough of these removal efforts. They held ongoing talks about white perfidy and the problems they faced from the treaties. Benjamin Armstrong, who reported that he attended some of these discussions, said he feared that "if something was not quickly done trouble of a serious nature would soon follow." Great Buffalo, then about ninety-three years old, led a small contingent of Ojibwe to the nation's capital to personally lobby the president to allow the Wisconsin and Michigan Ojibwe to remain in their homelands. In Armstrong's recounting of events, he proposed the trip to Washington with the Ojibwe leaders so that "they could meet the great father and tell their troubles to his face."[57] Other sources say the Ojibwe leaders initially asked Leonard Wheeler, a Protestant minister on Madeline Island, to accompany them to Washington. They accepted Armstrong only when Wheeler proved unable or unwilling to make the trip.[58]

Decades later, Armstrong wrote a lengthy—and some believe, fanciful—account of that excursion to Washington, DC. He described a hasty canoe trip to Sault Ste. Marie, then a steamer journey to New York, with delays along the way as government officials sought to block the trip. Once they reached Washington, Armstrong said, both Lea and Secretary of Interior Alexander H. H. Stuart refused to meet with the Ojibwe and ordered them to return home. Only a happenstance encounter with New York congressman George Briggs led to two meetings with President Fillmore and his reversal of Zachary Taylor's removal order.[59]

Unfortunately, no documents recording the reversal of Taylor's removal order, signed by President Millard Fillmore, have been found by scholars.[60] Furthermore, Leonard Wheeler later claimed nothing of consequence was achieved on the journey. Also, once they had returned to Wisconsin, Great Buffalo and Oshogay, the younger Ojibwe leader who made the journey to Washington, sent a letter to Ramsey, acknowledging it was his decision whether or not the Ojibwe should be removed to Minnesota. That seems inconsistent with a presidential decree rescinding the removal order.[61]

However, historian Ronald Satz, who has studied the Ojibwe treaties, wrote, "Several contemporaneous events . . . reinforce Armstrong's contention that Fillmore revoked Taylor's order, and demonstrate that such a suspension by Fillmore is consistent with his handling of Indian affairs." These contemporaneous events include Fillmore's treatment of other Native nations in Wisconsin and nations from Texas to California. Other sources also suggest that Great Buffalo, Armstrong, and the others *did* meet with Fillmore and present a petition seeking to have Taylor's removal order overturned.[62]

Regardless of the precise political actions, the Wisconsin and Michigan Ojibwe remained in their homelands, in spite of the unrelenting efforts of Governor Ramsey and John Watrous. Those two continued to plan for the removal of the Ojibwe to Minnesota and to insist their annuity payments would be disbursed only in Minnesota. However, before they could arrange another Sandy Lake event, President Franklin Pierce replaced Fillmore, and he soon appointed a new governor of the Minnesota Territory. Additionally, the Wisconsin Legislature urged federal officials to allow the state's Ojibwe to remain in Wisconsin. Whether in response to the legislature or other factors, discussions regarding a new treaty began.[63]

Ojibwe leaders from Wisconsin and Michigan talked of how they could obtain what they most desired in a new treaty with the government—the right to remain in their homeland. The Lake Superior Ojibwe, along with those in Minnesota, were aware that the government and white citizens of the region were eager to win control of the mineral-rich Ojibwe lands along the northwest coast of the lake. The area in question runs from Fond du Lac (today's Duluth) to the old fur-trading site at Grand Portage, just south of the Canadian border. Today, the area is known as Minnesota's North Shore.

In September of 1854, scores of Ojibwe leaders gathered at La Pointe on Madeline Island to receive annuity payments and goods but also to negotiate what became known as the Treaty of 1854. Great Buffalo and other Ojibwe demanded that Benjamin Armstrong review treaty language and advise them during the negotiations, which he did.[64]

The Treaty of 1854 included thirteen articles, the first two of which were the most important. In Article I, the Ojibwe agreed to cede those mineral-rich lands on the North Shore to the US government. But the Ojibwe were no longer interested in giving away land in exchange for promises of future action by the government or a few years of annuities. Because of that attitude, Article I was entirely dependent on the simultaneous approval of Article II, in which the government agreed to permanently set aside six reservations in Wisconsin and Michigan as homes for the Ojibwe. As Treaty Commissioner Henry Gilbert put it in a summation of the negotiations: "[T]he points most strenuously insisted upon" by the Ojibwe were "first the privilege of remaining in the country where they reside and next the appropriation of land for their future homes. Without yielding these points, it was idle for us to talk about a treaty."[65]

The treaty was approved by those gathered at La Pointe in September of 1854, but it was not ratified by Congress until January 10, 1855.[66] The reservations set aside were roughly described in the treaty but were to be formally surveyed later. In Wisconsin, they included what became the Red Cliff Reservation, on the mainland west of Madeline Island and north of the present-day town of Bayfield. This was initially known as the Buffalo Estate and involved land set aside in the treaty specifically for Great Buffalo and his heirs.[67] There was also the Bad River Reservation at the southern end of Chequamegon Bay and east of the current city of Ashland as well as reservations south of Lake Superior for the Lac du Flambeau, Lac Court Oreilles, and St. Croix bands of Ojibwe. Additionally, there were reservations for the L'Anse and Vieux De Sert bands in Michigan and for the Grand Portage band in Minnesota.[68] Other Ojibwe bands in the three states did not obtain their own reservations until later treaties were concluded, in some cases decades later.

Additional provisions of the Treaty of 1854 established the payment for the ceded land: five thousand dollars a year in cash for twenty years, plus eight thousand dollars a year in household goods and farming supplies for the same twenty years. An additional ninety thousand dollars was to be divided by chiefs of the tribe "in open council." There were provisions to hire government blacksmiths for each reservation, to prohibit the sale of "spirituous liquors" on any of the lands set aside, and to bring up to date all payments the Ojibwe were due from previous treaties.

Importantly, the treaty also granted the La Pointe band of Ojibwe the right to two hundred acres "on the northern extremity of Madeline Island, for a fishing ground." That was the opposite end of the island from the Cadotte compound and the town of La Pointe. Equally important, the treaty said each mixed-ancestry head of a family or single person over twenty-one years old was entitled to eighty acres of land "to be selected by them under the direction of the President."[69]

The Treaty of 1854 didn't solve all problems for the Ojibwe; indeed, there were later attempts to overturn some of its provisions. The Ojibwe suffered, as did most Native nations, from the Dawes General Allotment Act of 1887, which allowed reservation lands to be broken up into individual parcels, then sold by the Native people who owned them. In times of crushing poverty, the Dawes Act became a means for many whites to gain control of Native lands. Moreover, some of the hunting, fishing, and other rights recognized for the Ojibwe had to be relitigated in twentieth-century court cases.

In addition to these issues, it would take more than twenty years after approval of the treaty for the mixed-ancestry land provisions to be implemented, despite their importance to families like the Cadottes.

CHAPTER 23

NEW GENERATIONS

In 1907, Mary Warren English began working as an interpreter for Frances Densmore, who was conducting a study of Anishinaabe customs for the Smithsonian Institution's Bureau of Ethnology. English, the daughter of Lyman Warren and granddaughter of Michel and Equaysayway Cadotte, was seventy-two at the time. She'd already had a distinguished career as a teacher and school administrator in both Native and non-Native schools. She would go on to interpret for Densmore for another fourteen years.[1]

English drew accolades from Densmore for her work as an interpreter, but that's not surprising. In translating Ojibwe for non-Indians, Mary Warren English was carrying on a family tradition that stretched back to the days of her great-grandfather Jean-Baptiste Cadot Sr., and perhaps earlier. Cadot Sr. served as an interpreter between the Ojibwe and the French. Later he translated Ojibwe for British merchants and government officials.

That tradition continued with English's uncles, cousins, and siblings. Surprisingly, given this long family tradition, Michel Cadotte never joined the cadre of well-known Cadotte interpreters. It's clear from the family account books and North West Company documents that he could read and write French, and he apparently understood some English. But he never developed the reputation of an interpreter that his father, his brother, and several of his children did.

Even so, linguistic skill seemed to come naturally to Michel and Equaysayway's descendants. Their sons Michel Jr. and Augustin served as interpreters for the British during the War of 1812, as did their brother, who was named Jean-Baptiste Cadotte, like his uncle. In 1804, when Jean-Baptiste was thirteen years old, his father sent him to work with trader François

Victor Malhiot. In his journal, Malhiot described the arrangement: "He comes to spend the winter with me to learn to read, and serve me as interpreter when necessary. If I teach him French, he will teach me Saulteux [Ojibwe] in return."[2] By late December 1804, Malhiot was extolling the virtues of his young pupil-interpreter: "I take this opportunity to say that the child promises well. . . . When he came here in the autumn he did not know a single letter of the alphabet, and could barely pronounce a few words in French, and now he can read as well as a child who has been 4 years at school. He knows his prayers and his catechism; but one step more and he will be a prodigy."[3]

Other, more distant, relations also used their linguistic skills to bridge the language barrier between Ojibwe- and English-speakers. For example, a distant cousin of the Madeline Island Cadottes, Alexander Cadotte—a grandson of Le Petit Michel Cadotte—served as an interpreter before Queen Victoria during a visit by Ojibwe men from Canada that was arranged by painter George Catlin.[4]

All of these members of the next generations of Cadottes lived in a time of great change for the Ojibwe and their mixed-ancestry relatives. Not only was the fur trade winding down, but the status of French Canadians and those of mixed ancestry had fallen considerably under the largely Protestant American regime.

For many Cadotte family members, interpreting for government entities or private concerns was one way to navigate through these troubling times. But they found other occupations as well—whether it was teaching as Mary Warren English and her sister, Julia Warren Spears did; or operating sawmills and farms as Mary and Julia's brothers and cousins did; joining a traveling troupe of Native entertainers as Alexander Cadotte did; or working for the government as several of the male Warrens did.

For the grandchildren of Michel and Equaysayway, dexterity with languages may have been a necessity. They grew up speaking Ojibwe as their "mother tongue," according to grandson William Warren, but they had to survive in an English-speaking world.[5] Their father, Lyman Warren, made sure they were educated in the language of the Americans.

Mary Cadotte Warren, Lyman Warren's wife, was Michel and Equaysayway's fourth daughter, and like her parents, she spoke very little English. She accompanied her children to Clarkson, New York, in 1838 when they went east to attend school there and live with their grandparents. Mary spent seven months in the home of her father-in-law, Lyman Warren Sr. Although she reportedly could understand some English, she was never able to carry on a conversation with her in-laws.[6] The Reverend Alfred Brunson, who visited the Warrens later when they lived on the Chippewa River, said of Mary Cadotte Warren, "She was an excellent cook, and a neat housekeeper, though she could not speak a word of English."[7]

Nevertheless, several of Mary's children became skilled interpreters. The most famous of the group, William Whipple Warren, began his career early. "When Rev. Alfred Brunson visited the Indians at La Pointe in the winter of 1842–3, on an embassy for the government, he selected my brother . . . a boy of 17 years as interpreter and found him very efficient and skilled," Julia Warren Spears wrote in 1924. "He was appointed United States interpreter and continued to act as such until he died."[8] Actually, William's employment by the US government was interrupted on several occasions, most notably in June of 1847, when he was suspended from his duties by the Department of Indian Affairs subagent for La Pointe, James P. Hays. This came after the drunken Hays had attacked both William and his wife in their home on Madeline Island.[9]

William was not reinstated as the official interpreter at La Pointe, but he did receive support from fur trader Henry M. Rice, who was appointed to assist in negotiating a new treaty with the Lake Superior Ojibwe. Rice encountered William on his way to Madeline Island, and he heard William's account of his suspension. After arriving at La Pointe, Rice wrote a letter to Commissioner of Indian Affairs William Medill in which he noted, "The Sub Agent Mr Hays, left here three days ago, after having been beastly intoxicated for three weeks. . . . He suspended the Govt interpreter, Mr William W. Warren after shamefully abusing and assaulting his family." Rice added, "Mr Warren is a young man of irreproachable character, and the only correct interpreter in the Chippewa nation." Rice said he brought William back to La Pointe because he knew William's "services would be indispensable."[10]

Later that year, William again provided his services as an interpreter while a treaty with the Minnesota Ojibwe was being negotiated at Fond du Lac. During that effort, he supported the idea of moving the site of annuity payments for the Lake Superior Ojibwe away from La Pointe in order to reduce the ability of the American Fur Company and other traders to make profits off the Ojibwe. As a result, William became the target of attacks by American Fur Company officials and their supporters, while he won praise from others for standing up to the company.[11]

William Warren was born on Madeline Island on May 27, 1825, after his father and uncle had purchased the fur-trade business from his grandfather Michel Cadotte. William said he learned much of his Ojibwe history and Cadotte family stories from his grandmother Equaysayway.[12] He also noted that his fluency in the Ojibwe language gave him "every advantage" in learning stories of tribal history from Ojibwe elders.[13]

William played a critical role, both as an interpreter and advocate for the Indians, in several of the treaty negotiations between the Ojibwe and the US government. During his time as an interpreter, he also began interviewing Ojibwe leaders on Madeline Island and in Minnesota Territory to learn all he could about Ojibwe history. He later worked as a clerk for Henry Rice on the Crow Wing River in Minnesota Territory. William married Matilda Aiken, the daughter of his father's friend and fur-trading colleague William Aiken.

William spent time as a farmer for the Indians on a reservation in Minnesota Territory, and he began writing letters to Minnesota newspapers, advocating on behalf of the Ojibwe in treaty negotiations. Sometimes he offered insights about the people's history, based on what he had learned from the tribal elders. He submitted information about Ojibwe history to Henry Rowe Schoolcraft when he learned that Schoolcraft was preparing an in-depth study of the Indian nations of the United States.

With the encouragement of D. A. Robertson, editor of the *Minnesota Democrat*, William began to write a series of articles on Ojibwe history, which he would eventually turn into his book, *History of the Ojibway People*. However, despite his tenacious efforts to get it published, the book didn't appear in print until three decades after his death.[14]

William was also deeply involved in the efforts to get the Wisconsin and Michigan Ojibwe removed to Minnesota, although he supported the removal reluctantly. He "was convinced that the Wisconsin bands would never be happy in the northern forests of Minnesota, sharing resources with so many other Anishinaabeg," according to author Theresa M. Schenck, "yet as an agent of the Indian Department and an opponent of the sale of liquor to the Indians, he would still try to assist in their removal."[15]

In the fall of 1850, working at the behest of Minnesota Territorial Governor Alexander Ramsey, William accompanied more than eight hundred Ojibwe from Wisconsin to Sandy Lake, in the prelude to the Sandy Lake Tragedy. Because William was seriously ill then—he suffered much of his adult life from tuberculosis—his eighteen-year-old sister Julia (later Julia Warren Spears) accompanied him on the trip. She recalled the journey seventy-five years later.

> My brother was in poor health and my mother urged him not to go, fearing the trip would be too hard for him, but he said he had started and did not wish to turn back. I then told my brother to let me go. Then if he got sick I could help take care of him and I could cook for him and I told him he would not be sorry. He was afraid I could not stand the walking; but finally consented to let me go. . . . In September we started from our Uncle James Ermatinger's home at what is now Jim Falls [near present-day Chippewa Falls, Wisconsin], went first to Lac Court de Oreilles, where we had to wait a day for the Indians to gather. A great many came with their canoes. Then we started from Lac Court de Oreilles walking through the woods, the Indians packing their canoes on their backs, some others with big packs of provisions. My brother had two men hired to pack our canoe and tent. We walked all day and did not come to any lake or river to cross. . . . [Then we] started for the mouth of the St. Louis river, near Lake Superior and camped near the sand bar near where the city of Duluth now stands. Some more Indians were waiting for us there. . . . That night my brother was taken sick with hemorrhage of the lungs, and was not able to travel for four days. . . . From there we traveled toward Sandy Lake, and that was the hardest part of our journey, as we had to walk for about six days. . . . In all there were several thousand [Ojibwe] waiting to receive their payments. We had to wait three weeks for the money to come. It was then late in the fall. The measles broke out and many children died and some of the grown folks as well. It was a sad time for us all.[16]

William, in addition to being ill himself, feared for the safety of Matilda and their children, who had met him at Sandy Lake. Therefore, he chose not to linger long there, leaving the lake with most of his family in late

November. His sister Sophia came down with the measles, so she and Julia remained at Sandy Lake until December, when their brother Truman came for them.[17] The following January, William spoke at a public meeting at a church in St. Paul, which also featured Ojibwe leader Hole in the Day the Younger and was attended by members of the Minnesota Territorial Legislature, about the tragedy at Sandy Lake. William laid the blame largely on Congress rather than on Governor Ramsey and his colleagues.[18]

Prior to the Sandy Lake Tragedy, in September of 1850, William had been elected as one of four representatives from Minnesota's Sixth District to the Minnesota Territorial Legislature. He took his seat as a Democrat in January 1851 at the Capitol in St. Paul and served on the Committee on Territorial Affairs and the Committee on the Militia.[19] When William sought reelection the following year, however, he lost by six votes. He contested the election, claiming with solid evidence that at least thirteen votes had been invalid because they weren't cast by legal residents. But his challenge ultimately failed.[20]

Throughout these years, William continually sought to obtain additional money he believed was owed to him for his work as an interpreter, as well as money he was convinced was still owed to his father by the American Fur Company or through treaties. He also got into a public spat, trading angry newspaper letters with his former friend and prominent Minnesota Ojibwe leader, Hole in the Day the Younger, over who was to blame for the problems at Sandy Lake the previous winter.

John Watrous, who worked with Governor Ramsey to try to force the Lake Superior Ojibwe to migrate to Minnesota, condemned William in 1851. Watrous and Ramsey then were renewing their effort to remove the Ojibwe of Lake Superior to Minnesota, and Watrous claimed that William tried to sabotage the effort. Actually, even after the Sandy Lake Tragedy, the evidence shows William continued to work reluctantly on behalf of the removal.[21]

William also worked hard to complete his book and to get it published. In 1853, he traveled to New York and Chicago in search of a publisher. He returned to Minnesota in May exhausted and soon after suffered a hemorrhage and died at the home of his sister Charlotte Warren Price, in St. Paul on June 1, 1853, at just twenty-eight years of age.[22]

William's siblings did not achieve his level of fame, but they accom-

plished much in their lives nonetheless. Julia Warren Spears married twice
and was widowed within a few years each time. After her second husband,
Andrew J. Spears, died in 1861, Julia began a teaching career at Indian
schools in Minnesota—first at the Crow Wing Agency, then at Leech Lake,
and finally at White Earth. She was reportedly the first schoolteacher
in Becker County, Minnesota.[23] She also assisted Frances Densmore in
Densmore's study of Ojibwe culture by gathering Ojibwe songs.[24]

When Julia's health began to fail, she moved in with her daughter at
Detroit (now Detroit Lakes), Minnesota, where she died on June 21, 1925.
Before her death, she wrote a detailed series of letters about her life and
her family to Wisconsin businessman and amateur historian William W.
Bartlett. The letters were published in the *Eau Claire Leader* in the summer
and fall of 1925. Four years later, Bartlett republished them in book form
along with other historical information about northern Wisconsin.[25]

Mary Warren English also died in 1925, about two months after Julia.
Frances Densmore thought enough of Mary to include a brief account of
her life in her ethnological exami-
nation of Ojibwe customs.[26]

Another sister, Sophia Warren,
survived until 1933, while Charlotte
Warren Price died in 1884.[27] Brother
Truman A. Warren served as a government farmer at several different
Ojibwe Indian agencies, including
the one at Bad River, Wisconsin, at
the south end of Chequamegon Bay.
He died in 1888.[28]

As noted earlier, the children
of Truman Warren Sr., brother of
Lyman Warren, were also raised
as part of Lyman Warren's family
after Truman Sr. died in 1825. So,

Truman A. Warren, brother of William W.
Warren, undated. PHOTOGRAPHER UNKNOWN.
WHI IMAGE ID 28289

although they were cousins, they were effectively raised as siblings of Lyman's children. One of these cousin siblings, Nancy Warren Beaumont,
lived in Wisconsin and Minnesota and died in 1887.[29] Her brother Edward
Warren died in a hunting accident in 1849. His twin brother, George War-

ren, served with the 36th Wisconsin Volunteers during the Civil War, was honorably discharged after being injured at the Battle of Cold Harbor and served as an interpreter for the Ojibwe on several trips to Washington, DC. He also operated a trading post and a sawmill in northern Wisconsin. He died in 1884.[30]

It was George Warren who accomplished one of the most important acts of historical preservation involving his family. Although it's not clear how he came into possession of the Cadotte family account book that his great-grandfather Jean-Baptiste Cadot Sr. and then his grandfather Michel Cadotte had kept for decades, he preserved the ledger for historical purposes. Multiple pages were missing and others were out of order, but it still contains invaluable information about the family and its fur-trade business. In 1848, George Warren donated the account book to a Dr. Goldsmith of Chippewa Falls, Wisconsin. Goldsmith, in turn, donated the ledger to Bishop's Memorial Hall at Notre Dame University in Indiana. It is archived at the university today.[31]

These and other descendants of Michel and Equaysayway Cadotte found ways to survive through difficult times as they attempted to stand with one foot in the Ojibwe world and the other in the European.

CHAPTER 24

BIG CHANGES ON THE BIG LAKE

The treaties that the Ojibwe signed with the US government, culminating in the Treaty of 1854, significantly altered their lives and those of their mixed-ancestry relatives living near Lake Superior. But land cessions and reservation life weren't the only major changes that occurred near the middle of the nineteenth century.

On June 18, 1855, less than six months after Congress ratified the Treaty of 1854, the steamer *Illinois* pushed into the first set of locks at Sault Ste. Marie while a crowd of more than a thousand people watched. Later that day, the *Illinois* passed from the highest of the locks into the waters of Lake Superior, becoming the first ship to make the trip between Lake Huron and Lake Superior without having to be unloaded, partially dismantled, and hauled by ropes and animals around the falls of St. Mary.[1]

A half-century earlier, while lying on his deathbed, Jean-Baptiste Cadot Sr. had told his family that this strip of land with St. Mary's River running through it—Sault Ste. Marie—had been given to him by Ojibwe leaders and it now belonged to his descendants. But members of the Cadotte family were not able to find documents to prove that claim.[2] Instead, the waterway between the two Great Lakes, along with the land that surrounds it, became crucial to the industrial development of the United States and Canada. The locks that opened in 1855 allowed ships hauling copper and iron ore, as well as wheat from the plains, to pass from Lake Superior to the other lakes and to manufacturing centers beyond.[3]

Copper around Lake Superior had been identified and valued since prehistoric times. In fact, the earliest known metalworking in North America is believed to have occurred roughly seven thousand years ago by people

The locks at Sault Ste. Marie ca. 1898. PHOTOGRAPHER UNKNOWN. LIBRARY OF CONGRESS

extracting copper on the lake's Keweenaw Peninsula. Those early artisans constructed bracelets, fishhooks, beads, and other items, many of which they traded with other Native nations. Copper from Keweenaw has been found in ancient sites in locations across North America.[4] When Europeans arrived, they also became enamored with the copper ore near the lake and the wealth it might provide. The first sailing ship on Lake Superior was probably constructed about 1731 to haul copper from planned mining enterprises that never materialized.

Later, Alexander Henry, Jean-Baptiste Cadot Sr., and others engaged in a partnership to search for and recover copper from around the lake.[5] Henry even had his own ship built for the effort, but he later said, "The copper ores of Lake Superior can never be profitably sought but for local consumption."[6] Without a means to get ore-carrying vessels from Lake Superior to the lower Great Lakes, it was simply not economical to mine and sell the copper.

That all changed with the opening of the locks in 1855. By 1871, a single mine on the Keweenaw Peninsula, the C&H, produced 16.2 million pounds of copper and paid $2.4 million to its stockholders.[7] Other copper mines were working in different locations along the southern shores of Lake Superior. Meanwhile, valuable deposits of iron ore had also been discovered in Michigan, Wisconsin, and Minnesota.[8]

By World War II, the nation was desperate for copper and iron ore for the war effort and grain from the northern plains states to help feed the troops. Protecting the shipping of those materials was critical. Consequently, Sault Ste. Marie with its locks—which had been rebuilt several times since 1855—was reportedly "the most heavily guarded place in North America."[9]

When the first locks opened, the southern shore of Lake Superior experienced frenetic growth. The year 1855 was "A Year of 'Booming'" for the town of Superior, Wisconsin, a municipality that hadn't even existed five years previously, when Julia Warren Spears accompanied her brother William Warren on the trek to Sandy Lake.[10] Superior and its sister city, Duluth, Minnesota, were built on either side of the St. Louis River at the west end of Lake Superior, the site that fur traders called "Fond du Lac." Both towns boomed briefly, then stalled with the Panic of 1857. They regained their economic strength later, with the Civil War and the postwar industrial boom, which required the hauling of more and more copper, iron, and grain by Lake Superior's ships.

The first census for Superior, Wisconsin, conducted in the summer of 1855, counted 385 residents, 93 of whom were unidentified women or children. Among the 292 adult males listed were two Cadottes: John and Augustus.[11] It's possible that "John" was actually Jean-Baptiste Cadotte, the son of Michel Cadotte Jr. and grandson of Michel and Equaysayway Cadotte. "Augustus" may have been Augustin, another son of Michel and Equaysayway, or perhaps a different Augustin Cadotte who was a grandson of Michel's brother Jean-Baptiste Jr.

Later, there would also be a Cadotte Avenue in Superior, named for Benjamin Cadotte, "an early French-Chippewa trader."[12] He was a distant cousin of Michel Cadotte. Benjamin worked as a clerk for Michel for a time and later was employed by the American Fur Company. His daughter Elizabeth was the first person baptized at La Pointe on Madeline Island by Father Frederick Baraga. Benjamin Cadotte and his family were among the first arrivals in the new town of Superior, Wisconsin.[13]

In 1865, the town of Cadott was founded on the Yellow River in north-central Wisconsin, not far from the Chippewa River where Michel and Equaysayway had conducted early fur-trading expeditions almost eighty years earlier. There are several theories about which Cadotte was the source of the town's name. Some say Jean-Baptiste Cadotte, the son of Michel and

Equaysayway, established a trading post in the area in the early 1800s, and so the town was named for him. Others attribute the trading post and the town's name to Michel and Equaysayway's son Augustin. In any event, the town traces its roots back to the Cadotte family's fur-trading endeavors, even if town founders didn't spell the name correctly.[14]

Another event occurred in the town of Superior in 1855 that was important for the Ojibwe and their mixed-ancestry relatives. On August 8, the General Land Office opened a branch in the burgeoning village of Superior.[15] The General Land Office was in charge of public-domain lands throughout the United States and the disposal of those lands under a variety of laws. White settlers went to the Land Office to file claims for property on former Ojibwe lands. People of mixed descent like the Cadottes also used the Land Office to file for 80-acre allotments that were due them under the Treaty of 1854. The first entry at the Superior General Land Office was filed by a man named Benjamin Thompson for a lot in what is now the town of Bayfield, west across Chequamegon Bay from La Pointe on Madeline Island.[16] This was land that, until 1854, had belonged to the Ojibwe.

Meanwhile, Madeline Island and the community of La Pointe, once so prominent in the fur-trade era and later during treaty negotiations, found their fortunes deteriorating even as communities on the mainland were developing. Throughout the 1840s and early 1850s, La Pointe had remained the most important community at the west end of Lake Superior. It served as the primary receiving and assembly point for regional commerce. Even though its docks were not large, La Pointe was the port of call for vessels on the west end of Lake Superior. According to author Hamilton Ross, "Boats, both great and small, ran for it when bad weather portended."[17] But that would soon change, as larger ships, plying the lake after the locks opened at the Sault, began to use the docks at Duluth, Superior, and the new town of Ashland, at the south end of Chequamegon Bay.

The 1850 census showed 485 people residing in La Pointe, 40 of them with the surname Cadotte. The same census listed a total of 596 people in all of La Pointe County, which then encompassed what are now Bayfield and Ashland Counties, plus parts of two others.[18] Therefore, more than 80 percent of the non-Indian population of this part of northwestern Wisconsin at the time lived on Madeline Island.

By 1860, there were only 307 people at La Pointe and 73 deserted houses.[19] By the 1890s, the village was largely deserted, with only a handful of buildings still standing.[20] There were a few fishermen, farmers, and loggers living on the island then, eking out a meager living. However, by the end of the nineteenth century, a new invasion commenced and would continue through the twentieth century and into the twenty-first. Tourists began to arrive from other parts of the country, mostly building summer homes and later camping or renting cottages, to enjoy the pleasures of the island during the warm seasons.[21]

While the fortunes of La Pointe and Madeline Island fluctuated, settlers created farms and sawmills on lands that had once belonged to the Ojibwe. Descendants of Michel and Equaysayway Cadotte were among the sawmill operators. William Warren was convinced there were more opportunities to be had for him and his relatives. He noted in an early 1850 letter to his cousin George Warren that recent government action prohibited whites from buying or cutting timber on Indian lands: "Now all this operates to our benefit," he wrote. "By the Treaty of Fond du Lac [of 1847] Half Breeds are allowed the same right & privileges to the soil and annuities as Indians, and no law can prevent us from cutting *our own* logs and selling them to Whites. We can monopolize the business and make money like dirt."[22] Events conspired to keep William Warren out of the timber business, but George Warren operated a sawmill for a time near the Chippewa River.[23]

Meanwhile, those people of mixed European and Ojibwe descent found it difficult to acquire and hold the lands they were due under the terms of the 1854 treaty. As one historian put it, the land-allotment program for those of mixed ancestry became "a lurid tale of thievery and deceit."[24] A commission appointed by the Interior Department to look into the land allotments issued a report to Congress in 1874 that detailed some of that "thievery and deceit." For example, although the government struggled to define which mixed-ancestry families and individuals were eligible for eighty acres under the terms of the Treaty of 1854, some people, including several Indian agents, took a very expansive view of the terms. One Indian agent, L. E. Webb of the Red Cliff Ojibwe Reservation on the mainland just west of Madeline Island, concocted a scheme under which he sent out people working for him to pay mixed-ancestry individuals to apply for scrip—legal tender for the land that was due under the treaty—whether or not the individuals were eligible. "In addition, the names of parties whom they [Webb and his cohorts] failed to find were used without permission, and also the names of some full-bloods," the report to Congress said. "In some cases, moreover, names were used where the persons bearing them had been dead for years."[25]

Webb then personally certified the veracity of these claims, 199 in all, "which he disposed of to other parties," presumably whites, "realizing from such transaction the sum of $2.50 per acre."[26] So, from each claim for eighty acres that Webb "disposed of to other parties," he received two hundred dollars. That amounts to almost forty thousand dollars for all 199 parcels, a very nice sum in 1870 dollars.

The report to Congress listed the names of several other individuals believed to be involved in fraudulent schemes involving scrip and/or claims for mixed-ancestry land under the Treaty of 1854. Some people even went to Canada to obtain the signatures of mixed-ancestry individuals, despite the fact that people living there were not eligible, according to the treaty.[27]

Even when there were no overt plans to defraud the government or those who were due land under the treaty, it was clear that whites either misunderstood or intentionally ignored some of the treaty provisions regarding the mixed-ancestry allotments. According to the report to Congress, "[I]n 1864, Chippewa scrip began to be considered desirable property." Although the treaty expressly forbade the transfer of allotment rights from eligible people of mixed descent to others who were ineligible, the scrip "nevertheless became an article of trade, and was kept on sale by brokers and at the principal banks of Saint Paul [Minnesota]."[28]

Even if they weren't dealing with outright fraud and white people eager to obtain their allotments under the treaty, the mixed-ancestry families faced an uphill bureaucratic slog. Government officials and members of Congress argued for years over whether scrip could even be issued for the allotments and whether those eligible had to show up in person to claim their land. They also debated exactly which people of mixed-ancestry from which regions were eligible and how they were to demonstrate their eligibility. Lists of applicants deemed eligible were submitted to the Interior Department, initially accepted, and then rejected after some politician or government official objected. New rules were drafted, and new lists of eligible applicants were drawn up. In most cases, the changes resulted in a substantial expansion of those deemed eligible.[29] In one eighteen-month period in 1864 and 1865, the commission reported that the number of mixed-ancestry people issued scrip grew by 565 individuals.[30]

Special instructions were sent out to General Land Office stations (such as the one in Superior, Wisconsin, which later was moved to Bayfield, then Ashland) about how to deal with scrip or other applications for mixed-ancestry allotments under the treaty, only to have the instructions rescinded in a few months, then reversed again in subsequent years. An agent for the Interior Department would be appointed to look into these issues and then his authority would be revoked. A four-member commission was appointed in 1871, followed by a second three-member commission the following year.[31]

Despite all of this confusion, by the time the first commission issued its report, the General Land Office had processed 1,168 applications for mixed-ancestry allotments under the treaty. It had issued land patents, or titles, for 558 parcels of land.[32] At least 17 Cadottes (with some misspelled as "Cardotte") are listed among the 1,168 people "to whom scrip or certificates of identity have been issued, showing them to be entitled to eighty acres of land," under the Treaty of 1854. They include one Michael Cadotte (probably Michel Cadotte Jr.), several John B. Cadottes, and others with the first name of Augustus and Joseph. The initial lists gave no indication of where they lived, and so it is difficult to determine which branches of the family they represent. Later documents show some Cadottes from Superior, Wisconsin, applying for treaty allotments, as well as some from Minnesota and others living as far away as California.[33]

Females were not allowed to apply unless they were widowed heads of households. Nevertheless, Mary Warren—later Mary Warren English—was among the applicants, as were her brother William and cousin George. Julia and Sophia Warren were part of a separate group who made later applications through a special commission.[34]

The commission examined late applications and rejected many because they were from ineligible parties or were downright fraudulent. One of the few late applications it upheld was that of Marie Cadotte of Superior, Wisconsin.[35]

Tracing those allotments into the twenty-first century is all but impossible because they have been sold, inherited by people with different family names, or otherwise transferred. It would take an army of title agents to sort them all out. But some titles can be partially tracked. For instance, John B. St. John, who was included on the first list of mixed-ancestry people eligible for land under the 1854 treaty, was issued an eighty-acre parcel near Bayfield in 1877. He sold it in 1904 to a member of the Red Cliff band of Ojibwe. The witnesses to that sale included a woman named Katie Cadotte.[36]

One group of mixed-ancestry people decided to take matters into their own hands late in the nineteenth century to ensure a safe, secluded home for themselves and their descendants, a home removed from the official reservations. In 1884, Frank Belanger, a mixed-ancestry man from La Pointe, and his wife, Elizabeth Morreau or Morrow, homesteaded 160 acres on wild lands in the vicinity of Bayfield and the Red Cliff Reservation. But it was isolated enough that it required a twelve-mile hike to the nearest town. It became known as the Belanger Settlement.[37]

Over the next several decades, the Belanger Settlement continued to grow, with other families of mixed ancestry joining the community, including several Cadottes. A man named Ben VanderVendt, who had married Madeline Cadotte of La Pointe, moved to the settlement in about 1890. This Madeline Cadotte is believed to have been a great-great granddaughter of the original Magdeline, or Equaysayway Cadotte. There were also Butterfields, Gordons, and several more Belangers at the settlement. By 1899, the community included a church, cemetery, and school. And by the 1920s, there were about ten families living there.[38]

The settlement is still going strong today, with people such as Roger Cadotte, several of his siblings, and their children living there, along with descendants of the Belangers and other families. There is a Belanger Settlement reunion every summer and a Belanger Settlement Historical Society and Facebook page.

It's possible the Belanger settlement had its origins in the 1854 treaty provision for land allotments to people of mixed heritage. Francis Belanger was listed among those eligible for eighty acres under the provision.[39] But it's not clear whether Frank Belanger used treaty allotments to establish the settlement or simply acquired the land under federal homestead rules that were available to all United States citizens at the time.

With or without the treaty allotments, descendants of the fur-trading

Cadottes survived the industrialization of the late nineteenth century, as well as times of extreme poverty and bigotry in the twentieth century. Land on Madeline Island that was once claimed by Michel and Equay-sayway Cadotte survived in Cadotte family ownership into the twentieth century, but it was sold sometime prior to 1960.[40] Many Cadotte descendants left the region to seek careers elsewhere, but a number returned to the region later. Others remained in the area. Like their ancestors from centuries earlier, all have demonstrated remarkable resiliency.[41]

Epilogue

This book has traced the history of key members of the Cadotte family and their involvement in the development of the fur trade, as coureurs de bois, interpreters, traders, and businessmen, especially around Lake Superior. As this story has unfolded, I hope readers have come to an understanding, as I did, of just how adaptable and resilient members of the Cadotte clan—and, indeed, other people of mixed French and Native ancestry—had to be to survive the constant social, political, and economic changes to their world.

Consider the trajectory of the patriarch of this branch of the family, Jean-Baptiste Cadot Sr. The British first arrived at Sault Ste. Marie in 1762 in the person of twenty-one-year-old adventurer Alexander Henry and, a few months later, a small garrison of soldiers from Fort Michilimackinac. And, just like Chevalier De Repentigny, who came to the Sault in 1750 to establish a French military presence, they found Jean-Baptiste Cadot Sr. and his Ojibwe wife, Athanasie, living there.[1] Also like the French, the British soon found a trustworthy ally in Cadot. This proved critical because many of the French Canadians in the region were reluctant to abandon their loyalty to the French king. The same year that Henry arrived at the Sault, British authorities at Fort Michilimackinac, roughly sixty miles from Sault Ste. Marie, blamed French Canadians for creating obstacles to British control of the region and for promoting unrest among the Indians.[2]

Whether Cadot agonized over his decision to work with the British instead of the French is not known. Perhaps he just understood sooner than his colleagues what the outcome would be. He and other French Canadians had little choice but to work with the British once the Treaty of Paris was signed in February 1763 and France ceded all its territory in North America to England. But even before then, it was clear the British were winning in Canada and the Great Lakes region. Québec had fallen in 1759, and the governor of New France ceded control of Montreal and most of Canada a year later. Although some Native nations and French Canadians refused to accept this defeat, the British were asserting their military authority through a string of small forts, including Michilimackinac, which the British occupied in the autumn of 1761. In 1762, when Cadot first met Henry, he must have understood that his future was with the British. So he made the transition and soon became a favorite of the British, as he had previously been with the French.

Cadot's family in 1762 consisted of his wife, Athanasie, daughters Marie Renée and Charlotte, and a year-old son, Jean-Baptiste Jr.[3] He was thirty-nine years old, pragmatic, and adaptable. He seized opportunities when he found them, such as partnering with Henry in the fur trade, then later joining an expedition to territories west of Lake Superior with men who would become leaders in the North West Company. But he also had significant influence with Ojibwe in the region, in part through Athanasie and her relatives. That made it possible for him to discourage violence, such as persuading the Ojibwe of the Sault Ste. Marie area not to join Odawa leader Pontiac in the fight against the British or, with Athanasie's help, saving Henry's life on several occasions. Those qualities, along with his skills as an interpreter, made him a significant force in the industry and the region in the last decades of the eighteenth century. One twentieth-century writer described him as "one of the most influential people in the Upper Lakes."[4]

It's likely that Cadot's grandfather Mathurin Cadot and his father, uncles, and brothers who briefly participated in the fur trade shared these character traits, but there aren't enough records of their activities to be certain. However, those characteristics were clearly passed on to his descendants. Although the fur-trade career of his son Jean-Baptiste Jr. ended abruptly because of his drinking, he displayed his ability to prevent violence on several occasions. And when his career in the fur trade ended, he demonstrated his adaptability by using his linguistic skills to obtain a job as an interpreter with the Canadian government.

However, it was Michel Cadotte, with Equaysayway beside him, whose character was most similar to that of his father. He saved fellow trader Jean-Baptiste Perrault from a near attack by Ojibwe warriors and dissuaded other Ojibwe from joining Tecumseh's early-nineteenth-century uprising against the Americans. He adapted by working with new trading companies as old alliances disappeared, by obtaining United States citizenship when that was the only way he could continue trading on the southern shores of Lake Superior, and by formalizing his marriage with Equaysayway under American rules when that became important.

Their son Michel Jr. helped prevent Indian violence against the Americans during the War of 1812, even though he was allied with the British forces. And, like his father, once the war was over, he put his talents to work on behalf of the Americans. Brother Augustin joined him in that regard, while another brother, Jean-Baptiste, moved to Canada rather than join the Americans.

Michel and Equaysayway's grandchildren also displayed their adaptability and their perseverance as treaties were enacted that, in many respects, diminished their social and economic status. Yet they worked with the treaty makers, helped explain the changes to their Ojibwe relatives and other Indians, and even encouraged Ojibwe to move when they believed it was best. They assisted the missionaries and the scientists who moved into their homeland, and they worked with lumber and fishing companies. They were educators who taught non-Indians, Ojibwe, and those of mixed ancestry, and they provided important information to the public about Ojibwe history and that of their own family. Over many generations, the Cadotte family has demonstrated noteworthy resiliency in the face of rapidly changing social, political, and economic conditions. Members of the family have been tenacious in protecting their families and their interests, yet accommodating and diplomatic when need be. They have been leaders without being overbearing or authoritarian.

Many members of the Cadotte family lived long and productive lives during the fur-trade years, but their lives were by no means easy. Danger, hard work, and continually changing economic and social conditions were routine for them. When they began their fur-trading careers, they operated in what most people of European descent considered a wilderness. By the time Michel and Equaysayway's grandchildren were becoming influential, the Lake Superior region was on the cusp of the industrial revolution. They adapted to the changes and substantially altered their own lives when it became necessary.

Native people across this continent have continually had to accommodate to changes in their worlds as European-Americans overwhelmed their homelands and their cultures. Many are still doing so today. The people of mixed heritage—including those of French Canadian and Ojibwe ancestry—have had to adapt to numerous cultural and economic transformations as well. They have made significant contributions to the region over many centuries. The Cadottes were involved as long as any other family and exerted considerable influence on the region over multiple generations.

My first view of Michel Cadotte's grave marker piqued my interest in who he was and what his life was like. Now, having learned so much about the family, I am both awestruck and humbled by knowing what members of the Cadotte family endured, how they adapted and persevered, how they flourished sometimes and suffered setbacks at other times, and how they prepared the way for future generations. The legacy of the Cadottes has endured not in property and possessions, but in character, reputation, and renown. It is a history of resiliency and adaptability, of leadership and assistance to others, while discouraging violence, protecting family, and honoring culture. They occupy a significant place in the story of this region, of Wisconsin, and of the country as a whole.

ACKNOWLEDGMENTS

This book could not have been completed without the assistance of many people. The following list is no doubt incomplete, but it includes many who provided important aid:

- Howard Paap, author and retired professor of anthropology of Bayfield, Wisconsin, listened to my thoughts, read my manuscript, and offered valuable critiques and ideas. His book *Red Cliff, Wisconsin: A History of an Ojibwe Community* also provided important information and insight into Ojibwe history and culture. He is married to a member of the Red Cliff, Wisconsin, band of Ojibwe.

- Professor Theresa Schenck, Professor Emeritus Comparative Literature and Folklore Studies, University of Wisconsin–Madison, listened graciously to my initial ideas and pointed me toward numerous historical sources that were critical for my research. She also reviewed early drafts of what I wrote and helped keep me focused. I used several of her writings as key sources.

- Members of the Cadotte family, especially Roger Cadotte of Red Cliff, Wisconsin; Jack Cadotte of Duluth, Minnesota; Sister Grace Ann Rabideau of Bayfield, Wisconsin; and Kenneth Cadotte of La Pointe, Wisconsin, were willing to put up with an outsider delving into the history of their family, to offer information about that history, and to talk about their own lives.

- Marvin DeFoe, Ojibwe elder and teacher and a member of the Red Cliff band, offered invaluable perspectives about Ojibwe traditions and the cultural importance of rice gathering. He is working to preserve Ojibwe history for the Red Cliff band and to pass on traditions to young tribal members. He is related to the Cadotte family through marriage.

- Robert Garcia of Grand Junction, Colorado, prepared the maps for this book, met regularly with me to ensure we were both on track, and read the entire manuscript.

- John DuLong of Holt, Michigan, past president of the French-Canadian Heritage Society of Michigan, has done extensive research on the Cadotte family genealogy. He provided the Cadotte family tree used in this book and helped me better understand Cadotte family relationships, beginning with Mathurin Cadot, and also corrected some errors in my text.

- Peter David of Washburn, Wisconsin, helped me understand the science, history, and work involved in gathering wild rice.

- Erik Vosteen of Indiana provided insight into historic and modern animal trapping techniques.

- Howard Sivertson, of Grand Marais, Minnesota, allowed me to use several of his paintings about the fur trade around Lake Superior for illustrations in this book.

- Linda Mittlestadt, archivist with the Wisconsin Historical Society and based at the Northern Great Lakes Visitors Center in Ashland, helped me find important documents and maps related to the Cadotte and Warren families.

- Kevin Cawley, archivist, University of Notre Dame archives, South Bend, Indiana, arranged for me to have access to the Cadotte Family Papers in the university archives, which provided a treasure trove of information.

- Margie Wilson, owner, Grand Valley Books, Grand Junction, Colorado, helped me track down several out-of-print books related to the fur trade that weren't available online or through other readily accessible sources.

- Interlibrary loan personnel at Mesa County Libraries helped me find other books that weren't available locally but could be obtained on loan from other libraries around the country.

- Officials with the Library of Congress in Washington, DC, helped me track down rare images and obtain electronic copies to publish.

- Judy, my wife, read the manuscript and accompanied me on most trips to Lake Superior. Son Derek made a winter trip to Madeline Island and joined me in snowshoeing and research. Daughter Kara offered continuous encouragement. My siblings in Wisconsin also offered ideas, encouragement, and connections to people with knowledge of Lake Superior, the fur trade, and the Ojibwe.

- Finally, Kate Thompson, Rachel Cordasco, and others at the Wisconsin Historical Society Press not only were willing to publish this book, they offered encouragement, ideas for enhancing the narrative, and much-needed editing of the manuscript. Expert readers Rebecca Comfort, Thomas Krause, and Emily Mac-Gillivray also provided thoughtful comments and suggestions for ways to improve the manuscript.

Notes

Introduction

1. See Michael Witgen, *How the Native New World Shaped Early North America* (Philadelphia: University of Pennsylvania Press, 2013) and Erik M. Redix, *The Murder of Joe White: Ojibwe Leadership and Colonialism in Wisconsin* (East Lansing: Michigan State University Press, 2014).
2. Edmund Jefferson Danziger Jr., *The Chippewas of Lake Superior* (Norman: University of Oklahoma Press, 1979), 7.
3. Danziger, *The Chippewas of Lake Superior*, 7.
4. Theresa M. Schenck, *The Voice of the Crane Echoes Afar: The Sociopolitical Organization of the Lake Superior Ojibwa, 1640–1855* (New York: Garland Publishing, 1997), 17–18.
5. Alexander Henry, *Travels and Adventures in Canada and the Indian Territories between the Years 1760 and 1776* (New York: J. Riley, 1809), 197.

Chapter 1

1. Hamilton Nelson Ross, *La Pointe: Village Outpost on Madeline Island*, rev. ed. (1960; repr., Madison: State Historical Society of Wisconsin, 2000), 40–43.
2. William W. Warren, *History of the Ojibway People*, reprint (St. Paul: Minnesota Historical Society Press, 1984), 96.
3. Ross, *La Pointe: Village Outpost on Madeline Island*, 64.
4. David Dale Owen, *Report of a Geological Survey of Wisconsin, Iowa and Minnesota; and incidentally of a portion of Nebraska Territory, Made under instructions from the United States Treasury Department* (Philadelphia: Lippincott, Grambo & Company, 1852), xxxiv–xxxv.
5. Pierre-Esprit Radisson, "Radisson's Account of His Third Journey, 1658–1660," American Journeys Collection, Document No. AJ-045, Wisconsin Historical Society Digital Library and Archives, www.americanjourneys.org.
6. Alexander Mackenzie, *The Journals of Alexander Mackenzie. Voyages from Montreal, on the River St. Laurence, Through the Continent of North America, To the Frozen and Pacific Oceans; In the Years, 1789 and 1793. With a Pre-*

liminary Account of the Rise, Progress, and Present State of the Fur Trade of That Country, rev. ed. (1801; repr. Santa Barbara, CA: The Narrative Press, 2009), 39.

7. John J. Bigsby, *The Shoe and Canoe, or Pictures of Travel in Canada, Volume II* (London: Chapman and Hall, 1850), 187–188.

8. Grace Lee Nute, *Lake Superior*, rev. ed. (1994; Minneapolis: University of Minnesota Press, 2000), 9.

9. Michael Witgen, *An Infinity of Nations: How the Native New World Shaped Early North America* (Philadelphia: University of Pennsylvania Press, 2012), 35.

10. *The Ojibwe People's Dictionary*, http://ojibwe.lib.umn.edu.

11. Bigsby, *The Shoe and Canoe, Volume II*, 189–190.

12. Thomas L. McKenney, *Sketches of a Tour to the Lakes, of the Character and Customs of the Chippeway Indians, and Incidents Connected with the Treaty of Fond du Lac*, rev. ed. (1827; Barre, MA: Imprint Society, 1972), 177–178.

13. McKenney, *Sketches*, 178–179.

14. McKenney, *Sketches*, 179.

15. Mackenzie, *The Journals of Alexander Mackenzie*, 39.

16. David Thompson, *The Writings of David Thompson, Volume 1, The Travels, 1850 Version* (Toronto: The Champlain Society, 2009), 258.

17. McKenney, *Sketches*, 214–215.

Chapter 2

1. Geoffrey Chaucer, *The Canterbury Tales* (Garden City, NY: Anchor Books edition, Doubleday & Company, 1961), 20.

2. Eric Jay Dolin, *Fur, Fortune and Empire: The Epic History of the Fur Trade in America* (New York: W. W. Norton, 2010), 22.

3. William W. Warren, "Ojibwe Traditions," included in Henry R. Schoolcraft, *Historical and Statistical Information Respecting the History, Condition and Prospects of the Indian Tribes of the United States, Vol. II* (Philadelphia: Lippincott, Grambo & Company, 1851), 138.

4. William D. Fitzwater, "Trapping: The Oldest Profession," *Proceedings of the 4th Vertebrate Pest Conference (1970)*, http://digitalcommons.unl.edu/vpcfour/20.

5. David Thompson, *The Writings of David Thompson, Volume 1, The Travels, 1850 Version* (Toronto: The Champlain Society, 2009), 190–191.

6. Dolin, *Fur, Fortune and Empire*, 48–56.

7. Jim Spencer, "A History Lesson: Ancient Traps and Mountain Men," *Athlonoutdoors*, www.realworldsurvivor.com/2015/07/14/ a-history-lesson-ancient-traps-and-mountain-men.

8. Spencer, "A History Lesson."

9. Elizabeth Hart Bennett and Evan A. Hart, "Translation of the Cadotte Account Book, 1772–1794," *Cadotte Family Papers*, University of Notre Dame Archives, 68–70. For instance, on August 12, 1779, the account book listed dozens of items, including clothing, axes, three barrels of rum, and "2 beaver traps."

10. Eric Vosteen, email correspondence with the author, March 2018.

11. "Animals Skinned for Fur," *American Humane Society Position Statements*, August 26, 2016.

12. North American Fur Auctions, www.nafa.ca/auctions-2.

Chapter 3

1. Michael Witgen, *An Infinity of Nations: How the Native New World Shaped Early North America* (Philadelphia: University of Pennsylvania Press, 2013), 89–90.

2. Some scholars have offered wildly conflicting dates for the beginning of the Ojibwe's permanent residence at the western end of Lake Superior. One timeline outlining Ojibwe history includes the entry: "1395—Approximate time that Ojibwe people reached Moningwunakauning [Madeline Island]." ("Waasa-Inaabidaa: We Look in All Directions," PBS series summary online, www.ojibwe.org/home. Moningwunakauning means "place of the golden-breasted woodpecker"); however, other scholars maintain that the arrival of Ojibwe on Lake Superior and their permanent settlement there are far more recent events. A 1970s-era history argues that the Ojibwe didn't live permanently in the Chequamegon region until approximately 1680, well after their first contact with the French: see Harold Hickerson, *The Chippewa and Their Neighbors, A Study in Ethnohistory*, rev. ed. (1970; Prospect Heights, IL: Waveland Press, 1988), 56. Also see Theresa M. Schenck, *The Voice of the Crane Echoes Afar: The Sociopolitical Organization of the Lake Superior Ojibwa, 1640–1855* (New York: Garland Publishing, 1997), 51, and Thomas Peacock, *Ojibwe Waasa Inaabidaa: We Look in All Directions* (Afton, MN: Afton Historical Society Press, 2002), 23.

3. Erik M. Redix, *The Murder of Joe White: Ojibwe Leadership and Colonialism in Wisconsin* (East Lansing: Michigan State University Press, 2014), 3.

4. Witgen, *An Infinity of Nations*, 66.

5. Howard Paap, *Red Cliff, Wisconsin: A History of an Ojibwe Community* (St. Cloud, MN: North Star Press, 2013), 41–42.

6. William W. Warren, *History of the Ojibway People*, reprint (St. Paul: Minnesota Historical Society Press, 1984), 131, 282; Theresa M. Schenck, *William W. Warren: The Life, Letters, and Times of an Ojibwe Leader* (Lincoln: University of Nebraska Press, 2007), 67–68.

7. Warren, *History of the Ojibway People*, 90, 79–82.

8. Warren, *History of the Ojibway People*, 80–83.

9. Basil Johnston, *Ojibway Heritage* (Lincoln: University of Nebraska Press, 1976), 78.

10. Peacock, *Ojibwe Waasa Inaabidaa*, 23; Johnston, *Ojibwe Heritage*, 77–78.

11. Warren, *History of the Ojibway People*, 89–90. Warren also wrote that he witnessed the burial of the copper plate with his great uncle and others in a well-hidden location. It could not be found, even when Warren wrote his history a decade later.

12. Anton Treuer, *The Assassination of Hole in the Day* (St. Paul: Minnesota Historical Society Press, 2011), 35.

13. Henry Rowe Schoolcraft, *Historical and Statistical Information Respecting the History, Condition and Prospects of the Indian Tribes of the United States, Vol. I* (Philadelphia: Lippincott, Grambo & Company, 1851), 306.

14. Henry Rowe Schoolcraft, *Historical and Statistical Information Respecting the History, Condition and Prospects of the Indian Tribes of the United States, Volume II* (Philadelphia: Lippincott, Grambo & Company, 1851), 135.

15. Schenck, *The Voice of the Crane Echoes Afar*, 51.

16. Warren, *History of the Ojibway People*, 96–97.

17. Brenda J. Child, *Holding Our World Together: Ojibwe Women and the Survival of Community* (New York: Penguin Books, 2012), 56.

18. Paap, *Red Cliff, Wisconsin*, 57.

19. Witgen, *An Infinity of Nations*, 27, 42, 94–95.

20. Paap, *Red Cliff, Wisconsin*, 41–42.

21. Redix, *The Murder of Joe White*, 5–7.

22. Witgen, *An Infinity of Nations*, 86.

23. Witgen, *An Infinity of Nations*, 86–90.

24. John DuLong, "Jean-Baptiste Cadotte's Second Family: Genealogical Summary—Part 1," *Michigan's Habitant Heritage (MHH)* 36, no. 4 (October 2015): 191; *Dictionary of Canadian Biography*, s.v. "Cadot, Jean-Baptiste," by David A. Armour, Accessed on February 1, 2019, www.biographi.ca/en/bio/cadot_jean_baptiste_5E.html.

25. Theresa M. Schenck, *All Our Relations: Chippewa Mixed Bloods and the Treaty of 1837* (Madison: Amik Press, 2010), 35.

26. Edmund Jefferson Danziger Jr., *The Chippewas of Lake Superior* (Norman: University of Oklahoma Press, 1979), 10–11.

27. Patty Loew, *Indian Nations of Wisconsin: Histories of Endurance and Renewal* (Madison: Wisconsin Historical Society Press, 2001), 8.

28. Warren, *History of the Ojibway People*, 44–45.

29. Loew, *Indian Nations*, 8.

30. Anton Treuer, *The Assassination of Hole in the Day* (St. Paul: Minnesota Historical Society Press, 2011), 15.

31. Treuer, *The Assassination of Hole in the Day*, 15, 29.

32. Treuer, *The Assassination of Hole in the Day*, 9.

33. Schenck, *William W. Warren*, 35–40.

34. "Waasa-Inaabidaa: We Look in All Directions," PBS series summary online, www.ojibwe.org/home.

Chapter 4

1. Hamilton Nelson Ross, *La Pointe: Village Outpost on Madeline Island*, rev. ed. (1960; repr., Madison: State Historical Society of Wisconsin, 2000), hand-drawn map, 140–141. Although Ross gave no source for his description of this and other historic trails, he mentioned in other writings that he personally knew Jean-Baptiste Cadotte III, a grandson of Michel Cadotte and resident of Madeline Island who died in 1913. This man told Nelson many stories about the history of the region.

2. Copy of map in undated record book, by H. N. Ross, June 1952, Wisconsin State Historical Society, Ashland, WI.

3. Ross, *La Pointe*, 140–141.

4. Matthew Timothy Bradley, "Snowshoes in New France/Les raquettes en Nouvelle-France," *Snowshoe Magazine* (Denver, CO), January 12, 2015.

5. Pierre-Esprit Radisson, "Radisson's Account of His Third Journey, 1658–1660," American Journeys Collection, Document No. AJ-045, Wisconsin

Historical Society Digital Library and Archives, www.americanjourneys.org.

6. Alexander Henry, *Travels and Adventures in Canada and the Indian Territories between the Years 1760 and 1776* (New York: J. Riley, 1809), 68.

7. Grace Lee Nute, *The Voyageur* (New York: D. Appleton, 1931; repr. St. Paul: Minnesota Historical Society, 1955), 97.

8. David Thompson, *The Writings of David Thompson, Volume 1, The Travels, 1850 Version* (Toronto: The Champlain Society, 2009), 12–13.

9. George Nelson, *My First Years in the Fur Trade: The Journals of 1802–1804*, eds. Laura Peers and Theresa M. Schenck (St. Paul: Minnesota Historical Society Press, 2002), 141.

10. Nelson, *My First Years*, 143.

Chapter 5

1. Olga Jurgens, "Brulé, Étienne," in *Dictionary of Canadian Biography, Vol. 1*.

2. Pierre-Esprit Radisson, *Radisson's Account of His Third Journey, 1658–1660*, American Journeys Collection, Document No. AJ-045, Wisconsin Historical Society Digital Library and Archives, www.americanjourneys.org, 51; Henry Colin Campbell, "Radisson and Groseilliers: Problems in Early Western History," *The American Historical Review* 1, no. 2 (January 1896): 1–8. Historians have long argued about whether or not Radisson actually accompanied his brother-in-law on this journey. Germaine Warkentin asserts instead that Groseilliers travelled with an unnamed companion, and that Radisson later inserted himself into the story: see *Pierre-Esprit Radisson, The Collected Writings, vol. 1*, Germaine Warkentin, ed. (Montreal: McGill-Queens University Press, 2012), 14, 35–36, 42–46.

3. Reuben Gold Thwaites, *The Colonies: 1492–1750*, published as part of The Epochs of American History series, (New York: Longman, Green and Co., 1894), 247.

4. Ancestry.com. *Quebec, Genealogical Dictionary of Canadian Families* (Tanguay Collection), *1608–1890*.

5. Ancestry.com; also, Theresa M. Schenck, "The Cadottes: Five Generations of Fur Traders on Lake Superior," *The Fur Trade Revisited, Selected Papers of the Sixth North American Fur Trade Conference, Mackinac Island, Michigan, 1991* (East Lansing: Michigan State University Press, 1994), 189.

6. Thwaites, *The Colonies*, 248.

7. Susan Sleeper-Smith, *Indian Women and French Men: Rethinking Cultural*

Encounter in the Western Great Lakes (Amherst: University of Massachusetts Press, 2001), 6–7.

8. Thwaites, *The Colonies*, 248–250.

9. Michael Witgen, *An Infinity of Nations: How the Native New World Shaped Early North America* (Philadelphia: University of Pennsylvania Press, 2013), 172–173.

10. "[The] Iroquois Confederacy, self-name Haudenosaunee ("People of the Longhouse"), also called Iroquois League, Five Nations, or (from 1722) Six Nations, [a] confederation of five (later six) Indian tribes across upper New York state that during the seventeenth and eighteenth centuries played a strategic role in the struggle between the French and British for mastery of North America. The five original Iroquois nations were the Mohawk (self-name: Kanien'kehá:ka ["People of the Flint"]), Oneida (self-name: OnΛyote?a·ká ["People of the Standing Stone"]), Onondaga (self-name: Onoñda'gega' ["People of the Hills"]), Cayuga (self-name: Gayogǫhó:nǫ' ["People of the Great Swamp"]), and Seneca (self-name: Onödowa'ga:' ["People of the Great Hill"]). After the Tuscarora (self-name: Skarù·rę? ["People of the Shirt"]) joined in 1722, the confederacy became known to the English as the Six Nations and was recognized as such at Albany, New York (1722)" *Encyclopedia Britannica Online*, Academic ed., s.v. "Iroquois Confederacy," accessed June 26, 2019.

11. Witgen, *An Infinity of Nations*, 233.

12. Howard D. Paap, *Red Cliff, Wisconsin, A History of an Ojibwe Community* (St. Cloud, WI: North Star Press, 2013), 16; Edmund Jefferson Danziger Jr., *The Chippewas of Lake Superior* (Norman: University of Oklahoma Press, 1979), 27.

13. Paap, *Red Cliff*, 16.

14. Michael G. Johnson, *North American Indian Tribes of the Great Lakes* (Bloomsbury Publishing, 2012), 7.

15. "New France's economic revival occurred when French entrepreneurs went to Lake Superior and traded directly with Native trappers," wrote historian Edmund Danziger.

16. Danziger, *The Chippewas of Lake Superior*, 28–29.

17. Paap, *Red Cliff*, 18.

18. Charles C. Mann, *1491: New Revelations of the Americas before Columbus* (New York: Knopf, 2005), 299.

19. Thwaites, *The Colonies*, 249–250.

20. "Our Company," Hudson's Bay Company website: http://www3.hbc.com/hbc/about-us/.

21. Witgen, *An Infinity of Nations*, 173–191.

22. The Treaty of Utrecht ended the Spanish War of Succession between France and England and forced France to give up its claim not only to Hudson Bay, but Newfoundland and Acadia as well. However, France was able to strengthen its hold on the St. Lawrence River. www.canadahistory.com/sections/eras/eras.html

23. Marjorie Wilkins Campbell, *The North West Company* (Vancouver, BC: Douglas & McIntyre, 1983), 4–5.

24. Thwaites, *The Colonies*, 249–257.

25. Jacques Mathieu, "Seigneurial System," *The Canadian Encyclopedia* online, 2013.

26. Schenck, "The Cadottes," 189.

27. Alexander Mackenzie, *The Journals of Alexander Mackenzie. Voyages from Montreal, on the River St. Laurence, Through the Continent of North America, To the Frozen and Pacific Oceans; In the Years, 1789 and 1793. With a Preliminary Account of the Rise, Progress, and Present State of the Fur Trade of That Country*, rev. ed. (1801; repr. Santa Barbara, CA: The Narrative Press, 2009), 9.

28. Mackenzie, *The Journals of Alexander Mackenzie*, 9.

29. W. J. Eccles and John E. Foster, "Fur Trade," *The Canadian Encyclopedia* online, 2011, 3.

30. *Geni genealogy* online, www.geni.com/people/Marie-Catherine-Durand/6000000012165958711.

31. Thwaites, *The Colonies*, 249.

32. Mackenzie, *The Journals of Alexander Mackenzie*, 12.

33. Grace Lee Nute, *The Voyageur* (New York: D. Appleton, 1931; repr. St. Paul: Minnesota Historical Society, 1955), 4.

34. Yves F. Zoltvany, "Greyson Dulhut, Daniel," *Dictionary of Canadian Biography, Vol. 2.*

35. Zoltvany, "Greyson Dulhut, Daniel."

36. Zoltvany, "Greyson Dulhut, Daniel."

37. Nicholas Perrot, *The Indian Tribes of the Upper Mississippi Valley and Region of the Great Lakes, Memoir on the Manners, Customs, and Religion of the Savages of North America*, tr. Emma Helen Blair, 2nd ed. (Cleveland: Arthur H.

Clark Company, 1911; Nabu Press, 2010), 15; Jean Hamelin, "Nicollet De Belleborne, Jean," *Dictionary of Canadian Biography, Vol. 1*; J. Monet, "Marquette, Jacques," *Dictionary of Canadian Biography, Vol. 1*; Céline Dupré, "Cavelier de La Salle, René Robert," *Dictionary of Canadian Biography, Vol. 1*. For new scholarship on Nicolet's journey, see Patrick Jung, *The Misunderstood Mission of Jean Nicolet: Uncovering the Story of the 1634 Journey* (Madison: Wisconsin Historical Press, 2018), 144–145.

38. Witgen, *An Infinity of Nations*, 77.

39. Perrot, *Indian Tribes*, 220–225.

40. Perrot, *Indian Tribes*, 224.

41. Perrot, *Indian Tribes*, 225.

42. William W. Warren, *History of the Ojibway People*, reprint (St. Paul: Minnesota Historical Society Press, 1984), 130.

43. Warren, *History of the Ojibway People*, 131.

44. Warren, *History of the Ojibway People*, 131.

45. Warren, *History of the Ojibway People*, 132.

46. Warren, *History of the Ojibway People*, 131, 212.

47. Perrot, *Indian Tribes*, 225.

Chapter 6

1. Edward Duffield Neill, *The History of Minnesota from the Earliest French Explorations to the Present Time* (Philadelphia: J. B. Lippincott, 1858), 117–119.

2. Hamilton Nelson Ross, *La Pointe: Village Outpost on Madeline Island*. rev. ed. (1960; repr., Madison: State Historical Society of Wisconsin, 2000), 37. The shifting nature of the area is reflected in the fact that in 1970, Chequamegon Point and Long Island—previously separated by water— were joined as one long landscape following a particularly violent November storm. E. J. Epstein, A. Galvin, and W. A. Smith, "Site Description for Long Island-Chequamegon Point," *A Data Compilation and Assessment of Coastal Wetlands of Wisconsin's Great Lakes*, Wisconsin Department of Natural Resources, PUBL ER-803 2002. https://dnr.wi.gov/files/PDF/pubs/er/ER0803.pdf.

3. A. Nasatir, "Le Sueur, Pierre," *Dictionary of Canadian Biography, Vol. 2*.

4. Ross, *La Pointe*, 40–43. See also, Reuben Gold Thwaites, "The Story of Chequamegon Bay," *Collections of the State Historical Society of Wisconsin, Volume 13* (Madison: Historical Society of Wisconsin, 1895), 138–140.

5. Neill, *The History of Minnesota*, 148.

6. Ross, *La Pointe*, 45.

7. Neill, *The History of Minnesota*, 148.

8. Neill, *The History of Minnesota*, 149.

9. Neill, *The History of Minnesota*, 149.

10. Nasatir, "Le Sueur, Pierre."

11. Ross, *La Pointe*, 46.

12. Neill, *The History of Minnesota*, 151–152. See also Reuben Gold Thwaites, *The French Regime in Wisconsin II—1727–1748, Collections of the State Historical Society of Wisconsin, Volume 17* (Madison: Historical Society of Wisconsin, 1906), 1–9.

13. Neill, *The History of Minnesota*, 180.

14. Thwaites, *The French Regime in Wisconsin*, xi–xii.

15. Neill, *The History of Minnesota*, 189–190.

16. Thwaites, *The French Regime in Wisconsin*, xiv.

17. "Mi'kmaq (Mi'kmaw, Micmac or L'nu, "the people" in Mi'kmaq) are Indigenous peoples who are among the original inhabitants in the Atlantic Provinces of Canada": Harold Franklin McGee Jr., "Mi'kmaq," in *The Canadian Encyclopedia. Historical Canada.* Article published August 13, 2008; Last Edited October 11, 2018. https://www.thecanadianencyclopedia.ca/en/article/micmac-mikmaq

18. Thwaites, *The French Regime in Wisconsin*, xv–xvi.

19. Ross, *La Pointe*, 50–52.

20. The Ontonagon River was where a famous five-ton copper boulder was discovered, then removed to Washington, DC, in the mid-nineteenth century. It now resides at the Smithsonian Institution. Hope Pantell, "The Story of the Ontonagon Copper Boulder," *The Mineralogical Record*, September–October 1976, http://www.michigan.gov/documents/deq/GIMDL-G-GOCB_302361_7.pdf, 1–3 (originally printed in the *Smithsonian Institution Press*, 1971).

21. Ross, *La Pointe*, 50–51.

22. Ross, *La Pointe*, 51.

23. Ross, *La Pointe*, 52.

24. Ross, *La Pointe*, 53.

25. Thwaites, *The French Regime in Wisconsin*, 477–478.

26. Thwaites, *The French Regime in Wisconsin*, 477–478.

27. Ross, *La Pointe*, 55–56.

28. William W. Warren, *History of the Ojibway People*, reprint (St. Paul: Minnesota Historical Society Press, 1984), 141–142.

29. William Morrison, "An Incident of Chegoimegon—1760," in *Report and Collections of the Historical Society of Wisconsin, Volume 8* (Madison: David Atwood, State Printer, 1879), 224–226. The newspaper article was actually written by Henry Rowe Schoolcraft, who heard the story from Morrison. Morrison, in turn, said he'd heard the tale from an elderly Ojibwe man who had been present at La Pointe when the events occurred.

30. Warren, *History of the Ojibway People*, 195. Warren spelled the leader's name "Ma-mong-e-se-da," but I have used the spelling most commonly found in various records.

31. Warren, *History of the Ojibway People*, 220.

Chapter 7

1. Alexander Mackenzie, *The Journals of Alexander Mackenzie. Voyages from Montreal, on the River St. Laurence, Through the Continent of North America, To the Frozen and Pacific Oceans; In the Years, 1789 and 1793. With a Preliminary Account of the Rise, Progress, and Present State of the Fur Trade of That Country*, rev. ed. (1801; repr. Santa Barbara, CA: The Narrative Press, 2009), 9.

2. Helen Hornbeck Tanner, "The Career of Joseph La France, Coureur de Bois in the Upper Great Lakes," in *The Fur Trade Revisited, Selected Papers of the Sixth North American Fur Trade Conference, Mackinac Island, Michigan, 1991* (East Lansing: Michigan State University Press, 1994), 171–172.

3. Tanner, "The Career of Joseph La France," 171–184.

4. Tanner, "The Career," 177–179.

5. Tanner, "The Career," 171–184.

6. Tanner, "The Career," 181.

7. Theresa M. Schenck, "The Cadottes: Five Generations of Fur Traders on Lake Superior," in *The Fur Trade Revisited, Selected Papers of the Sixth North American Fur Trade Conference, Mackinac Island, Michigan, 1991* (East Lansing: Michigan State University Press), 189.

8. Thomas L. McKenney, *Sketches of a Tour to the Lakes of the Character and Customs of the Chippeway Indians, and Incidents Connected with the Treaty of Fond du Lac*, rev. ed. (1827; Barre, MA: Imprint Society, 1972), 179.

9. Mackenzie, *The Journals of Alexander Mackenzie*, 41.

10. McKenney, *Sketches of a Tour of the Lakes*, 173.

11. McKenney, *Sketches*, 173.

12. Alexander Henry, *Travels and Adventures in Canada and the Indian Territories between the Years 1760 and 1776* (New York: J. Riley, 1809), 317.

13. David Thompson, *The Writings of David Thompson, Volume 1. The Travels, 1850 Version* (Toronto: The Champlain Society, 2009), 199.

14. Henry, *Travels and Adventures*, 219–222.

15. Grace Lee Nute, *The Voyageur* (New York: D. Appleton, 1931; repr. St. Paul: Minnesota Historical Society, 1955), 19.

16. Nute, *The Voyageur*, vi.

Chapter 8

1. Carolyn Gilman, "L'Anneeé du Coup: The Battle of St. Louis, 1780, Part 1," *Missouri Historical Review* (April 2009): 133–147.

2. Gilman, "L'Anneeé du Coup," 133–147.

3. Lt. Gov. Patrick Sinclair to Captain D. Brehm, October 29, 1779, "Haldimand Papers," *Collections of the Pioneer Society of the State of Michigan, Volume 9*, 542.

4. DuLong, "Jean Batiste Cadotte's Second Family: Genealogical Summary—Part 1," *Michigan's Habitant Heritage (MHH)* 36, no. 4 (October 2015): 197.

5. Theresa M. Schenck, "The Cadottes: Five Generations of Fur Traders on Lake Superior," in *The Fur Trade Revisited, Selected Papers of the Sixth North American Fur Trade Conference, Mackinac Island, Michigan, 1991* (East Lansing: Michigan State University Press, 1994), 189.

6. Schenck, "The Cadottes," 190.

7. "The United States v. Repentigny 1866," in *Cases Argued and Adjudged Before the Supreme Court of The United States, Volume 5* (Washington City: Published for John Conrad and Co., 1804–1861), 215–216.

8. Grace Lee Nute, *The Voyageur* (New York: D. Appleton, 1931; repr. St. Paul: Minnesota Historical Society, 1955), 14–15.

9. *Dictionary of Canadian Biography*, s.v. "Cadot, Jean-Baptiste," by David A. Armour, Accessed on February 1, 2019, www.biographi.ca/en/bio/cadot_jean_baptiste_5E.html.

10. Elizabeth Hart Bennett and Evan A. Hart, "Translation of the Cadotte Account Book, 1772–1794," *Cadotte Family Papers*, University of Notre Dame Archives, 76.

11. Armour, "Cadot, Jean-Baptiste"; DuLong, "Jean Batiste Cadotte's Second Family: Genealogical Summary—Part 1," *Michigan's Habitant Heritage* 36, no. 4 (October 2015): 190–193. DuLong says that the senior Cadot didn't marry his second wife, Catherine, a Native woman, in a formal Catholic ceremony as he had done with Athanasie. Rather, they lived only under the less formal Ojibwe marriage structure. Additionally, it appears that he didn't provide the same degree of education for the children of this second marriage, although he supported them and their mother during his lifetime. In a separate document, DuLong says that Marie-Renée handled her father's business details in Montreal until her death in 1786, at the age of thirty.

12. John DuLong, "Jean Baptiste Cadotte's First Family, Genealogical Summary," unpublished document e-mailed to the author, December 4, 2018. A second daughter, Charlotte, also apparently accompanied Athanasie and the children to Montreal, but Charlotte died in 1768 at the age of eight.

13. Bennett and Hart, "Translation of the Cadotte Account Book, 1772–1794," 4.

14. "The United States v. Repentigny 1866," 220.

15. "The United States v. Repentigny 1866," 221, 223.

16. "The United States v. Repentigny 1866," 225–226.

17. "The United States v. Repentigny 1866," 256–268.

18. William W. Warren, *History of the Ojibway People*, reprint (St. Paul: Minnesota Historical Society Press, 1984), 221.

19. Charles M. Sheridan, "Michael Cadotte Buried on Madeline Island. Picturesque Figure in Early Fur Trade," *The Washburn Times*, August 11, 1927.

20. Warren, *History of the Ojibway People*, 221; Theresa M., Schenck, "Who Owns Sault Ste. Marie?" *The Michigan Historical Review* (March 2002): 28, 109–120.

21. Armour, "Cadot, Jean-Baptiste"; DuLong, "Jean Batiste Cadotte's Second Family," 197.

22. Theresa M. Schenck, *The Voice of the Crane Echoes Afar, The Sociopolitical Organization of the Lake Superior Ojibwa, 1640–1855* (New York: Garland Publishing, 1997), 71.

23. Lt. Gov. Patrick Sinclair to Captain D. Brehm, October 29, 1779, "Haldimand Papers," 530.

24. Alexander Henry, *Travels and Adventures in Canada and the Indian Territories between the Years 1760 and 1776* (New York: J. Riley, 1809), 157.

25. Henry, *Travels and Adventures*, 158–162.

26. Henry, *Travels and Adventures*, 163–164.

27. Henry, *Travels and Adventures*, 164–165.

28. Henry, *Travels and Adventures*, 165–166.

29. Henry, *Travels and Adventures*, 165–166.

30. Armour, "Cadot, Jean-Baptiste."

31. Henry, *Travels and Adventures*, 191–193.

32. William Howard to Sir William Johnson, May 17, 1765, in Schenck, "The Cadottes, Five Generations of Fur Traders on Lake Superior," 191.

33. Presumably by Captain William Howard of Michilimackinac, though that's unclear: see David Armour, "Cadot, Jean Baptiste." However, he doesn't say who appointed Cadot as an interpreter, only that he held the position for more than a year.

34. Armour, "Cadot, Jean-Baptiste."

35. Henry, *Travels and Adventures in Canada*, 223–235; Armour, "Cadot, Jean-Baptiste"; DuLong, "Jean Baptiste Cadotte: His Life and Role in the Northwest Fur Trade, 1723–1803," paper prepared for *The French-Canadian Heritage Society of Michigan*, 1983, 23–24.

36. Henry, *Travels and Adventures in Canada*, 237–303. Armour, "Cadot, Jean-Baptiste"; DuLong, "Jean Baptiste Cadotte, His Life and Role," 23–29.

37. DuLong, "Jean Baptiste Cadotte: His Life and Role," 29.

38. Bennett and Hart, "Translation of the Cadotte Account Book, 1772–1794," *Cadotte Family Papers*, 72.

39. Bennett and Hart, "Translation of the Cadotte Account Book," 73.

40. Lt. Gov. Patrick Sinclair to Captain D. Brehm, October 29, 1779, 530, 542.

41. Lt. Gov. Patrick Sinclair to Captain D. Brehm, October 29, 1779, 542.

42. Gilman, "The Battle of St. Louis," 142–143.

43. Lt. Gov. Patrick Sinclair to Sir Frederick Haldimand, July 1780, 563.

44. Carolyn Gilman, "L' Anneé du Coup: The Battle of St. Louis, 1780, Part 2," *Missouri Historical Review* (July 2009): 195–211.

45. Lt. Gov. Patrick Sinclair to Sir Frederick Haldimand, July, 1780, "Haldimand Papers," 563.

46. DuLong, "Jean-Baptiste Cadotte's Second Family," 190; Lt. Gov. Patrick Sinclair to Captain D. Brehm, October 29, 1779, 196.

47. Schenck, "The Cadottes," 194.

48. Armour, "Cadot, Jean-Baptiste."

49. Bennett and Hart, "Translation of the Cadotte Account Book," 80; Schenck, "The Cadottes," 194.

50. Bennett and Hart, "Translation of the Cadotte Account Book," 55.

51. DuLong, "Jean-Batiste Cadotte's Second Family," 193.

52. DuLong, "Jean-Batiste Cadotte's Second Family," 190.

Chapter 9

1. Susan Sleeper-Smith, *Indian Women and French Men: Rethinking Cultural Encounter in the Western Great Lakes* (Amherst: University of Massachusetts Press, 2001), 5.

2. Brenda J. Child, *Holding Our World Together: Ojibwe Women and the Survival of Community* (New York: Penguin Books, 2012), 46.

3. Nicholas Perrot, *The Indian Tribes of the Upper Mississippi Valley and Region of the Great Lakes: Memoir on the Manners, Customs, and Religion of the Savages of North America*, tr. Emma Helen Blair, 2nd ed. (Cleveland: Arthur H. Clark Company, 1911; Nabu Press, 2010), 75–76.

4. Frances Densmore, *Chippewa Customs* (St. Paul: Minnesota Historical Society Press, 1979), 119–123.

5. Erik M. Redix, *The Murder of Joe White: Ojibwe Leadership and Colonialism in Wisconsin* (East Lansing: Michigan State University Press, 2014), 108–117.

6. Sylvia Van Kirk, *Many Tender Ties: Women in Fur-Trade Society, 1670–1870* (Norman: University of Oklahoma Press, 1983), 4.

7. Van Kirk, *Many Tender Ties*.

8. Sleeper-Smith, *Indian Women and French Men*, 4.

9. *The Ojibwe People's Dictionary*, University of Minnesota, http://ojibwe.lib.umn.edu.

10. Densmore, *Chippewa Customs*, 72.

11. Van Kirk, *Many Tender Ties*, 28–29.

12. *Dictionary of Canadian Biography*, s.v. "Cadot, Jean-Baptiste," by David A. Armour, Accessed on February 1, 2019, www.biographi.ca/en/bio/cadot_jean_baptiste_5E.html.

13. Child, *Holding Our World Together*, 46–49.

14. George Nelson, *My First Years in the Fur Trade: The Journals of 1802–1804*, eds. Laura Peers and Theresa M. Schenck (St. Paul: Minnesota Historical Society Press, 2002), 107.

15. Nelson, *My First Years in the Fur Trade*, 61–62.

16. Thomas L. McKenney, *Sketches of a Tour to the Lakes, of the Character and Customs of the Chippeway Indians, and Incidents Connected with the Treaty of Fond du Lac*, rev. ed. (1827; Barre, MA: Imprint Society, 1972), 262. Also see Henry R. Schoolcraft, *Narrative Journal of Travels Through the Northwestern Regions of the United States, Vol. II* (Philadelphia: Lippincott, Grambo & Company, 1851), 231.

17. Redix, *The Murder of Joe White*, 106–107.

18. Henry Rowe Schoolcraft, *Narrative Journal of Travels through the North-western Regions of the United States, Vol. II* (Philadelphia: Lippincott, Grambo & Company, 1851), 231.

19. Nelson, *My First Years in the Fur Trade*, 8–10, 18–19.

20. Robert Dale Parker, "Schoolcraft, Jane Johnston," *American National Biography*. Also see *Dictionary of Canadian Biography Vol. 6*, s.v. "Johnston, John," by David A. Armour, Accessed on February 1, 2019: http://www.biographi.ca/en/bio/johnston_john_6E.html; Witgen, *An Infinity of Nations*, 11–13.

21. Van Kirk, *Many Tender Ties*, 83.

22. Van Kirk, *Many Tender Ties*, 83.

23. Anton Treuer, *The Assassination of Hole in the Day* (St. Paul: Minnesota Historical Society Press, 2011), 25–26.

24. Redix, *The Murder of Joe White*, 102–104.

25. William W. Warren, *History of the Ojibwe People* (St. Paul: Minnesota Historical Society Press, 1984), 151, 202–204; Redix, *The Murder of Joe White*, 103–104.

26. Treuer, *The Assassination of Hole in the Day*, 26.

27. Redix, *The Murder of Joe White*, 104.

28. Theresa S. Smith, "Yes, I'm Brave: Extraordinary Women in the Anishinaabe (Ojibwe) Tradition," *Journal of Feminist Studies in Religion* 15, no. 1 (1999): 43.

29. Treuer, *The Assassination of Hole in the Day*, 27.

30. Redix, *The Murder of Joe White*, 104, 119–121.

31. McKenney, *Sketches of a Tour to the Lakes*, 150.

32. McKenney, *Sketches of a Tour*, 151.

33. McKenney, *Sketches of a Tour*, 259.

34. Child, *Holding Our World Together*, 46.

35. Van Kirk, *Many Tender Ties*, 54–72.

36. Child, *Holding Our World Together*, 46.

37. Reuben Gold Thwaites, ed., "Mackinac Register of Baptisms and Internments, 1695–1821," in *Collections of the State Historical Society of Wisconsin, Vol. XIX*, 65.

38. Thwaites, ed., "Mackinac Register," 69–70.

39. Thwaites, ed., "Mackinac Register," 112–113.

40. Van Kirk, *Many Tender Ties*, 28–29.

41. Van Kirk, *Many Tender Ties*, 13.

42. Van Kirk, *Many Tender Ties*, 26.

43. Sleeper-Smith, *Indian Women and French Men*, 41.

44. Van Kirk, *Many Tender Ties*, 26.

45. Van Kirk, *Many Tender Ties*, 51.

46. Nelson, *My First Years in the Fur Trade*, 19.

47. David Thompson, *The Writings of David Thompson, Volume I. The Travels, 1850 Version* (Toronto: The Champlain Society, 2009), xxxiv–xxxv.

48. Van Kirk, *Many Tender Ties*, 240–242.

49. Van Kirk, *Many Tender Ties*, 240–242.

50. Van Kirk, *Many Tender Ties*, 240–242.

51. Child, *Holding Our World Together*, 48.

Chapter 10

1. David Thompson, *The Writings of David Thompson, Volume 1, The Travels, 1850 Version* (Toronto: The Champlain Society, 2009), 147.

2. "Canoes," *Fort William Historical Park* website: http://fwhp.ca/our-collection/historic-collection/canoes; Grace Lee Nute, *The Voyageur* (New York: D. Appleton and Company, 1931; repr. St. Paul: Minnesota Historical Society, 1955), 24–25.

3. "Canoes," *Fort William Historical Park* website.

4. Alexander Mackenzie, *The Journals of Alexander Mackenzie from Montreal, on the River St. Laurence, Through the Continent of North America, To the Frozen and Pacific Oceans; In the Years, 1789 and 1793. With a Preliminary Account of the Rise, Progress, and Present State of the Fur Trade of That Country*, rev. ed. (1801; repr. Santa Barbara, CA: The Narrative Press, 2009), 32.

5. Mackenzie, *The Journals of Alexander Mackenzie*, 31.

6. Mackenzie, *The Journals of Alexander Mackenzie*, 33–34.

7. "Canoes," Fort Williams Historical Park website.

8. "Canoes," Fort Williams Historical Park website.

9. Grace Lee Nute, *The Voyager*, 62.

10. Mackenzie, *The Journals of Alexander Mackenzie*, 37.

11. Alexander Henry, *Travels and Adventures in Canada and the Indian Territories between the Years 1760 and 1776* (New York: J. Riley, 1809), 226.

12. Henry, *Travels and Adventures in Canada*, 234–235.

13. Grace Lee Nute, *Lake Superior*, rev. ed. (1994; Minneapolis: University of Minnesota Press, 2000), 117. Hamilton Nelson Ross, *La Pointe: Village Outpost on Madeline Island*, rev. ed. (1960; repr., Madison: State Historical Society of Wisconsin, 2000), 51.

14. Nute, *Lake Superior*, 115–116.

15. Nute, *Lake Superior*, 116.

16. Nute, *Lake Superior*, 116.

Chapter 11

1. Alexander Mackenzie, *The Journals of Alexander Mackenzie: Voyages from Montreal, on the River St. Laurence, Through the Continent of North America, To the Frozen and Pacific Oceans; In the Years, 1789 and 1793. With a Preliminary Account of the Rise, Progress, and Present State of the Fur Trade of That Country*, rev. ed. (1801; repr. Santa Barbara, CA: Narrative Press, 2009), 26.

2. Mackenzie, *The Journals of Alexander Mackenzie*, 25.

3. Elizabeth Hart Bennett and Evan A. Hart, "Translation of the Cadotte Account Book, 1772–1794," *Cadotte Family Papers*, University of Notre Dame Archives, 36–37.

4. W. Stewart Wallace, ed., *Documents Relating to the North West Company* (Toronto: Champlain Society, 1934), 63.

5. Wallace, *Documents Relating to the North West Company*, 63.

6. Marjorie Wilkins Campbell, *The North West Company* (Vancouver, BC: Douglas & McIntyre, 1983), 2.

7. Campbell, *The North West Company*, 1.

8. Wallace, *Documents*, 90–91.

9. Wallace, *Documents*, 170–171.

10. Wallace, *Documents*, 170–171.

11. Wallace, *Documents*, 176–178.

12. Campbell, *The North West Company*, 8.

13. Carolyn Gilman, *The Grand Portage Story* (St. Paul: Minnesota Historical Society Press, 1992), 55.

14. Gilman, *The Grand Portage Story*, 16.

15. Mackenzie, *The Journals of Alexander Mackenzie*, 20.

16. Mackenzie, *The Journals of Alexander Mackenzie*, 20–21.

17. Wallace, *Documents Relating to the North West Company* (Toronto: Champlain Society, 1934), 66.

18. Campbell, *The North West Company*, 92–96.

19. Wallace, *Documents*, 70–75.

20. Wallace, *Documents*, 73.

21. Wallace, *Documents*, 73.

22. Wallace, *Documents*, 73.

23. Grace Lee Nute, *The Voyageur* (New York: D. Appleton, 1931; repr. St. Paul: Minnesota Historical Society, 1955), 5, 51–54.

24. Campbell, *The North West Company*, 93–96.

25. *Wallace, Documents*, 256.

26. *Wallace, Documents*, 73.

27. Harry W. Duckworth, "British Capital in the Fur Trade: John Strettell and John Fraser," in *The Fur Trade Revisited, Selected Papers of the Sixth North American Fur Trade Conference, Mackinac Island, Michigan, 1991* (East Lansing: Michigan State University Press, 1994), 39.

28. Duckworth, "British Capital in the Fur Trade."

29. Duckworth, "British Capital," 42–43.

30. Duckworth, "British Capital," 44.

31. Duckworth, "British Capital," 46–48.

32. Duckworth, "British Capital," 48–49.

33. Duckworth, "British Capital," 50.

34. Wallace, *Documents*, 91–94.

35. Wallace, *Documents*, 91–94.

36. Campbell, *The North West Company*, 124–154.

37. Campbell, *The North West Company*, 149.

38. Campbell, *The North West Company*, 160.

39. Campbell, *The North West Company*, 170–197.

40. Campbell, *The North West Company*, 198–218.

41. Bruce M. White, "Cadotte, Joseph," in *Dictionary of Canadian Biography, Vol. 6*; John DuLong, "Jean-Baptiste Cadotte's Second Family: Genealogical

Summary—Part 1," *Michigan's Habitant Heritage* 36, no. 4 (October 2015): 190–196.

42. Campbell, *The North West Company*, 198–218.

43. Campbell, *The North West Company*, 254–277.

44. John S. Galbraith, "British-American Competition in the Border Fur Trade of the 1820s," *Minnesota History Magazine* (September 1959), 243.

45. Mackenzie, *The Journals of Alexander Mackenzie*, 22.

Chapter 12

1. Reviews on Trip Advisor from 2011 and 2012; www.tripadvisor.com/ ShowUserReviews-g43117-d143418-r173261438-Pigeon_River-Grand_ Portage_Minnesota.html.

2. Alexander Mackenzie, *The Journals of Alexander Mackenzie. Voyages from Montreal, on the River St. Laurence, Through the Continent of North America, To the Frozen and Pacific Oceans; In the Years, 1789 and 1793. With a Preliminary Account of the Rise, Progress, and Present State of the Fur Trade of That Country*, rev. ed. (1801; repr. Santa Barbara, CA: The Narrative Press, 2009), 41.

3. David Thompson, *The Writings of David Thompson, Volume 1, The Travels, 1850 Version* (Toronto: The Champlain Society, 2009), 176.

4. "Grand Portage Trail," Grand Portage National Monument website, National Park Service: https://www.nps.gov/grpo/learn/photosmultimedia/ grand-portage-trail.htm.

5. Carolyn Gilman, *The Grand Portage Story* (St. Paul: Minnesota Historical Society Press, 1992), 19.

6. Mackenzie, *The Journals of Alexander Mackenzie*, 41.

7. John Lundy, "Portion of Grand Portage Trail Rediscovered in Jay Cooke State Park," *Duluth News Tribune*, January 9, 2015.

8. William Warren, *History of the Ojibway People*, reprint (St. Paul: Minnesota Historical Society Press, 1984), 280–281.

9. Jean-Baptiste Perrault, "Narrative of the Travels and Adventures of a Merchant Voyageur in the Savage Territories of Northern America, Leaving Montreal the 28th of May 1783 (to 1820)," (Lansing: Historical Collections and Researches made by the Michigan Pioneer and Historical Society, Vol. XXXVII, 1909, 1910), 570.

10. Grace Lee Nute, *The Voyageur* (New York: D. Appleton and Company, 1931;

repr. St. Paul: Minnesota Historical Society, 1955), 17.

Chapter 13

1. John J. Bigsby, *The Shoe and Canoe, or Pictures of Travel in Canada, Volume I* (London: Forgotten Books, 2017), 242–243.
2. Bigsby, *The Shoe and Canoe*, 244.
3. Reuben Gold Thwaites, *Travels and Explorations of the Jesuit Missionaries in New France 1610–1791, Volume 48* (Cleveland: The Burrows Brothers Company, 1900), 137.
4. Thwaites, *Travels and Explorations of the Jesuit Missionaries*, 137.
5. Henry Rowe Schoolcraft, *Narrative Journal of Travels Through the Northwestern Regions of the United States, Vol. II* (Philadelphia: Lippincott, Grambo & Company, 1851), 270.
6. David Thompson, *The Writings of David Thompson, Volume 1, The Travels, 1850 Version* (Toronto: The Champlain Society, 2009), 25.
7. Thompson, *The Writings of David Thompson*, 25–26.
8. Thomas C. Keefer, "Montreal and the Ottawa: Two Lectures Delivered Before the Mechanics Institute of Montreal in January, 1853 and 1854," in *The Canals of Canada, their prospects and influence* (Montreal: Andrew H. Armour and Company, 1894), 34.
9. Keefer, "Montreal and the Ottawa," 34.
10. "The Voyageurs," McGill University Digital Library, http://digital.library .mcgill.ca/nwc/history/08.htm.
11. Elliott Coues, *New Light on the Early History of the Greater Northwest, the Red River of the North, Volume I. The Journals of Alexander Henry and David Thompson* (New York: F. P. Harper, 1897), 413.
12. Thompson, *The Writings of David Thompson*, 25–26.
13. Thompson, *The Writings of David Thompson*, 25–26.
14. Johnathon Webb, "Sweet-Smelling Secrets of Mosquito-Repellent Grass," *BBC News* online, August 19, 2015.
15. Webb, "Sweet Smelling Secrets." Also, Tony Bush, "Northern Sweetgrass," Plant Fact Sheet, U.S. Department of Agriculture, Natural Resources Conservation Service, 2010.
16. G. Mandela Fernandez-Grandon, Salvador A. Gezan, John A. L. Armour, John A. Pickett, and James G. Logan, "Heritability of Attractiveness to Mosquitoes," *PLoS ONE*, April 22, 2015.

Chapter 14

1. David Thompson, *The Writings of David Thompson, Volume 1. The Travels, 1850 Version* (Toronto: The Champlain Society, 2009), 229.

2. Thompson, *The Writings of David Thompson*, 229–231.

3. Thompson, *The Writings of David Thompson*, 323.

4. William Warren, *History of the Ojibway People*, reprint (St. Paul: Minnesota Historical Society Press, 1984), 280, 290.

5. *Dictionary of Canadian Biography*, s.v. "Cadot, Jean-Baptiste," by David A. Armour, Accessed on February 1, 2019, www.biographi.ca/en/bio/cadot_jean_baptiste_5E.html.

6. Reuben Gold Thwaites, ed., *Mackinac Register of Baptisms and Internments, 1695–1821*, in *Collections of the State Historical Society of Wisconsin, Vol. XIX* (Madison: Wisconsin State Historical Society, 1910), 65.

7. Elizabeth Hart Bennett and Evan A. Hart, "Translation of the Cadotte Account Book, 1772–1794," *Cadotte Family Papers*, University of Notre Dame Archives, 4. A note on the front cover of the translated copy of the Cadotte Account Book says, "Presentation notes written by James F. Edwards, Archivist of Notre Dame until 1911, according to Father McAvoy, Archivist, 1963."

8. Bennett and Hart, "Translation of the Cadotte Account Book."

9. Bennett and Hart, "Translation," 5.

10. Bennett and Hart, "Translation," 16.

11. Lt. Gov. Patrick Sinclair to Captain D. Brehm, October 29, 1779, *Haldimand Papers*, In *Collections of the Pioneer Society of the State of Michigan, Volume Nine*, 533.

12. Stuart R. J. Sutherland, Pierre Tousignant, and Madeleine Dionne-Tousignant, "Haldimand, Sir Frederick," in *Dictionary of Canadian Biography, Vol. 5*, 18–19.

13. Captain D. Brehm to Lt. Gov. Patrick Sinclair, April 17, 1780, *Haldimand Papers*, 537.

14. Warren, *History of the Ojibway People*, 279–280.

15. Bennett and Hart, "Translation," 80.

16. Theresa M. Schenck, "The Cadottes: Five Generations of Fur Traders on Lake Superior," in *The Fur Trade Revisited, Selected Papers of the Sixth North American Fur Trade Conference, Mackinac Island, Michigan, 1991* (East Lansing: Michigan State University Press), 194.

17. Bennett and Hart, "Translation," 51–57.

18. John DuLong, "Jean Baptiste Cadotte's First Family: Genealogical Summary," draft document given to the author, December 2018, 6.

19. Bennett and Hart, "Translation," 58, 100.

20. *Dictionary of Canadian Biography*, s.v "Campion, Étienne-Charles" by various authors, Accessed May 10, 2019, http://www.biographi.ca/en/bio/ campion_etienne_charles_4E.html.

21. Jean-Baptiste Perrault, "Narrative of the Travels and Adventures of a Merchant Voyageur in the Savage Territories of Northern America," *Historical Collections and Researches made by the Michigan Pioneer and Historical Society, Vol. XXXVII*, 536–538. Perrault said the senior Cadot was a founding member of the *Societé General*, although he called it the General Company of Lake Superior. Perrault's journal was written in French when he was about seventy years old. He wrote the journal at the request of Henry Rowe Schoolcraft when both were living at Sault Ste. Marie. The journal was discovered among Schoolcraft's papers at the Smithsonian Institute in 1905. It was edited by John Sharpless Fox and translated by Fox's wife.

22. Perrault, "Narrative of the Travels and Adventures of a Merchant Voyageur," 544–545. Perrault didn't say which "Mr. Cadotte" led the canoes of Objibwe at the ceremony. An early-twentieth-century editor's note in Perrault's journal says it was likely Jean-Baptiste Cadot Sr., then age sixty-five, because he had significant influence with the Ojibwe. But Jean-Baptiste Cadotte Jr. was already developing influence among the tribe, and it's not difficult to imagine that the father had turned to his eldest son, then twenty-six, to represent him by leading the canoe armada at the ceremony. Given the importance of the occasion and the fact that both Jean-Baptiste Jr. and Michel made their permanent homes at nearby Sault Ste. Marie at the time, it is likely both were present.

23. Perrault, "Narrative of the Travels and Adventures of a Merchant Voyageur," 555.

24. Perrault, "Narrative," 556–557.

25. Perrault, "Narrative."

26. Perrault, "Narrative," 561.

27. Warren, *History of the Ojibway People*, 290.

28. Warren, *History of the Ojibway People*, 280–281. Also, Joseph Tasse, *Les Canadiens De L'ouest* (Montreal, 1882), cited in *Cadotte Family Stories*, 109.

29. Warren, *History of the Ojibway People*, 280–282.

30. Warren, *History*, 280–281.

31. Warren, *History*, 282.

32. Warren, *History*, 282–283.

33. Warren, *History*, 283–287.

34. Warren, *History*, 288.

35. Marjorie Wilkins Campbell, *The North West Company* (Vancouver, BC: Douglas & McIntyre, 1983), 109.

36. Perrault, "Narrative," 569.

37. W. Stewart Wallace, ed., *Documents Relating to the North West Company* (Toronto: Champlain Society, 1934), 90.

38. Perrault, "Narrative," 570.

39. John Lundy, "Portion of Grand Portage Trail Rediscovered in Jay Cooke State Park," *Duluth News Tribune*, January 9, 2015. Also, Jim Umhoefer, "Jay Cooke State Park Log," *Minnesota Trails Magazine*, April 29, 2009.

40. Perrault, "Narrative," 570. Perrault said Cadotte's disaster at the falls occurred in the summer of 1795. However, if it was the summer after Cadotte spent his first winter under contract with the North West Company, as Perrault says at the beginning of this passage, then it had to be in 1796.

41. Wallace, *Documents Relating to the North West Company*, 91.

42. Warren, *History of the Ojibway People*, 290.

43. Perrault, "Narrative," 575.

44. Perrault, "Narrative," 575.

45. Perrault, "Narrative," 576.

46. Perrault, "Narrative," 576.

47. Warren, *History of the Ojibway People*, 290–291.

48. Warren, *History*, 292–294.

49. Warren, *History*, 293–294. The story of Mackenzie forgiving Cadotte's debt doesn't appear in either Mackenzie's journal or the extant documents of the North West Company. Several later sources recounted both that story and the one that follows about the murder, trial, and execution that occurred under Cadotte's watch. However, because the wording of these later accounts is so similar to that used by Warren, it's likely that they were derived from his narrative. His version almost certainly came directly from Equaysayway, who was present during the second event.

50. Warren, *History of the Ojibway People*, 294–295.

51. Warren, *History*, 295–297.

52. Wallace, *Documents Relating to the North West Company*, 170–171.

53. Wallace, *Documents*, 172.

54. Elliott Coues, ed., *New Light on the Early History of the Greater Northwest, the Red River of the North, Volume I. The Journals of Alexander Henry and David Thompson* (New York: F. Harper, 1897).

55. Arthur J. Ray, *Indians in the Fur Trade: Their Role as Trappers, Hunters and Middlemen in the Lands Southwest of Hudson Bay, 1670–1870* (Toronto: University of Toronto Press, 1974), 142–143.

56. Wallace, *Documents Relating to the North West Company*, 268–267.

57. Perrault, "Narrative," 577.

58. Wallace, *Documents Relating to the North West Company*,184, 185.

59. Wallace, *Documents*, 186.

60. Wallace, *Documents*, 182.

61. Wallace, *Documents*, 267–268.

62. DuLong, "Jean-Baptiste Cadotte's First Family," 13.

63. John DuLong, "The Cadottes, the Indian Department and the War of 1812, Part 1," *Michigan's Habitant Heritage* 37, no. 4 (October 2016): 185.

64. Wallace, *Documents Relating to the North West Company*, 428. DuLong, "Jean-Baptiste Cadotte's First Family," 13.

Chapter 15

1. Eliza Morrison, *A Little History of My Forest Life, An Indian-White Autobiography* (La Crosse, WI: Sumac Press, 1978), 60.

2. Frances Densmore, *Chippewa Customs* (St. Paul: Minnesota Historical Press, 1979), 123.

3. Morrison, *A Little History of My Forest Life*, 28; Theresa M. Schenck, *All Our Relations, Chippewa Mixed Bloods and the Treaty of 1837* (Madison: Amik Press, 2010), 39.

4. Morrison, *A Little History of My Forest Life*, 91–92.

5. Roger Cadotte, email correspondence with the author, April 2015.

6. Arent De Peyster to Gov. Haldimand, June 1, 1779, "Haldimand Papers," *Collections of the Pioneer Society of the State of Michigan, Volume 9*, 383.

7. Alexander Henry, *Travels and Adventures in Canada and the Indian Territories between the Years 1760 and 1776* (New York: J. Riley, 1809), 218.

8. "National Nutrient Database," U.S. Department of Agriculture: http://ndb .nal.usda.gov/ ; "Maple Nutrition," Wisconsin Maple Syrup Producers Association website: http://wismaple.org/maple-nutrition/.

9. George Nelson, *My First Years in the Fur Trade, the Journals of 1802–1804*, eds. Laura Peers and Theresa M. Schenck (St. Paul: Minnesota Historical Society Press, 2002), 154.

10. Alexander Mackenzie, *The Journals of Alexander Mackenzie Voyages from Montreal, on the River St. Laurence, Through the Continent of North America, To the Frozen and Pacific Oceans; In the Years, 1789 and 1793. With a Preliminary Account of the Rise, Progress, and Present State of the Fur Trade of That Country*, rev. ed. (1801; repr. Santa Barbara, CA: Narrative Press, 2009), 37.

11. Howard D. Paap, *Red Cliff, Wisconsin, A History of an Ojibwe Community, Volume 1* (St. Cloud, WI: North Star Press, 2013), 65.

12. Densmore, *Chippewa Customs*, 123.

13. Roger Cadotte, email correspondence with the author, April 2015.

14. Roger Cadotte, email correspondence with the author, April 2015.

15. Roger Cadotte, email correspondence with the author, April 2015.

16. Jane C. Busch, "People and Places: A Human History of the Apostle Islands, Historic Resource Study of the Apostle Islands National Lakeshore," National Park Service, prepared under contract to the Midwest Regional Office of the National Park Service, Omaha, 2008, 59.

17. Morrison, *A Little History of My Forest Life*, 123.

Chapter 16

1. William W. Warren, *History of the Ojibway People*, reprint (St. Paul: Minnesota Historical Society Press, 1984), 304.

2. Warren, *History of the Ojibway People*, 303.

3. Warren, *History of the Ojibway People*, 303.

4. Arthur J. Ray, *Indians in the Fur Trade: Their Role as Trappers, Hunters and Middlemen in the Lands Southwest of Hudson Bay, 1670–1870* (Toronto: University of Toronto Press, 1998), 14.

5. Warren, *History of the Ojibway People*, 298–304, 281.

6. Thomas McKenney, *Sketches of a Tour to the Lakes, of the Character and Customs of the Chippeway Indians, and Incidents Connected with the Treaty of Fond du Lac*, rev. ed. (1827; Barre, MA: Imprint Society, 1972), 215.

7. Elizabeth Hart Bennett and Evan A. Hart, "Translation of the Cadotte Ac-

count Book, 1772–1794," *Cadotte Family Papers*, University of Notre Dame Archives, 72.

8. Bennett and Hart, "Translation of the Cadotte Account Book," various pages.

9. Bennett and Hart, "Translation," 72, 108, 110.

10. W. Stewart Wallace, ed., *Documents Relating to the North West Company* (Toronto: Champlain Society, 1934), 176–178, 90–93.

11. Thomas Henry Tobola, *Cadotte Family Stories* (Milwaukee: Network Printers, 1974), 109; Theresa Schenck, *All Our Relations: Chippewa Mixed Bloods and the Treaty of 1837* (Madison: Amik Press, 2010), 35.

12. Schenck, *All Our Relations*, 38.

13. Thomas E. Randall, *History of the Chippewa Valley* (Eau Claire, WI: Free Press Print, 1875), quoted in Tobola, *Cadotte Family Stories*, 35–36. William Warren in *History of the Ojibway People*, 242–251, relates a more detailed story about the last conflicts between the Ojibwe and the Sauk, although he placed the battle at the falls of the St. Croix River, farther west than on the Chippewa River. His timeframe for the events meshes with that of Michel Cadotte Jr., as reported in Randall's account.

14. Warren, *History of the Ojibway People*, 301–302.

15. Warren, *History*, 301–302.

16. Jean-Baptiste Perrault, "Narrative of the Travels and Adventures of a Merchant Voyageur in the Savage Territories of Northern America, Leaving Montreal the 28th of May 1783 (to 1820)" (Lansing: Historical Collections and Researches made by the Michigan Pioneer and Historical Society, Vol. XXXVII, 1909, 1910), 547–551.

17. Perrault, *Narrative of the Travels and Adventures*, 551–552.

18. Perrault, *Narrative*, 552.

19. Perrault, *Narrative*, 552–553.

20. Perrault, *Narrative*, 564.

21. Perrault, *Narrative*, 571; Schenck, *All Our Relations*, 41. Keeping track of who's who in the Cadotte family is no easy task. One chart, prepared by Michigan scholar John DuLong, shows descendants of Mathurin Cadot who were active in the fur trade or the War of 1812. It lists five different men named Jean-Baptiste Cadotte (or Cadot), five named Augustin Cadotte, four named Michel Cadotte (including Michel *le grand* and Michel *le petit*), and several named Joseph and Charles.

22. Perrault, *Narrative*, 571–572.

23. Francois Victor Malhiot, *A Wisconsin Fur-Trader's Journal, 1804–1805* (Madison: State Historical Society of Wisconsin, 1910), 190.

24. Malhiot, *A Wisconsin Fur-Trader's Journal*, 203.

25. George Nelson, *My First Years in the Fur Trade: The Journals of 1802–1804*, eds. Laura Peers and Theresa M. Schenck (St. Paul: Minnesota Historical Society Press, 2002), 168.

26. Malhiot, *A Wisconsin Fur-Trader's Journal*, 179.

27. David Thompson, *The Writings of David Thompson, Volume 1. The Travels, 1850 Version* (Toronto: Champlain Society, 2009), 265; McKenney, *Sketches of a Tour to the Lakes*, 214–215; Hamilton Nelson Ross, *La Pointe: Village Outpost on Madeline Island*, rev. ed. (1960; repr., Madison: State Historical Society of Wisconsin, 2000), 96; Warren, *History of the Ojibway People*, 299.

28. Warren, *History of the Ojibway People*, 326.

29. Schenck, *All Our Relations*, 35; Tobola, *Cadotte Family Stories*, 110.

30. Wallace, *Documents Relating to the North West Company*, 176, 429. Cadotte is believed to have signed a number of three-year contracts with the North West Company, but this is the only one in the company documents Wallace compiled.

31. Theresa M. Schenck, *Grant's Point, Madeline Island, in the Historical Record* (Madison: Wisconsin State Historical Society, 2003), 8.

32. Warren, *History of the Ojibway People*, 299–300.

33. Tobola, *Cadotte Family Stories*, 52.

34. Thompson, *The Writings of David Thompson*, 265.

35. Ross, *La Pointe, Village Outpost on Madeline Island*, 96.

Chapter 17

1. W. Stewart Wallace, ed., *Documents Relating to the North West Company* (Vancouver, BC: Douglas & McIntyre, 1983), 176, 429.

2. Wallace, *Documents*, 222.

3. Wallace, *Documents*, 429.

4. Wallace, *Documents*, 219–221.

5. Wallace, *Documents*, 222.

6. Marjorie Wilkins Campbell, *The North West Company* (Vancouver, BC: Douglas & McIntyre, 1983), 159.

7. Wallace, *Documents*, 225.

8. Wallace, *Documents*, 226.

9. Robert S. Allen, *His Majesty's Indian Allies: British Indian Policy in the De-*

fence of Canada, 1774–1815 (Toronto: Dundurn Press, 1992), 108–110.

10. Allen, *His Majesty's Indian Allies*, 114.

11. Allen, *His Majesty's Indian Allies*, 109.

12. John Tanner, *A Narrative of the Captivity and Adventures of John Tanner (U.S. Interpreter at the Sault de Ste. Marie) during Thirty Years Residence among the Indians in the Interior of North America* (London: Baldwin and Cradock, 1830), 155.

13. Tanner, *A Narrative of the Captivity and Adventures of John Tanner*, 158.

14. William W. Warren, *History of the Ojibway People*, 2nd ed. (St. Paul: Collections of the Minnesota Historical Society, Vol. 5; 1885; St. Paul: Minnesota Historical Society Press, 1984), 322–323.

15. "History of the Battle of Tippecanoe," Tippecanoe County Historical Association.

16. Warren, *History of the Ojibway People*, 323.

17. Warren, *History of the Ojibway People*, 323.

18. Timothy D. Willig, *Restoring the Chain of Friendship: British Policy and the Indians of the Great Lakes, 1783–1815* (Lincoln: University of Nebraska Press, 2008), 235.

19. Tanner, *A Narrative of the Captivity and Adventures of John Tanner*, 158.

20. Warren, *History of the Ojibway People*, 320–321. Also see Theresa M. Schenck, "The Cadottes: Five Generations of Fur Traders on Lake Superior," *The Fur Trade Revisited, Selected Papers of the Sixth North American Fur Trade Conference, Mackinac Island, Michigan, 1991* (East Lansing: Michigan State University Press), 195.

21. Warren, *History of the Ojibway People*, 320–321; Schenck, "The Cadottes: Five Generations," 195.

22. Warren, *History of the Ojibway People*, 321, 325, 382, 383.

23. Warren, *History*, 325–326.

24. Schenck, "The Cadottes," 195–196.

25. David Lavender, *The Fist in the Wilderness* (Lincoln: University of Nebraska Press, 1998), 108–118; Warren, *History of the Ojibway People*.

26. Allen, *His Majesty's Indian Allies*, 109–122; Amanda Foreman, "The British View the War of 1812 Quite Differently Than Americans Do," *Smithsonian Magazine* (July 2014): http://www.smithsonianmag.com/history/british-view-war-1812-quite-differently-americans-do-180951852/?no-ist.

27. Allen, *His Majesty's Indian Allies*, 109–122; Foreman, "The British View

the War of 1812."

28. Allen, *His Majesty's Indian Allies*, 120–121.

29. Warren, *History*, 368.

30. John Askew Jr. letter to "The Hon. Col. Wm. Claus, &c. &c. Fort George," July 13, 1812; *The Edinburgh Advertiser*, Edinburgh, Scotland, October 2, 1812.

31. John Askew Jr. letter.

32. Warren, *History of the Ojibway People*, 372.

33. Theresa M. Schenck, *All Our Relations, Chippewa Mixed Bloods and the Treaty of 1837* (Madison: Amik Press, 2010), 37–38; John DuLong, "The Cadottes, the Indian Department and the War of 1812: Part 2," *Michigan's Habitant Heritage* 38, no. 1 (January 2017): 31–35.

34. Howard D. Paap, *Red Cliff, Wisconsin, A History of an Ojibwe Community, Volume 1* (St. Cloud, WI: North Star Press, 2013), 114–115; *Dictionary of Canadian Biography Vol. 6*, s.v. "Johnston, John," by David A. Armour, Accessed on February 1, 2019: http://www.biographi.ca/en/bio/johnston_john_6E.html.

35. Paap, *Red Cliff, Wisconsin*, 115.

36. With the Treaty of Ghent, signed in the city of Ghent in what's now Belgium, the British and Americans basically accepted the status quo as it was prior to the War of 1812, at least with regard to international borders. That meant the British had to accept the fact that they no longer had any authority on the southern shore of Lake Superior or on Michilimackinac. Sault Ste. Marie was split in half. Another provision attempted to restore to Native nations on both sides of the border "all possessions, rights and privileges which they may have enjoyed or been entitled to" in 1811. Most Indian nations in the region, including the Ojibwe, signed "peace and friendship" treaties with the Americans in the months following the signing of the Treaty of Ghent. But many of the treaties were soon broken by the United States, which violated the treaty by "invading the Indian country and building forts." See Allen, *His Majesty's Indian Allies*, 168–176.

37. "Astor used partnerships, pools, and mergers to limit competition and control trade across the continent. Although he was never able to establish a monopoly, most of his competitors eventually ended up working for him": Jane C. Busch, "People and Places: A Human History of the Apostle Islands," National Park Service, 90. Also see Bernard DeVoto, *Across the*

Wide Missouri (New York: Houghton Mifflin Harcourt, 1998), xx–xxi.

38. Campbell, *The North West Company*, 223–224.

39. Schenck, "The Cadottes," 196.

40. Schenck, "The Cadottes," 196–197.

41. Ross, *La Pointe*, 73.

42. Schenck, "The Cadottes," 197.

43. "Doc. No. 121, Licenses to Trade with Indians," *Executive Documents, Printed by Order of the House of Representatives at the First Session of the Twenty-Second Congress*, 4.

Chapter 18

1. Basil Johnston, *Ojibway Heritage* (Lincoln: University of Nebraska Press, 1976), 73.

2. Thomas Peacock, *Ojibwe Waasa Inaabidaa: We Look In All Directions* (Afton, MN: Afton Historical Society Press, 2002), 91.

3. Benjamin V. Burgess, "Elaboration Therapy in the Midewiwin and Gerald Vizenor's The Heirs of Columbus," *Studies in American Indian Literatures, Series 2*, 18, no. 1 (2006): 23, JSTOR.

4. Anton Treuer, *The Assassination of Hole in the Day* (St. Paul: Minnesota Historical Society Press, 2011), 7.

5. Michael Witgen, *An Infinity of Nations: How the Native New World Shaped Early North America* (Philadelphia: University of Pennsylvania Press, 2013), 13, 65.

6. Nicholas Perrot, *The Indian Tribes of the Upper Mississippi Valley and Region of the Great Lakes: Memoir on the Manners, Customs, and Religion of the Savages of North America*, tr. Emma Helen Blair, 2nd ed. (Cleveland: Arthur H. Clark Company, 1911; Nabu Press, 2010), 75–76.

7. Edmund Jefferson Danzinger Jr., *The Chippewas of Lake Superior* (Norman: University of Oklahoma Press, 1979), 16–17; William W. Warren, *History of the Ojibway People,* reprint (St. Paul: Minnesota Historical Society Press, 1984), 118–119.

8. Johnston, *Ojibwe Heritage*, 47-48.

9. *Encyclopedia Britannica Online*, "Grand Medicine Society," accessed June 1, 2019, http://www.britannica.com/topic/Grand-Medicine-Society.

10. Frances Densmore, *Chippewa Customs* (St. Paul: Minnesota Historical Society Press, 1979), 86.

11. Densmore, *Chippewa Customs*, 86.

12. Densmore, *Chippewa Customs*, 87.

13. Johnston, *Ojibwe Heritage*, 83.

14. Warren, *History of the Ojibwe People*, 66.

15. Warren, *History*, 66–67.

16. Christopher Vescey, *Traditional Ojibwa Religion and Its Historical Changes* (Philadelphia: American Philosophical Society, 1983), 176; Harold Hickerson, *The Chippewas and Their Neighbors: A Study in Ethnohistory* (Prospect Heights, IL: Waveland Press, 1988), 59–63.

17. Warren, *History of the Ojibwe People*, 67.

18. Jennifer S. H. Brown and Laura L. Peters, "The Chippewa and Their Neighbors: A Critical Review," in *The Chippewa and Their Neighbors: A Study in Ethnohistory*, ed. Harold Hickerson (Prospect Heights, IL: Waveland Press Inc., 1988), 142.

19. Anton Treuer, "Full Circle: From Disintegration to Revitalization of Otterskin Bag Use in Great Lakes Tribal Culture," *The Princeton University Chronicle* 67, no. 2 (2006): 362, JSTOR.

20. Treuer, "Full Circle," 362. Also see Brown and Peters, "The Chippewa and Their Neighbors," 142.

21. Edmund F. Ely, *The Ojibwe Journals of Edmund F. Ely, 1833–1849* (Lincoln: University of Nebraska Press, 2012).

22. Ely, *The Ojibwe Journals*, 186.

23. Ely, *The Ojibwe Journals*, 158.

24. Theresa M. Schenck, "Lyman Marcus Warren" (unpublished manuscript, April 2013), 9.

25. John P. Dulong, *Jean-Baptiste Cadotte's First Family: Geneaological Summary*, 2018, draft report given to author, 28.

26. Reuben Gold Thwaites, *The Jesuit Relations and Allied Documents: Travels and Explorations of the Jesuit Missionaries in New France, 1610–1791, Volume 61* (Cleveland: Burrows Bros. Co., 1896–1901), 153–155.

27. Thwaites, *The Jesuit Relations*, 153–155.

28. Hamilton Nelson Ross, *La Pointe: Village Outpost on Madeline Island*, rev. ed. (1960; repr., Madison: State Historical Society of Wisconsin, 2000), 77–78, 90.

29. Reuben Gold Thwaites, "Mackinac Register of Baptisms and Interments—1695–1821," *Collections of the State Historical Society of Wisconsin, Volume 19* (Madison: Historical Society of Wisconsin, 1910), 1–160.

30. Ronald N. Satz, *Chippewa Treaty Rights: The Reserved Rights of Wisconsin's Chippewa Indians in Historical Perspective* (Wisconsin Academy of Sciences, Arts and Letters, 1991); also see Howard D. Paap, *Red Cliff, Wisconsin, A History of an Ojibwe Community, Volume 1* (St. Cloud, WI: North Star Press, 2013), 130–264.

31. Rev. Stephen R. Riggs, "Protestant Missions in the Northwest," *Collections of the Minnesota Historical Society, Vol. 6* (St. Paul: The Pioneer Press, 1894), 122.

32. Riggs, "Protestant Missions in the Northwest," 123–124.

33. Riggs, "Protestant Missions," 123–124.

34. Ross, *La Pointe*, 86.

35. Ross, *La Pointe*, 86.

36. Ross, *La Pointe*, 87.

37. Ross, *La Pointe*, 76.

38. Ross, *La Pointe*, 90–91. Ross did not explain the relationship of Benjamin Cadotte to Michel and Equaysayway Cadotte. Theresa M. Schenck said he was a distant cousin in *All Our Relations: Chippewa Mixed-Bloods and the Treaty of 1837* (Madison: Amik Press, 2010), 42. John DuLong traced that lineage back to John-Baptiste Cadot's uncle in *Jean-Baptiste Cadotte's Second Family: Genealogical Summary—Part 1, Michigan's Habitant Heritage* 36, no. 4 (October 2015): 198.

39. Ross, *La Pointe*, 91.

40. Frederic Baraga, *The Diary of Bishop Frederic Baraga, First Bishop of Marquette, Michigan* (Detroit, MI: Wayne State University Press, 2001), 26.

41. Ross, *La Pointe*, 97.

42. Treuer, "Full Circle," 364.

Chapter 19

1. *Marriage Register, Church of Ste. Anne de Michilimackinac* (English translation) from August 1, 1823 to October 1836, no. 28, 3.

2. Frances Densmore, *Chippewa Customs* (St. Paul: Minnesota Historical Press, 1979), 72–73.

3. Densmore, *Chippewa Customs*, 73.

4. John DuLong, email correspondence with the author, December 2018.

5. Jacqueline Peterson, "The Founders of Green Bay: A Marriage of Indian and White," *Voyageur, Historical Review of Brown County and Northeast Wisconsin* (Spring 1984): 1.

6. Peterson, "The Founders of Green Bay," 1.

7. Ryan T. Schwier, "According to the Custom of the Country: Indian Marriage, Property Rights and Legal Testimony in the Jurisdictional Formation of Indiana Settler Society, 1717–1897" (Master's thesis, Indiana University, 2011), 289–319.

8. President John Quincy Adams, "Treaty Between the United States of America and the Chippeway tribe of Indians; concluded August 5, 1826," included as an appendix in Thomas McKenney, *Sketches of a Tour of the Lakes, of the Character and Customs of the Chippeway Indians, and Incidents Connected with the Treaty of Fond du Lac*, rev. ed. (1827; Barre, MA: Imprint Society, 1972), 398.

9. McKenney, *Sketches of a Tour to the Lakes*, 402–404.

10. McKenney, *Sketches of a Tour to the Lakes*, 402–404.

11. Theresa M. Schenck, "Lyman Marcus Warren," (unpublished manuscript April 2013), 9.

12. Theresa M. Schenck, *Grant's Point, Madeline Island, in the Historical Record* (Madison: Wisconsin State Historical Society, 2003), 13–14.

13. *Marriage Register*, 3.

14. *Marriage Register*, 3.

15. *Marriage Register*, 3.

16. Schenck, *Grant's Point*, 30.

17. Michel Cadotte grave marker, Madeline Island.

18. Warren, *History of the Ojibway People*, 282.

19. Ancestry.com report on Equaysayway; Roger Cadotte, email correspondence with the author, January 2016.

Chapter 20

1. Lyman Warren to William Aiken, September 1838, Henry Hastings Sibley Papers, 1826–1848, Wisconsin Historical Society.

2. Theresa Schenck, *William W. Warren: The Life, Letters and Times of an Ojibwe Leader* (Lincoln: University of Nebraska Press, 2007), 1.

3. Schenck, *William W. Warren*, 3.

4. Schenck, *William W. Warren*, 3.

5. Schenck, *William W. Warren*, 3–4.

6. Hamilton Nelson Ross, *La Pointe: Village Outpost on Madeline Island*, rev. ed. (1960; repr., Madison: State Historical Society of Wisconsin, 2000), 73.

7. Ross, *La Pointe*, 8.

8. Schenck, *William W. Warren*, 3. The relationship between Truman and Bazinet is unclear in the records. Truman may have married Bazinet "in the custom of the country," then later abandoned her. It is highly unlikely there was a formal divorce. Bazinet went on to marry another trader a few years later.

9. Ross, *La Pointe*, 74.

10. Julia Warren Spears to William Bartlett, "Interesting Sidelights on the History of Early Fur Trading Industry in Chippewa Valley," *Eau Claire Leader*, August 9, 1925.

11. William W. Warren, *History of the Ojibway People*, reprint (St. Paul: Minnesota Historical Society Press, 1984), 384; also see Schenck, *William W. Warren*, 5.

12. Spears to Bartlett, letter October 26, 1924.

13. Schenck, *William W. Warren*, 9–15.

14. "Extracts from Journal of J. Allen, Lieut. 5th Inf. Visit to La Pointe in 1832," in "Interesting Sidelights on the History of Early Fur Trading Industry in Chippewa Valley," *Eau Claire Leader*, June 10, 1925; also see Schenck, *William W. Warren*, 9.

15. "Extracts from Journal of J. Allen."

16. Edmund F. Ely, *The Ojibwe Journals of Edmund F. Ely, 1833–1849* (Lincoln: University of Nebraska Press, 2012), 17.

17. Ely, *The Ojibwe Journals of Edmund F. Ely*, 17.

18. Ross, *La Pointe*, 75.

19. Ross, *La Pointe*, 75.

20. Ross, *La Pointe*, 76.

21. Theresa M. Schenck, "Lyman Marcus Warren" (unpublished manuscript April 2013), 11.

22. Schenck, "Lyman Marcus Warren," 12.

23. Schenck, "Lyman Marcus Warren," 12.

24. Schenck, "Lyman Marcus Warren," 15.

25. Ross, *La Pointe*, 78.

26. Lawrence Taliaferro, *Autobiography of Maj. Lawrence Taliaferro* (St. Paul: Collections of the Minnesota Historical Society, 1894), 216. Although Taliaferro was known for his integrity, he was also notorious for his ego. His autobiography is filled with great deeds he allegedly performed on be-

half of Indians, along with disparagement of other Indian agents, notably Henry Rowe Schoolcraft. He had little good to say about nearly all traders, and he argued that all of the Lake Superior Ojibwe should be under his agency in Minnesota, rather than Schoolcraft's agency at Sault Ste. Marie or the subagency at La Pointe.

27. Anton Treuer, *The Assassination of Hole in the Day* (St. Paul: Borealis Books, 2011), Chapter 3.

28. Treuer, *The Assassination of Hole in the Day*.

29. Ross, *La Pointe*, 78–79.

30. Schenck, "Lyman Marcus Warren," 13.

31. Schenck, *William W. Warren*, 13.

32. Fred R. Gowans, *Rocky Mountain Rendezvous, A History of the Fur Trade, 1825–1840* (Layton, UT: Gibbs Smith, 2005). The Rocky Mountain Rendezvous was held along or near the Green River each year for more than a decade. Historian Bernard DeVoto described the rendezvous as "the annual season of supply, trade and saturnalia at which the brigades which had spent the year in the mountains outfitted afresh and turned over their pelts for transportation to the States." Also see DeVoto, *Across the Wide Missouri* (New York: Houghton Mifflin Harcourt, 1998), 47.

33. Spears to Bartlett letter, October 26, 1924.

34. Schenck, "Lyman Marcus Warren," 17.

35. Schenck, "Lyman Marcus Warren," 18.

36. Gabriel Franchère to Aiken, August 1838, Henry Hastings Sibley Papers.

37. Schenck, *William W. Warren*, 15.

38. Lyman Warren to Henry Sibley, August 18, 1838, Henry Hastings Sibley Papers.

39. Schenck, "Lyman Marcus Warren," 7.

40. Schenck, "Lyman Marcus Warren," 20.

41. Schenck, "Lyman Marcus Warren," 20, 23.

42. Lyman Warren to William Aiken, September, 1838, Henry Hastings Sibley Papers.

43. Schenck, "Lyman Marcus Warren," 15–16.

44. Schenck, "Lyman Marcus Warren," 16.

45. Schenck, "Lyman Marcus Warren," 23–24.

46. Lyman Warren to William Aiken, April 1838, Henry Hastings Sibley Papers.

47. Lyman Warren to William Aiken, September 1838, Henry Hastings Sibley Papers.

48. Schenck, *William W. Warren*, 18.

49. Schenck, "Lyman Marcus Warren," 20

50. Spears to Bartlett, letter, November 10, 1924.

51. Schenck, "Lyman Marcus Warren," 24.

52. Spears to Bartlett, letter, October 26, 1924.

53. Spears to Bartlett, letter, October 26, 1924.

54. Spears to Bartlett, letter, October 26, 1924.

Chapter 21

1. Peter David, telephone interview with the author, September 12, 2018.

2. Marvin Defoe, telephone interview with the author, October 29, 2018.

3. Peter David, telephone interview with the author.

4. David and Defoe, telephone interviews with the author.

5. Thomas Vennum, Jr., *Wild Rice and the Ojibway People* (St. Paul: Minnesota Historical Society Press, 1988), 113.

6. Vennum, *Wild Rice and the Ojibway People*, 118–120.

7. Vennum, *Wild Rice*, 123–132.

8. Vennum, *Wild Rice*, 132–133.

9. "Wild Rice," *Alternative Field Crops Manual*, University of Wisconsin-Extension, Cooperative Extension, University of Minnesota Center for Alternative Plant & Animal Products and the Minnesota Extension Service, December 2, 1997, 2; Peter David, telephone interview with the author.

10. Vennum, *Wild Rice*, 5–6.

11. Vennum, *Wild Rice*, 6.

12. Albert Ernest Jenks, *The Wild Rice Gatherers of the Upper Lakes, A Study in American Primitive Economics*, Extract from the Nineteen Annual Report of the Bureau of American Ethnology (Washington, DC: Government Printing Office, 1901), 82.

13. Vennum, *Wild Rice*, 39.

14. "Wild Rice," *Alternative Field Crops Manual*, 1.

15. Vennum, *Wild Rice*, 58.

16. Defoe, telephone interview with the author.

17. David Thompson, *The Writings of David Thompson, Volume 1, The Travels, 1850 Version*, ed. William E. Moreau (Toronto: The Champlain Society,

2009), 146.

18. Thompson, *The Writings of David Thompson*, 145–146.

19. "Zizania palustris/aquatic," in "Wild Rice (Zinzania) Nutrition," *Gramene*. Vennum suggested that either name was acceptable; Vennum, *Wild Rice*, 12; David, telephone interview with the author.

20. Reuben Gold Thwaites, *The Jesuit Relations and Allied Documents, Vol. 59* (Cleveland: The Burrows Brothers Company), 95.

21. Jenks, *The Wild Rice Gatherers of the Upper Midwest*, 21.

22. William W. Warren, *History of the Ojibway People History of the Ojibway People*, reprint (St. Paul: Minnesota Historical Society Press, 1984), 309.

23. David, telephone interview with the author.

24. Defoe, telephone interview with the author.

25. Thompson, *The Writings of David Thompson, 1850 version*, 246.

26. Jean-Baptiste Perrault, "Narrative of the Travels and Adventures of a Merchant Voyageur in the Savage Territories of Northern America," *Historical Collections and Researches made by the Michigan Pioneer and Historical Society, Vol. XXXVII*, 555.

27. Perrault, "Narrative of the Travels," 583.

28. Perrault, "Narrative of the Travels," 592.

29. Eliza Morrison, *A Little History of My Forest Life* (La Crosse, WI: Sumac Press, 1978), 145; Defoe, telephone interview with the author.

30. "Kakagon and Bad River Sloughs Recognized as Wetlands of International Importance," the Bad River Band of Lake Superior Chippewa Tribe website: http://www.badriver-nsn.gov/tribal-news/200-kakagon-and-bad -river-sloughs-recognized-as-a-wetland-of-international-importance

31. Warren, *History of the Ojibway People*, 309.

32. "Wild Rice: An Economic Assessment of the Feasibility of Providing Multi-Peril Crop Insurance," Economic Research Service, U.S. Department of Agriculture, 1996, 2.

33. David, telephone interview with the author.

34. Vennum, *Wild Rice and the Ojibway People*, 240.

35. Vennum, *Wild Rice*, 239.

36. "White Earth Wild Rice: Hand Harvested and Naturally Organic," White Earth Nation website: http://realwildrice.com/.

37. David, telephone interview with the author.

38. Defoe, telephone interview with the author.

Chapter 22

1. Ronald Satz, *Chippewa Treaty Rights: The Reserved Rights of Wisconsin's Chippewa Indians in Historical Perspective* (Madison: Wisconsin Academy of Sciences, Arts and Letters, 1991), 56.

2. Satz, "Chippewa Treaty Rights," 58. The death numbers are from Ojibwe leaders who petitioned the U.S. government the following year. Although there is no official account of the number who died, Protestant missionaries who were in the region confirmed that the death toll was horrendous and that graves could be found everywhere along the trail.

3. Brenda J. Child, *Holding Our World Together, Ojibwe Women and the Survival of Community* (New York: Viking, 2012), 66. Satz, *Chippewa Treaty Rights*, 51.

4. Edmund Jefferson Danziger Jr., *The Chippewas of Lake Superior* (Norman: University of Oklahoma Press, 1979), 88. Satz, *Chippewa Treaty Rights*, 52–53.

5. Child, *Holding Our World Together*, 66.

6. Satz, *Chippewa Treaty Rights*, 53–54.

7. Anton Treuer, *The Assassination of Hole in the Day* (St. Paul, MN: Borealis Books, 2011), 100.

8. Treuer, *The Assassination of Hole in the Day*, 102–107.

9. Benjamin G. Armstrong, *Early Life Among the Indians, Reminiscences from the Life of Benjamin G. Armstrong, as told to Thomas P. Wentworth* (Ashland WI: Press of A. W. Bowron, 1892), 10–12.

10. Satz, *Chippewa Treaty Rights*, 54–56.

11. Satz, *Chippewa Treaty Rights*, 56.

12. Howard D. Paap, *Red Cliff, Wisconsin, A History of an Ojibwe Community, Volume 1* (St. Cloud, WI: North Star Press, 2013), 212–213.

13. Child, *Holding Our World Together*, 74.

14. Satz, *Chippewa Treaty Rights*, 58.

15. Armstrong, *Early Life Among the Indians*, 17.

16. Theresa M. Schenck, *All Our Relations, Chippewa Mixed Bloods and the Treaty of 1837* (Madison: Amik Press, 2010), 1–2.

17. There are many different spellings of Bizhiki. This is from the "Ojibwe People's Dictionary," Department of American Indian Studies, University of Minnesota.

18. "Biography of Be Sheekee, or Buffalo": Chief Buffalo and Benjamin Armstrong, http://www.chiefbuffalo.com/buffalo/Their_lives.html.

19. Obituary published in La Pointe, Madeline Island newspaper, September 1855, republished in *Wisconsin Historical Collections, Volume III*.

20. Armstrong, *Early Life Among the Indians*, 196–197.

21. Schenck, *All Our Relations*, 35. Schenck reported that according to Lyman Warren's papers, Buffalo was a first cousin of Michel Cadotte. Several other sources, including an ancestry.com Cadotte Family Tree, show Buffalo as a first cousin of Equaysayway.

22. Paap, *Red Cliff, Wisconsin*, 130.

23. Paap, *Red Cliff, Wisconsin*, 130.

24. Thomas L. McKenney, *Sketches of a Tour to the Lakes, of the Character and Customs of the Chippeway Indians, and Incidents Connected with the Treaty of Fond du Lac*, rev. ed. (1827; Barre, MA: Imprint Society, 1972), 242.

25. McKenney, *Sketches of a Tour to the Lakes*, 379–380.

26. McKenney, *Sketches*, 379–380.

27. McKenney, *Sketches*, 379–380.

28. McKenney, *Sketches*, 399.

29. Paap, *Red Cliff, Wisconsin*, 136.

30. Michael Witgen, *An Infinity of Nations: How the Native New World Shaped Early North America* (Philadelphia: University of Pennsylvania Press, 2013), 124.

31. Cary Miller, "Gifts as Treaties: The Political Use of Received Gifts in Anishinaabeg Communities, 1820–1832," *American Indian Quarterly*, 26, no. 2 (Spring, 2002): 5, 21, JSTOR.

32. McKenney, *Sketches of a Tour to the Lakes*, 398.

33. McKenney, *Sketches*, 398, 402–403.

34. Paap, *Red Cliff, Wisconsin*, 137.

35. Paap, *Red Cliff, Wisconsin*, 138.

36. Danzinger, *The Chippewas of Lake Superior*, 87.

37. Erik M. Redix, *The Murder of Joe White: Ojibwe Leadership and Colonialism in Wisconsin* (East Lansing: Michigan State University Press, 2014), 35.

38. Redix, *The Murder of Joe White*, 37.

39. Armstrong, *Early Life Among the Indians*, 11.

40. Danziger, *The Chippewas of Lake Superior*, 87.

41. Satz, *Chippewa Treaty Rights*, 31.

42. Redix, *The Murder of Joe White*, 33–34.

43. Theresa M. Schenck, "Lyman Marcus Warren" (unpublished manuscript, April 2013), 15, 20.

44. Schenck, *All Our Relations*, 8.

45. Schenck, *All Our Relations*, 5, 35–39.

46. Satz, *Chippewa Treaty Rights*, 41.

47. Redix, *The Murder of Joe White*, 39–40.

48. Satz, *Chippewa Treaty Rights*, 40.

49. Satz, *Chippewa Treaty Rights*, 37–38.

50. Theresa M. Schenck, *William W. Warren* (Lincoln: University of Nebraska Press, 2007), 35–41.

51. Redix, *The Murder of Joe White*, 49.

52. Paap, *Red Cliff, Wisconsin*, 205.

53. Satz, *Chippewa Treaty Rights*, 51–52.

54. Paap, *Red Cliff, Wisconsin*, 221–226.

55. Armstrong, *Early Life Among the Indians*, 16.

56. Paap, *Red Cliff, Wisconsin*, 234.

57. Armstrong, *Early Life Among the Indians*, 18–32.

58. Satz, *Chippewa Treaty Rights*, 67. Paap, *Red Cliff, Wisconsin*, 241–242.

59. Schenck, *William W. Warren*, 161–162, 195.

60. Satz, *Chippewa Treaty Rights*, 67. Paap, *Red Cliff, Wisconsin*, 241–242.

61. Satz, *Chippewa Treaty Rights*, 68. Paap, *Red Cliff, Wisconsin*, 248.

62. Patty Loew, *Indian Nations of Wisconsin: Histories of Endurance and Renewal* (Madison: Wisconsin Historical Society Press, 2001), 63.

63. Satz, *Chippewa Treaty Rights*, 68.

64. Paap, *Red Cliff, Wisconsin*, 256.

65. "History of the Red Cliff Tribe," Red Cliff Band of Lake Superior Chippewa website, http://redcliff-nsn.gov/Heritage&Culture/history.htm.

66. Paap, *Red Cliff, Wisconsin*, 259.

67. Paap, *Red Cliff, Wisconsin*, 260.

Chapter 23

1. Frances Densmore, *Chippewa Customs* (St. Paul: Minnesota Historical Press, 1979), 4–5.

2. François Victor Malhiot, *A Wisconsin Fur-Trader's Journal, 1804–1805* (Madison: State Historical Society of Wisconsin, 1910), 189–190.

3. Malhiot, *A Wisconsin Fur-Trader's Journal*, 206.

4. "Descendants of Francois Xavier Cadotte," *Sneakers* website: http://members.shaw.ca/hjarmstrong/FranXCadotte.htm. Also see Benita Eisler, *The*

Red Man's Bones: George Catlin, Artist and Showman (New York: W. W. Norton, 2013), 295, 300–301.

5. Theresa M. Schenck, *William W. Warren: The Life, Letters, and Times of an Ojibwe Leader* (Lincoln: University of Nebraska Press, 2007), 66.

6. Schenck, *William W. Warren*, 15–16.

7. William W. Warren, *History of the Ojibway People*, reprint (St. Paul, Minnesota Historical Society Press, 1984), 11.

8. Julia Spears letter to William Bartlett, October 26, 1924, "Interesting Sidelights on the History of Early Fur Trading Industry in Chippewa Valley," *Eau Claire Leader*, August 9, 1925.

9. Schenck, *William W. Warren*, 32–33.

10. Schenck, *William W. Warren*, 36–37.

11. Schenck, *William W. Warren*, 39–40.

12. Warren, *History of the Ojibway People*, 12, 282, 296.

13. Schenck, *William W. Warren*, 66.

14. Author's note: I present an abbreviated account of William Warren's life here because so much has been written about him elsewhere. A good brief summary of his life is included at the beginning of Warren's book, *History of the Ojibway People*. It is titled "Memoir of William W. Warren" by J. Fletcher Williams, Secretary of the Minnesota Historical Society in 1885, when the book was first published. The most complete account of Warren's life is Schenck, *William W. Warren*.

15. Schenck, *William W. Warren*, 86.

16. Julia Spears letter to William Bartlett, May 12, 1925.

17. Schenck, *William W. Warren*, 92.

18. Schenck, *William W. Warren*, 101–102.

19. Schenck, *William W. Warren*, 98–99.

20. Schenck, *William W. Warren*, 156–157.

21. Schenck, *William W. Warren*, 101–110, 136–150.

22. Schenck, *William W. Warren*, 170.

23. Julia Warren Spears obituary, *Detroit* (Minnesota) *Tribune*, June 25, 1925, "Interesting Sidelights on the History of Early Fur Trading Industry in Chippewa Valley."

24. Densmore, *Chippewa Customs*, 5.

25. Julia Warren Spears obituary, June 25, 1925.

26. Densmore, *Chippewa Customs*, 4–5.

27. Schenck, *William W. Warren*, 2.

28. Schenck, *William W. Warren*, 2; Julia Warren Spears obituary.

29. Schenck, *William W. Warren*, 2; Julia Warren Spears obituary.

30. Schenck, *William W. Warren*, 2; Julia Warren Spears obituary.

31. Elizabeth Hart Bennett and Evan A. Hart, "Translation of Cadotte Account Book," inside front cover, *Cadotte Family Papers*, University of Notre Dame Archives.

Chapter 24

1. F. Clever Bald, "The Story of the Sault," *The Beaver* (Autumn 1955): 48. Also see Bernie Arbic and Nancy Steinhaus, *Upbound Downbound, the Story of the Soo Locks* (Detroit: Priscilla Press, 2005), 21.

2. See Chapter 8: Jean-Baptiste Cadot Sr.

3. Bald, "The Story of the Sault," 52.

4. "Timeline of Michigan Copper Mining Prehistory to 1850," Keweenaw National Historical Park, U.S. National Park Service, 2.

5. *Dictionary of Canadian Biography*, s.v. "Cadot, Jean-Baptiste," by David A. Armour, Accessed on February 1, 2019, www.biographi.ca/en/bio/cadot_jean_baptiste_5E.html.

6. "Timeline of Michigan Copper Mining, Prehistory to 1850," 3.

7. "Timeline of Michigan Copper Mining, 1851 to 1900," Keweenaw National Historical Park, U.S. National Park Service 4.

8. "Pre-eminence of the Iron Ore Trade," *History of the Great Lakes Volume I, Maritime History of the Great Lakes*, http://www.maritimehistoryof thegreatlakes.ca/GreatLakes/Documents/HGL/default.asp?ID=c030.

9. Bald, *The Story of the Sault*, 52.

10. Frank A. Flower, *Eye of the North-west, First Annual Report of the Statistician of Superior Wisconsin* (Milwaukee: King, Fowle & Co., 1890), 73.

11. Flower, *Eye of the North-west*, 73–74.

12. Flower, *Eye of the North-west*, 194.

13. Theresa M. Schenck, *All Our Relations, Chippewa Mixed Bloods and the Treaty of 1837* (Madison: Amik Press, 2010), 42–43.

14. Thomas Henry Tobola, *Cadotte Family Stories* (Madison: University of Wisconsin, 1974), inside cover–9; Schenck, *All Our Relations*, 37.

15. Flower, *Eye of the North-west*, 74–76.

16. Flower, *Eye of the North-west*, 76.

17. Hamilton Nelson Ross, *La Pointe: Village Outpost on Madeline Island*, rev. ed. (1960; repr., Madison: State Historical Society of Wisconsin, 2000), 110.

18. Ross, *La Pointe*, 113–114.

19. Ross, *La Pointe*, 122.

20. Eliza Morrison, *A Little History of My Forest Life* (La Crosse, WI: Sumac Press, 1978), 135.

21. Ross, *La Pointe*, 153.

22. Theresa M. Schenck, *William W. Warren: The Life, Letters, and Times of an Ojibwe Leader* (Lincoln: University of Nebraska Press, 2007), 60–61.

23. Obituary from a Chippewa County, Wisconsin, newspaper for George Warren from 1884; "Interesting Sidelights on the History of Early Fur Trading Industry in Chippewa Valley," *Eau Claire Leader*, August 2, 1925.

24. Edmund J. Danziger Jr., "They Would Not Be Moved: The Chippewa Treaty of 1854," *Minnesota History Magazine* (Spring 1973): 184.

25. "Half Breed Scrip. Chippewas of Lake Superior. The Correspondence and Action under the 7th Clause of the 2nd Article of the Treaty with the Chippewa Indians of Lake Superior and the Mississippi, Concluded at La Pointe, in the State of Wisconsin, September 30, 1854," House Ex. Doc. 193, 42d Congress, 2d session, 15.

26. "Half Breed Scrip," 15.

27. "Half Breed Scrip," 15.

28. "Half Breed Scrip," 14.

29. "Half Breed Scrip," 4–17.

30. "Half Breed Scrip," 7.

31. "Half Breed Scrip," 4–17.

32. "Half Breed Scrip," 17.

33. "Half Breed Scrip," 20–28.

34. "Half Breed Scrip," 28–32.

35. "Half Breed Scrip," 320.

36. Title search performed in 2016 at the request of the author by Don Cedric, retired title analyst, Washburn, Wisconsin.

37. Bruce Burnside, "The Settlement," produced November 3, 2008, audio story, beta.prx.org/stories.

38. Burnside, "The Settlement."

39. "Half Breed Scrip," 21.

40. Author's telephone conversation with Sister Grace Ann Rabideau (a Cadotte

descendant), Bayfield, WI, December 21, 2015.

41. Author's conversations with Jack Cadotte, Duluth, Minnesota; Roger Cadotte, Red Cliff, Wisconsin; Sister Grace Ann Rabideau, Bayfield, Wisconsin; and Kenneth Cadotte, La Pointe, Wisconsin, from 2013 to 2019.

Epilogue

1. Alexander Henry, *Travels and Adventures in Canada and the Indian Territories between the Years 1760 and 1776* (New York: J. Riley, 1809), 58; "The United States v. Repentigny 1866," in *Cases Argued and Adjudged Before the Supreme Court of The United States, Volume 5*, 215–216. French traders and priests had been visiting Sault Ste. Marie since the early 1600s, and there had at various times been small communities and missions there. However, Repentigny established the French military fort there in 1750, and Cadot and his family were apparently the only people of European descent then living at the Sault.

2. Keith R. Widder, "After the Conquest: Michilimackinac, a Borderland in Transition, 1760–1763," *Michigan Historical Review* (Spring 2008): 55.

3. John DuLong, "Jean-Baptiste Cadotte's Second Family, Part 1," *Michigan's Habitant Heritage* 36, no. 4 (October 2015): 193.

4. *Dictionary of Canadian Biography, Vol. 5*, s.v. "Cadot, Jean-Baptiste" by David A. Armour, Accessed on February 1, 2019: www.biographi.ca/en/bio/cadot_jean_baptiste_5E.html.

INDEX

ABOUT THE AUTHOR

Robert Silbernagel studied journalism at the University of Wisconsin and was the editorial page editor for *The Daily Sentinel* newspaper in Grand Junction, Colorado, for nineteen years. Now retired, he continues to write a history column for the newspaper. He is the author of *Troubled Trails: The Meeker Affair and the Expulsion of Utes from Colorado* and *Historic Adventures on The*  *Colorado Plateau*. He has also written articles for a number of periodicals, including the *Wisconsin Magazine of History* and *Colorado Heritage*. He and his wife, Judy, live near Palisade, Colorado.

CHRISTOPHER TOMLINSON